I0069043

The Massacre of Political Prisoners in Iran, 1988

REPORT OF AN INQUIRY CONDUCTED
BY GEOFFREY ROBERTSON QC

Published by
The Abdorrahman Boroumand Foundation

About the Author

Geoffrey Robertson QC is founder and Head of Doughty Street Chambers, London. He has appeared in many countries as counsel in leading cases in constitutional, human rights, criminal and international law and served as the first President and Appeal Judge in the UN War Crimes Court in Sierra Leone, where he authored landmark decisions on the limits of amnesties, the illegality of recruiting child soldiers and other critical issues in the development of international criminal law. In 2008, he was appointed by the UN Secretary-General as one of the "distinguished jurist" members of the UN Internal Justice Council.

In the UK, he sits as a Recorder (part-time judge) and is a Master of the Middle Temple and a visiting Professor in Human Rights Law at Queen Mary College.

His books include *Crimes Against Humanity – The Struggle for Global Justice* (Penguin and New Press, 3rd edn, 2006), *The Justice Game* (Vintage, 1998), *Robertson and Nicol on Media Law* (Sweet & Maxwell, 5th edn, 2008), *The Levellers: The Putney Debates* (Verso, 2007), *Freedom, the Individual and the Law* (Penguin, 7th edn, 1993), *The Tyrannicide Brief* (Vintage, 2006) and *Statute of Liberty* (Random House, 2009). He has made many television and radio programmes in the UK and Australia, notably, *Geoffrey Robertson's Hypotheticals*. His scholarly and journal articles can be found at www.geoffreyrobertson.com.

About the Abdorrahman Boroumand Foundation

The Abdorrahman Boroumand Foundation (ABF) is a non-governmental, non-profit organisation dedicated to the promotion of human rights and democracy in Iran. ABF is an independent organisation with no political affiliation. It is named in memory of Dr Abdorrahman Boroumand, an Iranian lawyer and pro-democracy activist who was assassinated in Paris on 18 April 1991. ABF believes that promoting human rights awareness through education and the dissemination of information are necessary prerequisites for the establishment of a stable democracy in Iran. ABF was founded in 2001 by Ladan and Roya Boroumand, the daughters of Dr Boroumand, who were recently awarded the Lech Walesa Institute Foundation Prize to honour their work to promote human rights, freedom of expression and democracy in Iran.

ABF is committed to the values enshrined in the Universal Declaration of Human Rights and in other internationally recognised human rights instruments. ABF seeks to ensure that human rights in Iran are promoted and protected without discrimination. Guided by the belief that impunity and unremedied human rights violations are major obstacles to the establishment of a stable democracy, ABF is committed to the rights of all victims of human rights abuse to justice and public recognition.

The work of ABF is enabled through the support of a diverse range of funders, including private foundations in Europe and the US, and individual donors. It has received funding from the National Endowment for Democracy (NED), which is funded by US Congress but is governed by an independent Board of Directors. ABF has never received funding from governments.

www.iranrights.org

Publisher's Note

In January 2009 Iranian authorities undertook to destroy hundreds of unmarked graves in Khavaran cemetery, south Tehran. The attempt to destroy evidence was the latest episode of a political drama which began in the summer of 1988, with the secret killing of thousands of Iranian political prisoners. Months before, in August 2008, security forces had prevented anyone from gathering in Khavaran on the anniversary of the killings, as victims' families had often done. As a human rights NGO mandated to protect and honor the memory of all victims of state violence in Iran and to promote fair trial and due process of law in that country, the Abdorrahman Boroumand Foundation (ABF) felt compelled to bring to the attention of the international community Iran's policy of systematic denial, historical falsification, and destruction of evidence of the mass executions.

Beginning with its creation in 2001, ABF has collected the names of thousands of political prisoners killed in the 1988 "prison massacres" and documented hundreds of their cases. It has interviewed relatives, friends, and the cellmates of scores of victims and has received through its website hundreds of electronic messages confirming or adding to existing cases. ABF researchers have also gathered a large body of survivor testimonies, published memoirs, as well as official statements by Iranian political and judicial authorities relevant to the understanding of the killings' ideological and political background.

In early 2009, ABF brought this body of evidence to Geoffrey Robertson QC, the highly-respected international legal expert, to investigate the 1988 secret executions and provide an independent legal opinion on the crime. As author, Mr Robertson is the sole judge of the evidence, be it testimony, an official statement, or a key historical event. Although it publishes this report, which it considers to be a significant contribution to legal and historical scholarship, ABF does not necessarily agree with all of Mr Robertson's comments or historical analyses. It does, however, endorse his overall findings and conclusions.

ABF is grateful to the survivors and victims' relatives who testified and who, by doing so, have courageously undermined the state's campaign to obliterate the truth about the 1988 prison massacre. Their testimonies have strengthened this report's narrative and its legal analysis. These witnesses come from various political backgrounds and do not necessarily share the author's analysis of the historical circumstances surrounding the prison massacre or his views on the organizations with which they were affiliated in 1988. They have contributed their testimonies (published separately) to this investigation only to promote justice and accountability. ABF hopes that Mr Robertson's legal opinion will be of help to the victims' quest for justice owed to them by the Iranian state and the international community, which has committed itself to fighting genocide and crimes against humanity.

Contents

1: A Failure to Investigate

Late in July 1988, as the war with Iraq was ending in a truculent truce, prisons in Iran crammed with government opponents suddenly went into lockdown. All family visits were cancelled, televisions and radios switched off and newspapers discontinued; prisoners were kept in their cells, disallowed exercise or trips to the infirmary. The only permitted visitation was from a delegation, turbaned and bearded, which came in government BMWs and Mercedes to outlying jails: a religious judge, a public prosecutor, and an intelligence chief. Before them were paraded, briefly and individually, almost every prisoner (and there were thousands of them) who had been jailed for adherence to the *Mojahedin Khalq* Organisation – the MKO. This was a movement which had taken its politics from Karl Marx, its theology from Islam, and its guerrilla tactics from Che Guevara: it had fought the Shah and supported the revolution that brought Ayatollah Khomeini to power, but later broke with his theocratic state and took up arms against it, in support (or so it now says) of democracy. The delegation had but one question for these young men and women (most of them detained since 1981 merely for taking part in street protests or possession of 'political' reading material), and although they did not know it, on the answer their life would depend. Those who by that answer evinced any continuing affiliation with the *Mojahedin* were blindfolded and ordered to join a conga-line that led straight to the gallows. They were hung from cranes,

four at a time, or in groups of six from ropes hanging from the front of the stage in an assembly hall; some were taken to army barracks at night, directed to make their wills and then shot by firing squad. Their bodies were doused with disinfectant, packed in refrigerated trucks and buried by night in mass graves. Months later their families, desperate for information about their children or their partners, would be handed a plastic bag with their few possessions. They would be refused any information about the location of the graves and ordered never to mourn them in public. By mid-August 1988, thousands of prisoners had been killed in this manner by the state – without trial, without appeal and utterly without mercy.

The regime did not stop at this extermination of *Mojahedin* supporters. The killings were suspended for a fortnight's religious holiday, but began again when the "Death Committee" (as prisoners would later call the delegation) summoned members of other left-wing groups whose ideology was regarded as incompatible with the theocratic state constructed by Imam Ruhollah Khomeini after the 1979 revolution. These groups included the communist *Tudeh* party, aligned with Moscow, the Marxist-Leninist *Fadaiyan Khalq* Organisation – the FKO (which had split into majority and minority factions), *Peykar* (orthodox Marxist-Leninist), and various other smaller leftist groups. Their interviews were longer, trickier and the chance of survival (albeit in most cases after torture) somewhat higher. This time the issue was not their political affiliation, but their religion and their willingness to follow the state's version of Islam: in short, whether they were apostates. This time there was a kind of brief trial, ending with a sentence of death for those atheists and agnostics whose parents were practising Muslims, whilst women in that category and others from secular families were instead ordered to be whipped five times a day until they agreed to pray, or else died from the lash. So there followed, in late August, September and October a second wave of executions, genocidal in intention (because the victims were selected on religious criteria) although more confused and arbitrary in implementation, with torture as an alternative sentence. This second wave of killings was accompanied by the same secrecy that had attended the extermination of the *Mojahedin* – families were not informed for several weeks and sometimes months, and were not told where their sons and husbands had been secretly buried. There was a news blackout over all these prison executions: the regime controlled all media.

Nevertheless, mass murder will out. Reports of an increase in political executions in Iran appeared in *The Financial Times* and *The New York Times* in mid-August 1988 and on 2 September 1988 Amnesty International put out an *Urgent Action* telegram evincing its deep concern that "hundreds of political prisoners may have been executed."[1] There was no conception of the scale of the massacres, but in September, the Human Rights Commission's Special Representative for Iran, the El-Salvador Professor Reynaldo Pohl, was deluged with oral and written complaints about a "wave of executions." He raised this with Iran's permanent representative at the UN, at a meeting

on 27 September 1988, only to be told that the "killings" were merely those which had occurred on the battlefield after the *Mojahedin's* small Iraq-based army had attempted to invade Iran in mid-July (this quickly-defeated incursion was known as the "Mersad Operation" to the Iranian state, and as "Operation Eternal Light" to the *Mojahedin*). Iran's position was complete denial, with a refusal to answer Professor Pohl's questions on the grounds that his information had been provided to him from *Mojahedin* sources and was therefore unreliable propaganda.[2] Professor Pohl nonetheless published in October credible allegations that 860 bodies of political prisoners had been dumped in a mass grave in a Tehran cemetery between 14 and 16 August 1988. (This interim report may have prompted the speaker of the Parliament, Ali Akbar Hashemi Rafsanjani, to admit unguardedly in February 1989 that "the number of political prisoners executed in the last few months was less than one thousand"[3] – a number he appeared to think was commendably low.)

Prime Minister Mir Hossein Mousavi (who twenty years later would be the defeated candidate in the 2009 presidential election) was asked in December 1988, when news of the prison killings had reached the West, by an Austrian television reporter what he had to say about the allegations made by the Western media concerning the human rights violations in Iran. He evaded the question by referring to the Mersad Operation that crushed the Mojahedin's attack. Mousavi condemned them as hypocrites and claimed that "they had plans to perpetrate killings and massacres. We had to crush the conspiracy... in that respect we have no mercy." He added, dishonestly, "we respect human rights and oppose the torture of individuals." He went on to urge Western intellectuals to acknowledge the right of Third World governments to take "decisive action" against their enemies – if only Allende in Chile had done so, Mousavi lamented, he would have survived.[4] (Mousavi must have known that anyone in Tehran in 1988 who promoted Allende's leftist views would have been immediately executed). In February 1989 Khomeini delivered an "historical message" about his former left-wing supporters: "We are not sorry that they are not with us. They never were with us. The revolution does not owe anything to anyone." He inveighed against "the liberals" who had criticised him for "enforcing God's sentence" against the *Mojahedin,* whom he described by using the Persian word *Monafeqin* ("the hypocrites") and he warned against feeling pity for "enemies of God and opponents of the regime." He went on, "as long as I exist I will not allow the regime to fall into the hands of liberals. I will not allow the hypocrites of Islam to eliminate the helpless people."[5] Although the Iranian stance at the UN was to deny all allegations about prison executions, these veiled but menacing under-statements by its leaders, for home consumption, can in retrospect be interpreted as a defiant justification for mass murder.

❧

It is important to appreciate that the UN was well aware of the massacres (if not that their victims numbered in the thousands) shortly after they had commenced and before they had concluded. Its Human Rights Commission had appointed an El Salvadoran law professor and diplomat, Reynaldo Galindo Pohl,

in 1986 as its Special Representative to report regularly upon the situation in this country, with particular concern to investigate the credible reports of executions and torture of political prisoners and the brutal repression of those who followed the Baha'i faith.[6] His first report, in 1987, confirmed the widespread use of *bastinado* and other torture techniques (medical examinations of escaped and released political prisoners had put this beyond doubt) but did no more than call on the Iranian government to set up a human rights commission to reply to what he described as "allegations" of mistreatment and summary executions, and to allow him into the country. He noted "with satisfaction" the government's agreement (on which it immediately resiled) to allow Red Cross visits with prisoners.[7] The government declined to address any of the allegations and instead diverted the Professor by raising academic questions about the compatibility of Sharia law with international human rights law, and historical quibbles about whether there had been sufficient input from Islamic jurists in the drafting of the Universal Declaration of Human Rights. Professor Pohl was more than happy to ponder these questions at length in his report in 1988: he made no effort to calculate the number of political prisoners in Iranian jails, who had by this stage run into many thousands, and he dropped his request to visit prisons (despite his awareness of information that "some prisoners were in danger of execution"). He merely suggested that "the government may wish to initiate an urgent investigation of these complaints in order to take measures of redress."[8] The measures of redress the government wished to take, namely the murder of all prisoners associated with the opposition, began in late July 1988 and lasted until November.

On 26 August 1988, Professor Pohl received information that 200 *Mojahedin* prisoners had been hanged in the assembly hall at Evin Prison. But not until 28 September ("having received information about a wave of executions that was allegedly taking place since the month of July 1988") did he write to Iran's Permanent Representative inviting the government's comments. He did, however, make an interim report to the General Assembly on 13 October 1988, in which he clearly set out information that "a large number of prisoners, members of opposition groups, were executed during the months of July, August and early September"[9] and reported that on 5 August the Chief Justice of Iran (Ayatollah Mousavi Ardebili) had announced that the judiciary was under pressure from public opinion to execute all members of the *Mojahedin* without exception and without trial, and had added a threat that more members of that organisation and "other groups" of oppositionists would be executed.[10] The UN Special Rapporteur on Summary Executions had already telegrammed the Iranian Minister for Foreign Affairs to the effect that the state was breaching Article 14 of the International Covenant on Civil and Political Rights by executing prisoners after "extremely summary, informal and irregular proceedings, failure to inform defendants of specific accusations against them, lack of legal counsel, absence of an appropriate instance of appeal and irregularities that contravene international standards on fair trial."[11] It is therefore quite clear that notwithstanding Professor Pohl's failure to take any urgent action during the massacre period, the General Assembly was provided on 13 October 1988 with evidence of mass murder in Iranian prisons. It did absolutely nothing, and nor did the Security Council.

Thereafter, credible and persistent reports of the "wave of killings" continued to reach Professor Pohl. In his next report in January 1989, he appended a list of the names of over 1,000 alleged victims and noted that his sources indicated that there had been several thousand, mostly from the *Mojahedin* but also from other left-wing groups. Many of the victims "had been serving prison sentences for several years, while others are former prisoners who were arrested and then executed... people witnessed large numbers of bodies being buried in shallow graves."[12] Professor Pohl concluded:

> The global denial [by the Iranian Government] of the wave of executions which allegedly took place from July to September of last year... is not sufficient to dismiss the allegations as unfounded... the allegations received from several sources, including non-governmental organisations, and reported in the media, referred to summary executions in places that were not affected by military operations. Many allegations contain names, places and dates of supposed executions, and some of them referred to persons arrested long before those events had taken place and to former prisoners who were re-arrested. These allegations deserve to be the subject of detailed investigation and information from the government concerned, in conformity with international practice. In particular, it may be expected that the application of the norms on fair trial with respect to each case should be

investigated and the result of that investigation reported.[13]

Notwithstanding this knowledge, Professor Pohl became lost in admiration for the ceasefire (he records "immense satisfaction and deep appreciation" to the Iranian government), which he is sure "will soon turn its positive attention to human rights problems" and will investigate abuses of power. With astonishing naivety, he assumed in this crucial report that the Iranian government would investigate its own abuses, despite meetings with the Iranian representatives to the UN who, with utter dishonesty, had assured him that all the *Mojahedin* deaths had occurred on the battlefield.[14]

No truthful information from the Iranian government was ever supplied to the UN Special Representative about the 1988 massacres. Professor Pohl is partly to blame: although his mandate was renewed by the Human Rights Commission, he seems to have lost interest in the prison massacres. His next report, in November 1989, records Iran's barefaced lie that most of the so-called massacre victims had been amnestied and released from prison and although he records, in passing, the massacres as a corroborated fact, he allows himself to be fobbed off with government promises of future further improvements in prison conditions. He made no real investigation of the massacre allegations, and at this stage (one year after the killings) the regime had not even permitted him to visit the country.

By the time of Professor Pohl's 1990 report, the government's campaign of assassinating its critics had achieved its terrorist purpose and the murder in Switzerland of Mr Kazem Rajavi, representative of The National Coun-

cil of Resistance (a coalition controlled by the *Mojahedin*) at the UN, and of other dissidents in Europe had chilled criticism and deterred potential witnesses. So had the outrageous death sentence *fatwa* which Supreme Leader Khomeini had pronounced on author Salman Rushdie in February 1989. The government felt sufficiently confident of Professor Pohl to allow him a 6 day visit, with 5 days of meetings with its officials and a half day visit to Evin Prison, where he was welcomed with a band concert (a tactic used by the Nazis for foreign visitors at Terezin and Auschwitz)[15] but denied access to the prisoners he requested to see.[16] They paraded before him instead some alleged inmates – they may not have been prisoners at all – who told him that "the treatment was satisfactory and the food superb"[17] and some stooges from state-backed women's organisations who explained that "women enjoyed freedom in absolute terms and without any limitations."[18] He was not, for unexplained reasons, able to meet Ayatollah Montazeri, one of the founders of the Islamic Republic who at the time of the alleged prison killings was Khomeini's designated successor, and who had specifically requested a visit – a mystery that Professor Pohl set no store by at the time.[19] The government told him it was "now in a position to refute the false allegations made by its political enemies"[20] and stressed "the role played by compassion in Islam."[21] Although he received a tip-off about some surviving *Mojahedin* secretly incarcerated in section 209 at Evin Prison, he did not follow this up.[22] His report ended not with a bang, but a whimper: he merely noted that allegations about human rights violations were too common to lack credibility and "government action to prevent and remedy such violations has not been sufficient to put an end to them."[23] According to Amnesty International, prior to his visit, the regime had removed flowers and memorial stones from the suspected site of a mass grave in the main Tehran cemetery, fearing that Professor Pohl would insist on visiting it.[24] He did not even ask permission to do so.

It is clear that the UN Human Rights Commission and the General Assembly had some evidence of the massacres shortly after they commenced, but no effective investigation was undertaken at that time or subsequently. Astonishingly, Professor Pohl's reports from 1991 onwards do not even mention them (although they note that execution of political prisoners without fair trial continues).[25] By this time, the reports are more concerned with Iran's overseas assassination campaign against its opposition leaders (the Shah's last Prime Minister, Shapour Bakhtiar, was killed in France, and other dissidents died in a hail of bullets in Germany, Switzerland and Turkey) and with the murder of one of Salman Rushdie's translators following the bloodthirsty call by the new (and current) Supreme Leader, Seyed Ali Khamenei, for Muslims throughout the world to carry out the *fatwa* on all connected with the publication of *The Satanic Verses*.[26] There can be little doubt that the Islamic Republic was emboldened to flout international law so outrageously as a result of the way in which it was able to avoid accountability, or even criticism, at the UN, for the brutal extermination of thousands of its prisoners. Why was it permitted to get away with the worst violation of prisoners' rights since the death marches of allied prisoners conducted by the Japanese at the end of the Second World War? This was, of

course, 1988 – five years before international tribunals were established to punish crimes against humanity in the former Yugoslavia and Rwanda. In March of that year Saddam Hussein had gassed the Kurds at Halabja, and had suffered no UN reprisals. The end of the Iran-Iraq war later in August 1988 produced a political climate in which other diplomats and UN officials wanted to give both countries the benefit of any doubt. But what they gave Iran was impunity, and the message that goes with it: if you can get away with murdering thousands of your prisoners, you can get away with other breaches of international law, like assassinating your enemies in other countries and even, eventually, with building nuclear arsenals. In 1988, the Islamic Republic of Iran learned the easy way, from the failure of the UN and its Commissions and its member states to investigate mass murders in Iranian prisons, that international law had no teeth for biting, or even for gnashing.

❧

The UN had failed to conduct an effective investigation, but in December 1990 Amnesty International stepped up to the plate by publishing a short but hard hitting account of "The Massacre of 1988." It recorded the names of over 2,000 victims, "including an unknown number of prisoners of conscience who...were in no position to take part in spying or terrorist activities...Many of the dead had been students in their teens or early twenties at the time of their arrest." The report gave some heart-wrenching examples of the cruelty towards bereaved parents who were forbidden from mourning and denied any information about their children's burial places. It claimed that Ayatollah Montazeri had written letters to Khomeini criticising the mass executions, which "showed that there was awareness at the highest level of the government that 'thousands' of summary executions were taking place without regard to constitutional and judicial procedures" and it surmised that "the massacre of political prisoners was a pre-meditated and co-ordinated policy, which must have been authorised at the highest level of government."[27]

Just how high was not conclusively revealed for 12 years. Then, in 2000, the "Montazeri letters" appeared in *The Diaries of Ayatollah Montazeri* compiled by his students in the holy city of Qom, where he lived (and where he died on 20 December 2009). He had been a formidable and radical theologian in the days of the Shah, when he was frequently imprisoned, and had been such a leading figure in the 1979 revolution that he was unanimously chosen by the Assembly of Experts to be Khomeini's successor as the nation's Supreme Leader. He certainly had no love for the *Mojahedin* – his son had been killed by a bomb attributed to them, in 1981 – but he alone of the regime's senior leaders refused to countenance the massacres. His memoirs reveal that on Thursday 28 July 1988, a few days after the *Mojahedin* "Eternal Light" invasion, Khomeini had issued a secret *fatwa* decreeing the execution of all remaining *Mojahedin* in Iranian prisons. The task of implementing this decree in Tehran was specifically entrusted to a three-man committee: Hossein Ali Nayyeri, a religious judge (later promoted to Iran's Deputy Chief Justice), Morteza Eshraqi, the city's chief prosecutor (now a Supreme Court Judge), and a representative from the Intelligence Ministry, a role usually taken by Mostafa Pourmohammadi, the Deputy Minis-

ter of Intelligence (later Interior Affairs Minister in Mahmoud Ahmadinejad's first Cabinet). This *fatwa* served as the death sentence for all *Mojahedin* who remained "steadfast" in their allegiance. The committee would not therefore be imposing a death sentence or making any sort of considered judgment upon each prisoner. It had simply to establish, on the basis of prison records and a simple question, whether the prisoner fell within its ambit. In so doing, the *fatwa* read, they "must not hesitate or show any doubt or be concerned with details," but be "ruthless to the unbelievers (Koran 48:29."

The Supreme Leader's decree was immediately questioned by the Chief Justice, Ayatollah Mousavi Ardebili, who asked whether it applied only to those who had already been tried and sentenced to death, or simply to everyone in prison, even if they had not been tried or were serving short sentences. "**To everyone**" came the Ayatollah's response: "**the sentence is execution for everyone who at any stage or at any time maintains his or her support for the *Monafeqin* organisation**." The Chief Justice asked whether local authorities could act independently or should refer decisions to a provincial centre: "**whichever is quicker**" came the response. "**Annihilate the enemies of Islam immediately**." Montazeri protested to Khomeini on 31 July, describing his *fatwa* as an "act of vengeance" and pointing out that execution without due process or any regard for judicial standards would damage the Republic and would make martyrs of the *Mojahedin*. His pleas for mercy fell on the deaf ears of the old man who had himself recently been given a finite time-frame by his doctors (he would die from cancer the following year). Soon Montazeri was writing despairingly to the Chief Justice that his judges had already killed up to 3,800 prisoners, and he feared "the judgment that posterity and history will pass upon us."

After the publication of the Montazeri letters, there were immediate demands for that judgment to be legal rather than historical. Lord Avebury and a number of British MPs called on the UN Human Rights Committee to conduct a proper investigation at last. This call for justice came in *Crime Against Humanity* – a 250-page publication in January 2001 urging the indictment of "Iran's ruling Mullahs for massacre of 30,000 political prisoners." It listed by name 3,208 *Mojahedin* victims, in many cases with their photographs, and gave graphic accounts from relatives of how they had been stopped from holding memorial services. It identified 20 officials and leaders whom it alleged to have played an active role in the massacres. The instigator, Imam Khomeini, had died in 1989, but the others still occupied senior positions in the government or judiciary. This publication, however, was attributed to the "Foreign Affairs Committee" of the *National Council of Resistance of Iran* – the organisation into which the *Mojahedin* had transmogrified. For all the convincing detail about the organisation's own victims, it was nonetheless a manifestly partisan account. The estimation of 30,000 victims appears to be an exaggeration,[28] and at least some of those characterised as "perpetrators" were not linked by evidence to the chain of command that must have implemented the *fatwa* (several were certainly connected to subsequent assassinations of overseas opponents but this does not, of course, prove that they were involved in the earlier crime). Although the booklet invoked,

by its title, the concept of the "crime against humanity," which was now being used in the new UN courts to prosecute political and military leaders responsible for atrocities in the Balkans and in Rwanda, there was no analysis of how or why these killings breached international criminal law as it existed in 1988 – a time, it must be remembered, when Saddam Hussein's use of chemical weapons to kill 8,000 Kurds at Halabja had passed without much international notice and without retribution.

As the years passed, survivors of the massacres gathered courage and came forward in books and on blog sites, and the families, of course, never forgot and never ceased in their attempts publicly to remember their children (as recently as January 2009 their gathering in a Tehran cemetery was disturbed by police, and the government attempted to destroy evidence by bulldozing a mass grave). But by 1999 Professor Ervand Abrahamian had been able to piece together the machinery of the "mass executions of 1988," (a chapter in his book *Tortured Confessions*[29]) and references to them appeared in the award-winning feature film *Persepolis* and in the widely acclaimed memoir *Reading Lolita in Tehran*, where Azar Nafisi writes:

> The victims of this mass execution were murdered twice, the second time by the silence and anonymity surrounding their executions, which robbed them of a meaningful and acknowledged death and thus, to paraphrase Hannah Arendt, set a seal on the fact that they had never really existed.[30]

Throughout these years, the government has maintained silence. In due course it permitted the establishment of an Islamic Human

Rights Commission which received complaints about the 1988 prison purges and submitted a lengthy list of victims to the judicial authority, only to receive a one-line response denying all knowledge. The prison officials said they had no records, so the Commission was unable to discover their burial places. Its secretary, bravely but despairingly, told the media the Commission was powerless: "Our work resembles that of a person attempting to use his nail to make a hole in the wall."[31]

In 2009 the Iran Human Rights Documentation Center, based in New Haven, published *Deadly Fatwa: Iran's 1988 Prison Massacre*, which summarised in compelling and grisly detail testimonies about the mass murders committed at twelve of the Iranian prisons and how government authorities had prohibited mourning and continued to deny information to families. It published some additional victim interviews and identified some prison administrators who had implemented the decree, but otherwise contained little new evidence. The Center is funded by the US government and so, although I judge its work to be reasonably reliable, others might think it compromised by financial support from the Bush administration (which had included Iran on its "Axis of Evil"). Its analysis of how the mass executions violated international human rights law concentrates on breaches of the International Covenant on Civil and Political Rights, which many state parties breach and which is not enforceable other than through a voluntary Human Rights Committee protocol which Iran (like the US and UK) has not ratified. Its anonymous authors conclude that "there is abundant evidence that the massacre of political prisoners was planned and prepared

long before Iran agreed to the cease-fire or the subsequent NLA [National Liberation Army of Iran] invasion,"[32] an important finding although the evidence it proffers is anything but abundant and my own investigation calls it into question. However the Center's work, supplemented in November 2009 by its publication of further evidence from survivors, does make credible allegations against many judges and clerics who remain in senior positions in Iran, that in 1988 they became accessories to a crime against humanity.

❧

It was against this background that I was approached by the Abdorrahman Boroumand Foundation and invited to conduct "an investigation of the alleged prison massacres in Iran in 1988, and to provide an opinion on the international law obligations of the state of Iran in relation to your findings." This Foundation was established in memory of Dr Boroumand, an Iranian lawyer, pro-democracy activist and advisor to the short-lived cabinet of Shapour Bakhtiar, who was later assassinated in Paris in 1991. It is a non-governmental and non-profit organisation, independent of the political groups which claim to be victims of the 1988 prison killings, and its work to date has mainly involved translating, archiving and publishing documents relevant to the human rights situation in Iran since the 1979 revolution.[33] Of course its scholarship – which includes documentation about victims of human rights abuses – must be highly uncongenial to the government of Iran. I have made use of the Foundation's files and of its translation services, but stipulated that my enquiry should be conducted with complete independence and that all opinions expressed in this published report are to be mine alone. As far as I am aware, there has been no involvement by any government, and funding for the enquiry and for the publication of my report has been provided by private organisations in the US and Europe.[34]

Since the Iranian government has always maintained a deliberate silence in respect of the mounting allegations, I decided that my first course would be to interview a number of persons who were in prison in Iran at the time, to hear their evidence and to test their credibility. In this exercise I have been assisted by Ms Jen Robinson, an Australian solicitor. We interviewed, together or separately, more than 40 former prisoners and their relatives – at my chambers in London and in Washington, Amsterdam, Paris, Cologne, Frankfurt and Berlin. Some had already published accounts of the massacre, whilst others had not been heard from before. It was necessary to factor into the evaluation of their evidence matters such as whether they continued to have a political affiliation or a bias which might skew or exaggerate their testimony; whether their memory had been affected by the passage of time or by repetition of their story or by retrospective embarrassment at any position they may have taken if they "repented" before the "Death Committee" back in 1988. It was important to distinguish between what they had seen with their own eyes, what they had inferred from events they had witnessed and what they had been told by others, often by Morse code communication through adjoining cells and wards. I considered that there were some discrepancies in their stories, a few cases of embroidery to fit facts described by others and some honest jumps to insecure conclusions (for exam-

ple, in relation to the interpretation of events in late 1987 and early 1988 as necessarily related to pre-planning for the massacre). However, making all such allowances, the gist of their narratives, which I summarise in the first two paragraphs above and in detail in Chapters 3-5 of this report, was remarkably consistent, and came across as the truth and little else but the truth. The quoted paragraphs of testimonies are verbatim or from published material; in the case of our interviewees, I have made some grammatical changes and paraphrases, which do not alter the gist of what was being said.

These massacres undoubtedly occurred, pretty much as alleged, in 1988, in prisons where political prisoners were detained. They took place, broadly speaking, in two waves: first, the Death Committee came for the unrepentant *Mojahedin* and then, after a short break, for atheistic or agnostic communists and for leftists it assessed as apostates. There was a good deal of confusion in complying with the *fatwa*, especially in provincial prisons, which may be explained by the fact that the massacres, whether or not planned in advance, were triggered by a furious malice against the *Mojahedin* for the "Eternal Light" invasion. The state destroyed all *Mojahedin* supporters it could lay its hands on, and then proceeded to eliminate, hurriedly and secretly, all male prisoners who refused to pray to the God whom the Supreme Leader represented on earth.

The former prisoners' accounts do not, of course, reveal the whole truth. They were potential victims – observers, survivors and in one case an escapee from a motorcade to the killing field. There has as yet been no public testimony by any prison official to explain how the orders were communicated and carried out, although this must be a knowledge gap that is capable of being filled: a few guards showed distress or tried to save prisoners to whom they had become attached, or to give warnings of what was about to happen. In any trial of perpetrators of international crimes, some direct testimony about the actual perpetration is relevant and may be essential. The other knowledge gap is how the *fatwa* was conceived and passed on: other than the inevitable inferences from the Montazeri letters, we can only speculate as to who was in this lethal loop. The National Council of Resistance of Iran has identified twenty leaders whom it claims were complicit, but allegations from this *Mojahedin* organisation need to be taken with a pinch of salt. Its allegations cannot be dismissed out of hand, however, because it still has unique access to intelligence: in 2003, for example, its dramatic claim that Iran was building a uranium enrichment plant in Natanz and a heavy water plant at Arak was confirmed by US satellite photographs.[36] (On the other hand its more recent propaganda coup, the photograph of the hostage taking at the American Embassy in 1979 which it claimed to show the young Ahmadinejad, seems to have been a case of mistaken identity.[36])

Eyewitness testimony from the survivors we have interviewed confirms the identity of the three Death Committee members before whom they appeared at the main Tehran prisons (Evin and Gohardasht) and further identifies several prison administrators who took a fanatically zealous part in the mass murder. One of them went so far as to pull at the legs of dangling prisoners to hasten their strangulation and so make way for a new set of victims. Evidence of leadership complicity at present relies mainly on inferences from the Montazeri letters and what can only be seen as "cover up" made by Ayatollahs Ali Khamenei (since 1989 the Supreme Leader) and Mousavi Ardebili (still a senior jurist), Ali Akbar Rafsanjani (Head of the Nation's Exigency Council) and, ironically, Prime Minister Mousavi (now the leader of opposition in Iran, although the "Green Movement" has always credited Grand Ayatollah Montazeri with its inspiration[37]).

Does a massacre that happened twenty years ago, at the very end of an eight year war that claimed about a million lives, and which targeted prisoners who were in some way sympathetic to terrorists, communists or Iraq (the national enemy) really matter today? More than ever, in my view. International law is the prisoner's only succour in times of war, when states are often especially prone to exploit popular hostility and unleash the lynch mob. Convicts make for particularly useful scapegoats, and if the temptation to slaughter them is to be kept at bay in the future, notorious cases in the recent past must be exposed and expiated. Otherwise, the weasel-worded "justifications" offered in 1988 by Mousavi and Rafsanjani will be heard again, from other statesmen at other times, and the moral courage of the more humane Montazeri will not be replicated for fear that the sacrifice will be in vain (Montazeri fell from grace partly as a result of his protest and spent some years under house arrest).[38] It is the utter vulnerability of the prisoner in times of war that makes common Article 3 of Geneva Conventions, requiring a basic minimum of humane treatment, of such importance, and imposes a duty on the state, and failing the state on the international community, to investigate and punish whenever credible allegations are made. That duty certainly fell on the UN and on its Human Rights Commission (now the Human Rights Council) from 1988 onwards: the General Assembly and Security Council chose to turn a blind eye, and although its Special Representative was aware of what was happening, his investigation was foiled by Iran and fizzled out through lack of will. It should be revived, while witnesses are still alive whose testimony might help to bring perpetrators to justice.

In this case, of course, exposure of the truth behind and about the mass killings would illuminate the nature of a regime which is still in place with many current leaders who connived in them at the time. Iran continues to test the patience of the world with its nuclear pretensions, its lies to the UN, and its intolerance of dissent. The street murders of protestors, the rigged television 'show trials' and the torture in its prisons are all reminders of what happens when the world fails to act over a massive human rights violation. It has become a recent requirement of international human rights law that nations should face up to, and make amends for, the atrocities of their past: there must be no "posthumous impunity." In the case of Iran where (with the exception of Supreme Leader Khomeini) the killers remain alive, there should be no impunity at all.

❧

I conclude this introductory section by thanking all those witnesses who have submitted themselves to questions by myself and Ms Robinson. Some are reluctant to be named, for reasons they have explained, and I have respected their wishes. Special thanks are due to those who shared their memories and experi-

ences. Without their courage in coming forward, this report would not have been possible, and I mention especially the work of Monireh Baradaran and Iraj Mesdaghi. I am grateful to Ms Roya and Ms Ladan Boroumand who have put the data collected by their Foundation at my disposal and have at my request assisted with arranging meetings with ex-prisoners and with translations. Ms Robinson has helped me with great dedication, expertise and discretion. Mrs Penelope Pryor and Mr Matthew Albert, my former PA and current research assistant respectively, have been invaluable and I am grateful to Doughty Street Chambers and to the Böhler Franken Koppe Wijngaarden law firm in Amsterdam which provided facilities for my enquiry.

This report will be read by many who have no special knowledge of Iranian history and politics, aspects of which are important to understand the situation of the country in 1988 and the behaviour of various parties in the lead up to the massacre, and certainly necessary to judge the explanations elliptically given by the regime for the actions it took against minority political groups at the end of the war with Iraq. For this reason I provide in the next chapter a thumbnail sketch of the political developments most relevant to the regime and its opponents in the lead up to 1988, before proceeding in the two following chapters to explain the situation of political prisoners in 1988, the preparation for their massacre and the procedures by which this was accomplished, first the *Mojahedin* and then the leftists. I then describe how the mass graves have been hidden and the families forbidden – even now – to mourn. Finally, I set out the international law that applies to hold the perpetrators accountable, and is available – even today – for deployment against them.

2: Back Story

Persepolis, in 1971, was the scene of the grandest of all *folies de grandeur*. The Shah of Persia had chosen to celebrate what he said was the 2,500th anniversary of the Peacock Throne. He claimed to be heir to a noble line which began with Cyrus the Great, Darius and Xerxes, leader of a people imbued with the poetry of Omar Khayyam and the philosophy of Zoroaster (hailed by Nietzsche in *Also Sprach Zarathustra* as first conceiver of the moral world). To celebrate this conceit came a plethora of potentates and plenipotentiaries: 9 Kings, 5 Queens, 16 Presidents, numerous Prime Ministers and even Haile Selassie, gallivanting for a fortnight in 70 ornate tents decorated by *Janson* of Paris, catered by *Chez Maxime* of Paris and served by royal courtiers dressed in uniforms designed by *Lanvin* of Paris. Thousands of the Shah's impoverished subjects were ordered to dress up and disport themselves as Medes and Persians, whilst guests consumed 25,000 bottles of French champagne to fortify themselves for speeches about his own and the nation's glorious past.[39] Whilst they caroused, 69 student activists, calling themselves the *Mojahedin Khalq* Organisation, prepared their first terrorist act – to blow up the power station that supplied all the electricity.

Persepolis symbolised the pretensions of the Shah of Iran, descended not from Darius but from Reza Khan, a Cossack general of unprepossessing birth, who dignified his military dictatorship in 1925 by adopting the name Pahlavi, with its pre-Islamic Persian resonance,

and by having himself crowned as Shah (i.e. king). The glories of Iranian history celebrated at Persepolis had actually been on the decline ever since the collapse of the Safavid Empire

Kayhan newspaper, 18 August 1979

Headline reads:

IMAM: WE MADE AN ERROR BY NOT BEING MORE REVOLUTIONARY

If we had acted in a revolutionary fashion when we brought the corrupt regime to its knees and tore down this evil barrier to our salvation;

If we had closed down the mercenary and corrupt newspapers and magazines and tried their editors;

If we had banned all corrupt parties and meted out just punishment to their leaders;

If we had erected hanging poles in our thoroughfares and gotten rid of the corrupt and the corruptors, then we would not have encountered the problems we are facing today...

I warn the corrupt elements still in our midst, wherever they are, that if they don't stop challenging us we shall deal with them in a most revolutionary manner as God has instructed us.

in the early 1700s, and Persia had entered the twentieth century as a backward backwater. Though the state was headed by an enfeebled dynasty known as the Qajars, it was effectively controlled by Britain and Russia, and its main resources – tobacco and then, crucially, oil – had been awarded by concessions to British corporations. A popular uprising produced some reform in 1905-7: a constitution (based on the Belgian model) which notionally survived until 1979 and an elected national assembly (the *Majlis*). Neither enjoyed much support from the *Ulema* – the country's powerful clergy, which was always nervous about the secular tendencies of liberal and nationalist politicians. The clerics themselves held sway over the intense spiritual lives of a people who were overwhelmingly Shia – members of the minority Muslim sect which believes that Mohammad's cousin Ali was the prophet's true heir ("Shia" is a contraction of Shi'at Ali, or "partisans of Ali"). According to their doctrines, the line of succession then passed to Ali's younger son Hossein, and after his martyrdom at Karbala (in modern-day Iraq), to a line of descendants which was extinguished at the end of the ninth century with the disappearance of the "Twelfth Imam."[40]

The First World War served to highlight the enormous importance of Iran's oil fields – "a prize from fairyland beyond our wildest dreams" as Winston Churchill described the concessions exploited by the Anglo-Iranian Oil Company. These were protected and extended by Reza Shah. He was a repressive dictator, much attracted in the late 1930s to fascism, but he did unite and to some extent modernise, or at least Westernise, this quiescent nation: to the concern of the *Ulema*, for

example, by banning the wearing of the veil and establishing schools for girls and sending bright students abroad to study. But in the end his fascist tendencies were too dangerous for Britain and Russia to risk as they hunkered down to the war against Hitler, so in 1941 they protected Allied oil supplies by invading Iran and requiring Reza to abdicate in favour of his son. Mohammad Reza Shah was a shy young man who had just finished at a Swiss finishing school and who was no match for a charismatic politician who by 1950 came to dominate the *Majlis*.

Mohammad Mossadeq was Iran's first, and in many eyes only, democratic hero. He was a doctor of laws from an aristocratic family who had served time in prison for opposing Reza Shah but was now the leader of the broad-based National Front, which demanded an end to the British oil concessions and a return to constitutional government by limiting the Shah's powers. He became a very popular Prime Minister, but outraged the British when he implemented the parliamentary will and nationalised the Anglo-Iranian Oil Company (later to change its name to British Petroleum), then the most profitable business in the world. It was a symbol of rampant and rapacious colonialism, paying little tax on its massive profits, which were extracted from the exertions of wretchedly paid local workers who lived in the company's slum housing, whilst British managers luxuriated in colonial mansions with swimming pools and tennis courts. The British Foreign Secretary, Herbert Morrison, blockaded Iran with gun-boats and insisted that its oil was British property. His efforts to "curb these insolent natives" (as Lord Mountbatten contemptuously characterised his attitude)[41] did not meet with Truman's approval, and Mossadeq was hailed by *TIME Magazine* as "Man of the Year" for 1951, chosen because he seemed the kind of politician devoted to the rule of law who might lead backward nations to democracy. His electrifying appearance at the International Court of Justice, where he defended in person his nationalisation of an oil company that treated Iranians "like animals" and had plundered their oil resources, turned into triumph when the court, albeit on a technicality, held in Iran's favour.

But democracy in the West proved a fickle friend to democracy in Iran: the British security services, unable to enlist the CIA to restore British profits, found a bait which quickly hooked the Eisenhower administration. Iran had a communist party – the *Tudeh,* which had fallen under Moscow's tutelage. MI6 played upon America's Cold War paranoia: "Mossadeqh is still incapable of resisting a coup by the *Tudeh* party, if it were backed by Soviet support" wrote "Monty" Woodhouse, the MI6 man in Tehran, to his CIA counterparts. His proposal for *"Operation Boot"* met favour with US Secretary of State John Foster Dulles and his brother, the new CIA boss, Allen Dulles. Renamed by humourless Americans *"Operation Ajax,"* it was implemented in August 1953 by Kermit Roosevelt. It took the form of massive bribes – to newspaper editors, clerics and army chiefs – and the fomenting of mob demonstrations against Mossadeq (whose belief in the rule of law was such that he naively ordered police not to interfere with the people's right to demonstrate against him). The Shah removed himself and his family from the country, leaving it to CIA-financed army generals to move in and arrest Mossadeq and his

government. When it was safe, he returned to a country controlled by his corrupted generals, backed by the US and Britain which justified their coup by declaring that Iran had not been ready for democracy. In fact, "Operation Ajax" had denied Iran any democratic future and implanted in the hearts and minds of its politically aware people an abiding hatred for "The Great Satan" (and contempt for Britain, "the Little Satan," which rewarded the US by allowing its oil companies a 40% shareholding in Anglo-Iranian). For all the self-congratulation (both Woodhouse and Roosevelt were permitted to write books glorifying their actions) history would demonstrate how counter-productive this 1953 putsch would prove.

The Shah at least spared Mossadeq's life: he was tried on trumped up charges by a military court, jailed and then released under house arrest until his death in 1967. His followers included the future Prime Ministers Bazargan, Bakhtiar and later Bani-Sadr, and the liberals who fought – and lost the fight – for a democratic constitution after the 1979 revolution. Mossadeq's photograph featured prominently on placards decorated by student activists in the street demonstrations that followed the presidential election of June 2009. Many clerics supported the National Front, although some who took CIA money were already opposed to Mossadeq because he refused to introduce Sharia law. One young Mullah who refused to join Mossadeq's coalition was Ruhollah Khomeini, who despised liberal democrats for their secular beliefs. He would, in due course, work out how to replace the rule of law by the rule of Shia jurists, and how to marginalise the *Majlis* by making everything it did subject to theologians, whose interpretation of the Sharia would become the law of the land after 1979.

After the coup, the Shah consolidated his power and built a strong centralised state, assisted by oil revenues that brought him – and a small upper class – unparalleled wealth. His arms deals were legendary (he bought more Chieftain tanks from Britain than its own army possessed) and he strengthened internal security by establishing the National Security and Intelligence Organisation, later to become infamous under its acronym, SAVAK. His obeisance to the Western powers inflamed the intellectual opposition – the Liberation Movement which had gingerly picked up Mossadeq's fallen banner. Mehdi Bazargan led its freedom movement at the head of a younger generation of Islamic militants – forerunners, in many respects, of the MKO. Their spiritual guide was a doctor of theology named Taleqani, who had been Mossadeq's most devoted clerical supporter. In contrast to Khomeini's theory of government by Islamic jurists, Taleqani would interpret the Koran consistently with democratic socialist ideals.[42] But both were in agreement about the corruption of the Shah's regime, and their denunciations inspired street demonstrations on 5 June 1963 which were brutally quelled by the army at the cost of hundreds of lives.[43]

Khomeini was briefly imprisoned and then expelled from the country. He made his base in the Shia seminary city of Najaf (in Iraq), where in 1970 he delivered a set of famous lectures on *velayat-e faqih* (the jurist's trusteeship – Islamic government). He utterly rejected democracy, and argued that political sovereignty under Islam resided in the *Ulema* – those learned in Islamic law. Ordinary people were required by God to live in accordance

with Sharia law as interpreted by clerics, who were expected to guide them until the Twelfth Imam eventually returned (he was in "occultation" – some form of hidden existence). Khomeini's theory was obviously attractive to members of the *Ulema*, because it gave them political as well as spiritual power, and its apparent orthodoxy was congenial to the mass of Shia believers who were used to looking to clerics for moral guidance. They were beguiled by Khomeini's teaching that Sharia law required particular care for the poor and oppressed – Islam, he insisted, not Marxism, would eliminate class differences and produce a just society no longer disfigured by the Shah's obscene luxury or his attachments to the big and little Satan. These beliefs spread beneath the surface, uncontrollably but unobtrusively, although some of their more radical exponents (like Ayatollah Montazeri) served terms in the Shah's prisons. SAVAK's attention, once it had demolished the old communists in the *Tudeh* network, turned to the armed resistance groups that formed in the 1960s and commenced their guerrilla struggle with an attack on a police station in Siahkal in Feburary 1971.

Most of these groups were Marxist-Leninist: the *Fadaiyan* (self-sacrificers) carried out the Siahkal attack and many more in the course of the decade, splitting after the revolution into a majority faction (which looked to Moscow and classic Marxist-Leninism) and a minority faction that refused to support the Islamic Republic. These groups were determinedly atheist, although an incipient anti-clericalism was put to one side whilst fighting the Shah's police state alongside revolutionary clerics. In prison, it was easy to sink differences with Islamists, although some jailed clerics (Montazeri, for example) complained about having to sit on toilets recently vacated by Marxist unbelievers.[44] There were jokes (much less amusing in later years) about how Mullahs farewelled Marxists at the gates of Evin Prison with promises to put them back when the Shah was overthrown.

These guerrilla movements which formed among youthful intellectuals in the aftermath of the unconscionable killings of the 5 June demonstrators were not original: they shared ideology and tactics with similar groups abroad – in Latin America in particular. But the heady fusion of Marxism and Islam that came to attract so many dedicated young martyrs to the *Mojahedin* was a distinctively Iranian development. It has been traced back to Bazargan's liberation movement, formed a decade after the fall of Mossadeq, infused with the teachings of two important intellectuals, Taleqani and Ali Shariati, who radically re-interpreted the sacred texts to argue that they stood for equality, socialism and scientific progress, and that they demanded armed struggle as an "historic necessity" to achieve these ends. To a new generation of educated teenagers (the Shah had at least invested some oil wealth in universal education) this had an obvious attraction: they could retain the passionate Shia heritage taught to them by their parents whilst embracing the class struggle and fighting the Shah's repressive state. The founders of the *Mojahedin* were students of engineering and law, who read Che Guevara, Debray and Fanon and paid special attention to a theoretician of the Algerian FLN, who argued that "Islam was a revolutionary socialist democratic creed and that the only way to fight imperialism was to resort to the armed struggle and appeal to the religious instincts of the masses."[45] With that grab-bag of principles

and an avowed aim "to synthesise the religious values of Islam with the scientific thought of Marxism" these new Shia Marxists prepared for martyrdom. It came rather more quickly than they had wished. Those sixty-nine students who formed the first *Mojahedin* detachment had just returned from a PLO training camp and were preparing to blow up a power station in order to plunge the Shah's 1971 Persepolis celebrations into darkness, when SAVAK struck. It arrested and tortured them and put them all on trial, with eleven leaders shot by firing squad after secret trial before a military tribunal, and the rest jailed. (Massoud Rajavi, a politics student from Tehran University who later became the charismatic leader of the organisation, survived with a prison sentence). The defiant rhetoric of the eleven executed leaders, as they courageously condemned the Shah at their closed court hearings, received a wide *samizdat* circulation. However jejune these *Mojahedin* theories now sound, they were enthusiastically discussed by students at universities and high schools, especially in the years following the 1979 revolution. As we shall see, most of the *Mojahedin* massacred in 1988 were arrested merely for distributing or possessing this literature after the organisation was banned in mid-1981.

In the intellectual ferment of the years just before and after the revolution, there were many shifts in ideological positions. Although a few radical clerics encouraged the *Mojahedin*, the conservative *Ulema* was overwhelmingly hostile to left-wing re-interpretations of Islamic texts. Khomeini himself, whilst welcoming allies against the Shah, said that he "smelled the distinct aroma of anti-clericalism" after meetings with Rajavi, who in turn found the Imam highly reactionary. The *Mojahedin* suffered its own ideological divisions as some adherents found that its Marxism made more sense than its Islamic fervour: many joined the *Fadaiyan* whilst others split and formed a Marxist wing of the *Mojahedin,* where they stopped praying and started reading the thoughts of Chairman Mao and further transmogrified after the revolution either into the *Peykar* Organisation ("the combat organisation for the emancipation of the working class") or the more orthodox Marxist *Rah-e Kargar* Organisation ("the worker's road"). These were some of the "leftist" groups whose members   were to become victims of the second wave of 1988 prison killings.

The 1970s was the decade of struggle between SAVAK and the militants. The Shah built new maximum security prisons on the American model, most notoriously Evin on the outskirts of Tehran and Gohardasht some thirty miles distant. It was the time of torture: random beatings were replaced by more scientific methods taught by the CIA or copied from General Pinochet, including solitary confinement, sleep deprivation, electrical shocks, mock execution and even an early form of water boarding.[46] The old-fashioned *bastinado,* however, remained the interrogators' favourite: all it required was that victims be tied to a metal bed or grille, and beaten on the soles of the feet with an electric cable. The technique had the great advantage of causing excruciatingly pain that was only exceptionally lethal: the highly sensitive nerve endings at the soles of the feet transmitted the shock of the beating through the whole nervous system. SAVAK used *bastinado* on newly captured guerrillas to extract information about accomplices and safe hous-

es, although even they did not use torture on peaceful opponents of the regime – a practice which only became commonplace in prisons after the overthrow of the Shah. Another SAVAK technique was the "public recantation," familiar from Stalin's show trials but capable of a new dimension with a television audience. This was to become a favourite of the Khomeini regime: its insistence that prisoners condemn their erstwhile comrades on prime-time television would manifest the sincerity of their recantations and it also served to promote their subsequent psychological break-down.

The last days of the Shah began, in 1978, when his tame press vilified Khomeini: street protests immediately elevated the absent cleric into the incarnation of resistance and of hope. SAVAK was blamed – wrongly, as it turned out – for starting a fire in a cinema in Abadan that incinerated around 380 civilians. The Shah's imperial guards massacred over a hundred protestors on "Black Friday" in September – an atrocity which served to unite all factions and classes against him, notwithstanding their disparate objectives. Even his US backers, somewhat sensitive to human rights violations during the Carter presidency, could not condone it. When in December the Shah in desperation turned to an old Mossadeq loyalist, Shapour Bakhtiar, it was too late: by now the martial law curfew was defied every night by a chorus of *Allah – o – Akbar* from the Tehran rooftops. The army was divided and the massive street demonstrations raised the chant "Death to the Shah," increasingly followed by "Long live Khomeini." The super-rich royal hangers-on had by now left with as much of their wealth as they could transfer to foreign banks. Bakhtiar ruled for 37 days during which he disbanded the political police and called for elections. As in 1953, the Shah fled the country and waited for the US to act, but this time there was no Kermit Roosevelt to engineer his return. Instead, on 1 February 1979, hailed by millions as if he was the de-occulting Twelfth Imam, it was Khomeini who returned, with a steely determination to introduce Islamic theocracy. As he told the nation shortly after his arrival, this was "not the republic of Iran, not the democratic republic of Iran, and not the democratic Islamic republic." Islam was not to be demeaned by the Western notion of democracy. Henceforth, it was simply "the Islamic Republic of Iran."[47]

It took eighteen months for Khomeini and his clerical colleagues, amongst whom Rafsanjani was prominent, to achieve this goal by thwarting and outmanoeuvring all their opponents. They were opposed by a significant conservative faction, which held to traditional Shia teachings about the separation of church and state, but the intoxication of political power soon overcame most doubters amongst the *Ulema*. The liberals, as in so many other revolutions, served as "useful idiots": caretakers who could not, in the end, take care of themselves, or of the democratic ideals that they forbore to impose by force. Bakhtiar went into hiding and was replaced by a "provisional prime minister" – another Mossadeq veteran, the 75 year old Bazargan. He did his best to rein in the revenge killings – virtual lynchings – of hated SAVAK officials, police chiefs and generals identified with the Shah's repression, but Khomeini denounced his proposal for open trials and defence lawyers as a reflection of "the Western sickness among us."[48] Khomeini was in charge – his authority was recognised by the

Revolutionary Council and the revolutionary committees and he was the idol of the masses. A constitution drafted by the liberal politicians was referred by Khomeini to the "Assembly of Experts," which re-drafted it to make him Supreme Leader, an authority superior to both the elected president and the prime minister of the majority party. His liberal and Marxist

Mohsen Khajehnuri, killed 1979

A senator under the Shah, Mr Khajehnuri was arrested in March 1979 and tried in September with two other senators. At the trial, the religious judge did not allow him to defend himself, or to summon his witnesses. He was shot by firing squad in Evin Prison in Tehran on 24 September 1979. He was 63 years old.

opponents were blindsided when his student supporters (reflecting the popular fury when the Carter administration allowed the Shah to enter America for cancer treatment) invaded the US embassy and held its male diplomats as hostages: in this "nest of spies" they found documents incriminating Bazargan by association, and his provisional Prime Ministership came to an early end. The hostage-taking served as a useful distraction from the crisis over the constitution.

In January 1980 Khomeini suffered a temporary setback in the presidential elections: although he used his position as Supreme Leader to veto the candidacy of Massoud Rajavi, the *Mojahedin* leader who had helped to topple the Shah but who had vocally opposed the re-drafted constitution and its incorporation of *velayat-e faqih*, the Supreme Leader had to suffer the election of Abolhassan Bani-Sadr, another ex-Mossadeq democrat. Khomeini asked everyone to support Bani-Sadr as long as he acted according to the principles of Islam, and such was his lukewarm welcome to the nation's first elected President. Bani-Sadr's first mistake was to go along with his clerical opponents' "cultural revolution," launched in April 1980 which marked the beginning of the end of political pluralism: universities were closed,

---

Farrokhru Parsa, M.D., killed 1980

Having served as Minister of Education under the Shah, Dr Parsa was arrested 6 days after the Monarchy fell on 11 February 1979. The Revolutionary Court did not allow her request to see the evidence of the charges brought against her even though part of her indictment states: "Based on other evidence in her file, it is clear that the accused has committed sins." She was found to be a "corruptor on earth." She was shot by firing squad on 8 May 1980 in Tehran's Evin Prison. She was 57 years old.

"un-Islamic" professors sacked, and clerically-organised vigilante thugs from *Hezbollah* ('the Party of God") organised attacks on the MKO and leftist groups.[49]

The Islamic Republic's defeat of its internal opposition by June 1981 can be briefly traced. President Bani-Sadr began well, showing genuine leadership in the face of a decision by Saddam Hussein, the Sunni Arab ruler of Iraq,

to declare war on his despised Persian neighbour. But the Islamists prevented the president from developing a power base in the army and built up their own dedicated armed force, the Revolutionary Guards. They replaced the old secular judicial system with Sharia judges, led by revolutionary radical Ayatollah Mousavi Ardebili. Women were sacked and attacked for not wearing veils, monarchists were executed and drug dealers lynched, and the stoning of adulterers began with the revolution's new judges throwing the first stones.[50] Backed by a propagandist media and patrolling Revolutionary Guards, Khomeini launched a verbal attack on the *Mojahedin* ("syncretic mixes of Marxism and Islam") and threatened those intellectuals who did not sever all ties with the West. Bani-Sadr was isolated, and eventually his only supporters with any armed clout were the *Mojahedin* whose ranks had swelled with recruits from schools and universities in the two years since the revolution. They clashed repeatedly with the Revolutionary Guards, and came out *en masse* for the elected President in a demonstration on 20 June 1981: a hundred of them were killed. Khomeini then deposed Bani-Sadr, who from his hiding place among the *Mojahedin,* called for a mass uprising. It did not happen, so Bani-Sadr and Rajavi together commandeered an air-force plane and were flown to Paris. On 28 June 1981 a massive bomb exploded at the headquarters of Khomeini's Islamic Republic Party in Tehran, killing 73 of its revolutionary leaders. The Republic's "war on terror" – especially on the *Mojahedin* and leftist dissidents – began in earnest.

3: Revolutionary Justice

The big MKO demonstration on 20 June 1981 and the bomb that blasted the Islamic Republic Party headquarters a week later set off a "reign of terror" in which, over the next few years of internecine urban violence, several thousand of the Islamic regime's youthful opponents, many of them high school students, would be gunned down, or executed after hasty trials, whilst *Mojahedin* terrorist reprisals would take their toll of Islamic judges, officials and Revolutionary Guards. Responsibility for the 28 June bombing is still uncertain: Khomeini blamed the *Mojahedin,* who were not averse to the accusation (describing the bombing as a "natural and necessary reaction to the regime's atrocities") although the first suspects were old SAVAK royalists and, years later, agents from Iraq.[51] The war against Iraq continued and created an atmosphere in which few were prepared to extend mercy to fifth columnists. From this point – June 1981 – the tensions between the forces that had overthrown the Shah emerged with bloodthirsty intensity. Khomeini beat his breast and blamed himself for tolerating the *Mojahedin* for two and a half years, during which they had spread their propaganda so effectively in the schools and universities: he called upon the moderates who had supported Bazargan to separate themselves from these Muslim deviationists whom he called "hypocrites" (*Monafeqin* – this label stuck) because they did not really believe in God: "they consider the afterlife to be here in this world."[52] (The label "hypocrites" was not merely an insult, but a Koranic term of deep and ominous significance: an entire chapter of the holy book (the 63rd) was devoted to exposing their perfidy, and centuries-old principles of Islamic jurisprudence established that they were liable to earthly punishment as well as divine retribution.) He appealed to the nation to support his policy of mass arrests and execution, and summary justice dispensed in

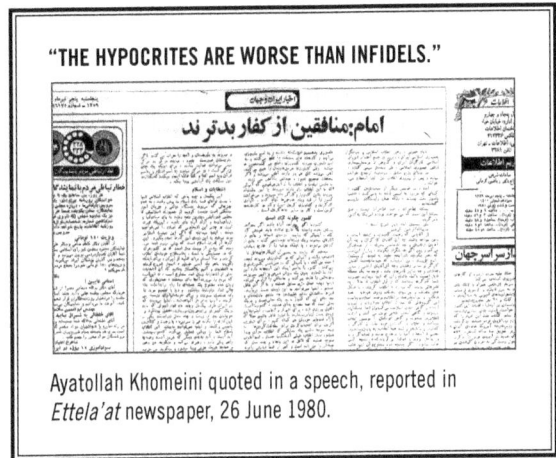

"THE HYPOCRITES ARE WORSE THAN INFIDELS."

Ayatollah Khomeini quoted in a speech, reported in *Ettela'at* newspaper, 26 June 1980.

the streets by Revolutionary Guards: "He who goes into streets armed and threatens people does not even have to kill anyone. Islam has ordained his fate. It has specified the punishment of [those] who scare believers and you surely know what it is."[53]

The Supreme Leader shed tears at the memory of his close friend Ayatollah Beheshti, the most notable casualty of the 28 June bombing, and promulgated Beheshti's theory that it was impossible to co-exist with 'warriors against God' (*mohareb*) a category which, according to

Rafsanjani, included all Marxist groups, Kurds and "hypocrites" i.e. "the so-called leftist Muslims or psuedo-Muslims with leftist tendencies who pray or fast and are regarded by their families as Muslims but who are hypocrites waging war against true believers and are no different from the Marxists." [54] At this point, the regime had not moved formally against the Marxist

---

Hojatoleslam Ali Akbar Hashemi Rafsanjani on the *Mojahedin Khalq* Organization

> ج – من رهبران این سازمان را که چهارم خرداد سالگرد شهادتشان است، از نزدیک ندیدم و هیچ وقت هم مستقیماً با آنها صحبت نکردم؛ اما از همان روزهای اول، به قسمتی از نتیجه، کارشان که همان ایدئولوژی باشد – و هنوز هم از آن دست برنداشته‌اند – اعتراض داشتم. پایه اصلی این انحراف را سازمان، از همان ابتدا گذاشت و کتابهای اصلی آنها – که حتی جوری است که اخیراً هم اینها ترویج شان نمی‌کنند – کاملاً براساس التقاط بین مارکسیسم و اسلام نوشته شد. من که خود آنها را ندیدم، ولی کسانی که آشنایی بیشتری

Excerpt from a speech published in the *Jomhuri Eslami* newspaper, 25 May 1981.

"I did not meet the leaders of this organization who were martyred on May 25 [1972]. I never spoke to them directly. However, from early on, I objected to their ideology—an ideology that they are still clinging to. Their misguided approach is rooted in the founding of the organization. Their main books, which they themselves are no longer promoting, were written for the purpose of creating an amalgam of Islam and Marxism."

---

groups that still supported it – *Tudeh* and the FKO (Majority) – but they had been warned. As for the liberals who once supported Mossadeq, they were infidels because of their loose morality, their contacts with the West, their opposition to the Islamisation of criminal and other laws and their social programmes.

The Friday sermons in this period set the ideological scene for the regime's approach to the punishment of political and religious deviation. Rafsanjani, who was Speaker of Parliament, in his sermon in October 1981 made a brutal call to exterminate the hypocritical warriors against God: "they must be killed, hanged, have their hands and feet cut off and be segregated from society." It fell to the religious judge to adopt one of these courses laid down by verse 5:33 of the Koran, because although 5:34 recognised that no punishment was due to those who repented, the *Mojahedin* had proved themselves to be incapable of reform after two and a half years of governmental effort. Their newspapers also achieved a high circulation, especially among schoolchildren. "Now they have turned into champions of human rights and accuse us of aggression for rightfully executing them!" Rafsanjani fumed. "As decreed by the Koran we have decided to eradicate the armed hypocrites." [55] Many were executed in this period for terrorist offences.

A few weeks later the religious judge who headed the Islamic Revolutionary Tribunals, Ayatollah Mohammadi Gilani, warned of a strict interpretation of the Sharia for religious rebellion. Death was the punishment for male apostates (i.e. those born into a family of practising Muslims who renounced Islam) and their repentance could not be accepted. But female Muslims and "innate" apostates (i.e. those not born into a Muslim family) were not to be sentenced to death: their "repentance" could be accepted if, after corporal punishment, they agreed to pray. [56] Again, this was drawn not from the Koran itself, which specifies no earthly punishment for apostates, but from conservative Shia jurisprudence that dated back to the tenth and eleventh centuries. [57] As for torture, Ayatollah Mohammadi Gilani assured the nation that religious punishment which is essentially torture is not torture because it is Islamic, explaining that at Evin Prison there were no breaches of Islamic rules: the floggings by cable on the soles of the feet were *tazir* (discretionary punishments permissible under Islamic jurisprudence).[58] Such treatment was mercilessly applied to most of those arrested during the years following 1981. As we shall see, even harsher beatings were meted out to left-wing "innate apostates" to force them to pray during the second wave of prison executions in 1988.

The authorities – the Ministry of Intelligence (which kept tabs on subversion) and the revolution's prosecutors – repeatedly asserted "we have no political prisoners in our courts. These are terrorists, conspirators, traitors and savages who will be prosecuted in an Islamic court, dealt with by Islamic laws, and punished accordingly."[59] Punishment was dispensed in prison by revolutionary courts headed by a religious judge appointed by Khomeini himself – in Tehran, this was Hossein Ali Nayyeri. The Shah's secular judiciary had been sacked (or had fled) shortly after the revolution and the Bar Association (an oasis of independence) had been disbanded because the concept of a defence attorney had been described by the Supreme Leader as a "Western absurdity."[60] The Justice Ministry insisted upon seminary training in Sharia for all magistrates.

In the initial shakedown period, from February to August 1979, death sentences were regularly imposed on drug dealers, homosexuals, prostitutes, SAVAK members and other officials of the Shah, who were condemned after short and usually secret hearings for "sowing corruption on earth." The list of executions soon expanded to include Kurds, Turkomans, Arab Iranians, and activists from various political groups who opposed the new

constitution or the Cultural Revolution. After the events of June 1981 – i.e. the *Mojahedin* demonstrations and the bombing of the Islamic Republic Party's headquarters – several thousand "hypocrites," many of them high-school and college students, were arrested and held in the prisons in which some had recently been incarcerated under the Shah. Those who

Ladan Bayani, killed 1981

A medical student at Tabriz Universty, Ms Bayani was last seen on 28 June 1981 at a safe house of the Red Star Organisation, a small anti-clerical leftist opposition group formed in 1980 when its members split from the *Peykar* Organization for the Liberation of the Working Class. For two months Bayani's mother visited the prisons of Tehran looking for her daughter to no avail. She learned of her daughter's execution on 3 Algust 1981 in the newspaper. She was 23 years old.

were implicated directly in armed terrorist activities were hanged after a short trial, while "sympathisers" (e.g. protestors or pamphlet distributors) were sentenced to jail terms of up to ten years. They were regularly subjected to *bastinado* before their interrogation; their trials were short and at Evin they were presided over by Nayyeri, whom they were to recognise again when he chaired their "Death Committee" proceedings in 1988.[61]

June 1981 marked the beginning of a period of revolutionary terror: its chief architect, Tehran prosecutor Asadollah Lajevardi, announced on 23 June (just two days after the demonstration) that 400 had been arrested and 25 already executed. Two days later Ali Khamenei (a previously undistinguished cleric who had recently become a member of the Supreme Defence Council) praised the people for "executing their enemies" so quickly. After the bombing of 28 June and over the following 9 months many "counter-revolutionaries" were executed – 250 MKO members in July 1981 alone.[62] These executions fed a vicious cycle: MKO terrorist attacks cost hundreds of lives, mostly of pro-government clerics and officials.

By the end of the year, Ali Khamenei had been elected as President. An editor of a government-supporting newspaper, Mir Hossein Mousavi, was nominated as Prime Minister.

In Paris, meanwhile, Rajavi and Bani-Sadr set up an opposition council (which also operated as a propaganda centre) denouncing the "medieval" regime and promising democratic freedoms of a kind that had never before been proposed by a semi-Marxist movement.[63] This helped to gather support from many socialist groups in Europe and, more dangerously, from Iraq, which sponsored their military operations and their radio station near the front lines of its ebbing and flowing war with Iran. This alignment was a Faustian bargain which gained the *Mojahedin* short-term advantage, but lost their last chance of mass support within Iran, where most families had men fighting in the patriotic battle against Saddam Hussein. *Mojahedin* guerrilla units in Tehran and other cities were frequently betrayed, most disastrously when Rajavi's wife and his second in command were killed in a shoot-out at a safe house that turned unsafe: their dead bodies were laid out in Evin Prison for prime-time television with the brutal Lajevardi cuddling Rajavi's baby son for the cameras. [64]

The regime was successful in inducing repentance from some *Mojahedin* prisoners, especially among youngsters faced with the alternative of execution or the spur of repeated *bastinado*. When the flurry of death sentences after the frenzy of 28 June 1981 abated, a new policy was duly promulgated by the Revolutionary Prosecutor. He announced that interrogations of MKO prisoners had produced a "miracle of the revolution," namely a widespread willingness to overcome Rajavi's brainwashing and welcome repentance. Henceforth, any judge convinced that a former armed revolutionary was sincerely penitent would grant a pardon. Those at liberty should therefore take the opportunity to turn themselves in and confess, because even those involved in military operations could now expect a reduced sentence.[65] This new penal policy had a less happy converse, however. Opposition to Khomeini was treated as a politico-religious thought crime capable of public expiation – but the flipside was that those who completed their sentence would no longer be released unless they were expressly repentant. By 1988, many prison wards were full of *mellikesh* – those who had served their sentences but had refused to recant.

The regime also became attracted to televised confessions, which helped to demoralise the opposition and rally its own supporters. (The technique's usefulness survives, as is apparent from the televised show trials of alleged plotters against the regime after the June 2009 protests.) They became all the rage after May Day 1983, when two *Tudeh* stalwarts were featured confessing to "horrendous crimes." This was the point at which Khomeini turned on the Communist Party and some of its Marxist-

EARLY VICTIMS

Vahid Hemmat Boland, killed July 1981

An avid math student, Mr Hemmat Boland was a sympathiser of the FKO (Majority), a Marxist-Leninist group that did not oppose the Islamic Republic. He was arrested while handing out leaflets in June 1981. During the twenty days Vahid was imprisoned in Evin, his mother's attempts to visit him remained unsuccessful. According to his sister, officials denied that he was in prison, insulted her mother, and threatened to arrest her. He was executed on 12 July 1981, at the age of 20. His family heard the news over the radio.

Shahin Dalvand, killed June 1983

Ms Dalvand, a member of the Baha'i Local Spiritual Assembly was arrested in November 1982, and taken to the Revolutionary Guards Detention Centre where on 2 December 1982 she was subjected to a mock execution as part of her initial processing and interrogation. Iranian authorities informed her that she would be subjected to four "sessions" in which she would be given the opportunity to recant her Baha'i faith and accept Islam. She was informed that if she did not sign a prepared statement rejecting her religion, she would be sentenced to death. She was hanged on 18 June 1983 at Adelabad Prison in Shiraz at age 27.

Shahla Hariri Motlaq, killed September 1982

Ms Hariri Motlaq [photo top right], affiliated with the MKO, was a secondary school teacher and a mother of two. She supported the revolution and Khomeini in 1979 and later joined the MKO. Hezbollah militias attacked her when, acting as an observer during the 1980 parliamentary election in a voting station, she protested against what she believed was a fraudulent election. She was hospitalised with a broken nose and bruises. She was detained for a short time in August 1981 but was released thanks to her husband, who was an influential official in the Islamic Republic. Her detention only strengthened her resolve. She was arrested for a second time in May 1982 and held incommunicado until her execution on 30 September 1982. She was 35.

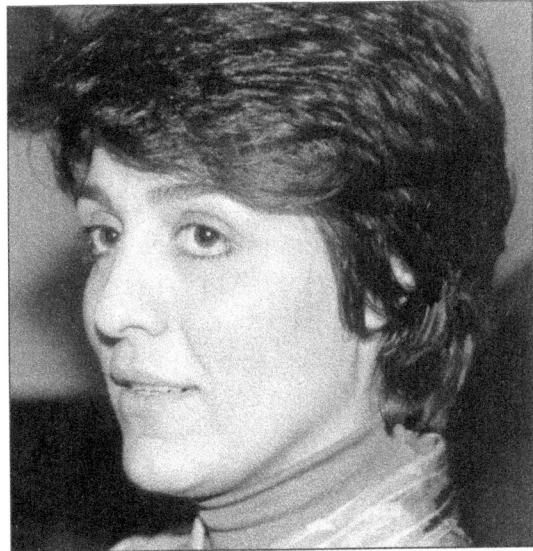

Latifeh Na'imi, killed October 1983

Ms Latifeh Na'imi, from the *Rah-e Kargar* Organisation, worked as a nurse. She was arrested in Shiraz in April 1983, and taken to Evin Prison, where she was executed by firing squad on 1 October 1983 at age 25. In her will, she addressed her parents saying, "I'm sorry to cause you pain. I hope you forgive me... Give my love to my brother and sister..."

Sa'id Sultanpur, killed June 1981

Mr Sultanpur, a member of the FKO (Minority), was a poet, writer, and play director. He was arrested by the Revolutionary Guards on his wedding night in April 1981. During his interrogation, officials demanded that he write a letter of repentance and participate in a TV interview, denouncing his political organisation and his own activities. He refused. The Islamic Revolutionary Court condemned him to death for waging war against God. He was executed in Evin Prison on 21 June 1981. He was 40 years old.

Leninist offshoots like the FKO (Majority) for having advocated a truce in the war with Soviet-backed Iraq. This served them right, the *Mojahedin* announced, because the Communists had "opportunistically supported – even spied for – his medieval bloodthirsty dictatorship."[66] This ideological spat did not help relations between the groups in prison, and the *Mojahedin* had to be separated from the Marxists. The latter were more readily broken, and in 1983-4 much of Iranian reality television comprised confessions from ideological penitents filmed in prison. Not that repentance meant release: of the 17 top *Tudeh* leaders who were arrested and appeared in a televised mass apology in 1983, nine were still available for execution in the second wave of the 1988 blood-bath.

The regime's true rationale for its war on ideological enemies began to become clear in the Friday sermons of speaker Rafsanjani. "Today, a person who disobeys the government is the same as a person who disobeys God and his messenger"[67] he explained. The statement amplified the Supreme Leader's proclamation that "There is always a war between Islam and non-Islam."[68] It was, for Iran's theocracy, a war not only against the satanic West and the godless Soviets, but against any perspective on the world that opposed its own religious viewpoint. The war against the MKO was therefore waged on grounds that were religious in principle, if political in result. The group was blasphemous first, and seditious consequentially: its members' basic crime was to be hostile unbelievers – "*moharebs,*" i.e. warriors against God. The point was crystallised by the Minister of Intelligence, in an important announcement which explained why the communist groups (which had previously supported the state and

opposed the *Mojahedin*) were just as evil: both Marxist-Leninist and Rajavi's brand of class-based Islam "confronted the political ideology of the state, denying Islam's pure (original) teachings and espousing an impure version of Islam... encouraging the society to seek the improvement of their standard of living and welfare, [as opposed to virtue and self-sacrifice for religious ideas]."[69]

These arrests of communists at last produced some sentencing guidelines. In February 1984, the regime announced that death sentences would be imposed on defendants who were in charge of training guerrillas or had delivered weapons or funds or information to clandestine military networks. Those who had paid membership dues or recruited or organised party members would be sentenced to 10-15 years; membership or financial support carried 5-10 years, while engaging in communist propaganda or cultural activities carried a 2-10 year sentence.[70] These gradations reflected the range of sentences that had crystallized in respect of *Mojahedin* prisoners, at least after the initial surge of executions in late 1981. The following years were marked by dissention over sentencing policy between Montazeri and his faction which favoured early release of repenters, and hardliners like Lajevardi who doubted whether any repentance by MKO members or Marxists would ever be genuine. As early as 1982, Lajevardi was denouncing pardons and extolling death sentences: "we execute because we care for humanity."[71]

Punishment for the crime of espionage remained in the discretion of the judge and usually involved execution after severe torture. Although there is no evidence that the Republic took any notice of the fact that Iran had ratified the International Covenant on Civil and Political Rights, and none of these "trials" and executions were carried out with the due process required by international law, it is noticeable that in dealing with public accusations in international fora at this time, Iran justified its executions of those whom it could not describe as "terrorists" on the grounds that they were "spies." This had a certain plausibility at a time of war when most of the opposition parties had some friendly connection with Iraq or with its Soviet backers. International law is notoriously unprotective of "spies" – a feature that is a hangover from the Cold War. But espionage was an accusation that could not be made against prisoners who had been no more than demonstrators or armchair enthusiasts for left-wing ideology. Another factor which explains the confused way in which prisoners were dealt with in this period was the understaffing and under-resourcing of the judiciary: the religious judges had little or no courtroom experience or training in legal procedures.

Prison conditions in Iran in the 1980s were cruel, and discipline was more severe than in SAVAK times. Overcrowding was extreme, certainly after all the arrests in mid 1981 and in 1983 when the arrests extended to communist groups that had previously supported the Islamic Republic, such as the *Tudeh* and the FKO (Majority). The prison guards were not the brightest (the best were needed at the front) and they brutally applied *bastinado,* which qualified as *tazir* – a discretionary religious punishment sanctioned by Islamic legal tradition. It was, however, torture, and was also applied in order to induce confessions prior to trial. Trials were delayed until any useful information had been beaten out of the defendant or (in cases where defendants had no or no further information to give) until they made an ideological confession (e.g. to "eclectism" – the doctrinal offence that Khomeini had detected in the MKO). Lajevardi, the infamous prosecutor of Evin, instituted a regime that was maintained throughout the 1980s and copied in other prisons. Inmates were blindfolded whenever they left their cells (if in a group, usually as a conga-line with hands on each others' shoulders). There were loudspeakers in all wards for announcements and government propaganda, and prisoners had access to state radio and television (especially when confessions were playing) and to the pro-government newspapers. This was for "re-education" purposes. A large group in every prison were "repenters," likely to inform on their former colleagues, although some of these recanters were mentally unstable and many were prone to suicide, especially after their confession had aired on state television.

Conditions in some prisons improved markedly after 1985, when Ayatollah Montazeri was put in control of penal policy. His officials permitted an increase in visits from relatives and ordered relaxation in some of the rules. In this period, the "mini-groups" (as the leftist organisations were dismissively called by government officials) were permitted to live in separate cell blocks and to organise (on democratic lines!) by electing representatives who would negotiate with prison administrators. Although maximum security restrictions were in force, they did not prevent "mini-group" members from maintaining solidarity or from contacting other wards by tapping messages in Morse code. The regime's prisons became a hypertensive microcosm of the political turmoil outside in the cities and in the war zones.

4: Countdown to the Killings

1988 began well for Iran's political prisoners, at least on the surface. A series of official announcements let it be known that "pardon committees" would soon be visiting prisoners to determine who was fit for early release. According to the High Judicial Council's spokesman, they would be headed by a religious judge and each would include a senior prosecutor and a prison governor. They would

Drawing by a prisoner of an open air cell at Evin Prison, section 209.

From the book *Memories from Prison*, by Sudabeh Ardavan, published in 2003 by Trydells Tryckeri AB in Laholm, Sweden.

review personal files and interrogate each penitent convict "to make sure that he has changed and is expressing regret and has genuinely become a supporter of the position of the Islamic Republic."[72] The committees would draw up a list to be submitted to Ayatollah Montazeri for a final decision: those who had previously displayed "tendencies to apostasy" would only be pardoned or have their sentences reduced if they constituted no danger to the public. Asked about *mellikesh* – political prisoners who had served their time but were still being kept inside because they had not repented – the spokesman admitted that they were treated differently than common criminals, who were released at the end of their sentences. He called on their families to use prison visits to explain to their children the error of their ways. At the end of January, it was reported that Montazeri had met the "pardon committee" at Qom and had instructed them that their recommendations on release should not be based on the length of a prisoner's sentence, but on whether he or she had truly repented.[73]

The regime had effectively imposed "preventive detention" on political prisoners, whose actual length of sentence became meaningless: their release back into society would depend not upon the expiry date of their sentence but upon their affirmation of faith in both Islam and the Islamic Republic. This *mellikesh* category were in most large prisons segregated from "repenters" (who were often informers and thus were assigned, as a result of hostility from other prisoners, to their own wards) and from the wards separately assigned (at their own insistence) to the *Mojahedin* and to the other leftist groups, although some wards (especially of women prisoners) were mixed. The classification had been confirmed in late 1987, when interviews and questionnaires were used to establish a prisoner's current political affiliation.

Some survivors have, with hindsight, seen this as a deliberate preparation for the August 1988 massacres. The "pardon committees" were three-man teams recognised as precursors to the Death Committees, and the increasingly bureaucratic classification of political prisoners certainly simplified the identification of the impenitent, and of those identified as *Mojahedin*. The National Council of Resistance of Iran claims that "there are numerous indications that the policy to exterminate political prisoners had been in the pipeline for a long time" although the only evidence it provides for this statement is the classification of political groups in late 1987 and some threats by prison guards in early 1988 to "settle scores in a bloody way." [74] (Lajevardi apparently threatened to lob hand grenades into the political-prisoner wards if the prison came under enemy attack.) I do not place much store by such evidence: "we'll get you one day" is exactly the kind of sledging that can be expected from prison guards. There was, however, a noticeably increased determination by prison authorities, aided by officials from the Ministry of Intelligence, to categorise prisoners in the year before the massacres, and to ascertain whether they were 'steadfast' in their group membership and whether any signs of repentance were genuine. For example, one ex-prisoner of Evin

recalls she was taken to meet the ubiquitous Mr Zamani from the Ministry of Intelligence in late 1987, who would say "This is a democracy. Why don't you tell me what is on your mind? What do you think of the Islamic Republic? Do you still approve of the position of the organisation you were active with?" [75] Reza Shemirani also recalls Zamani's presence at the Death Committee a year later, and a conversation with him after the massacres in which he admitted that mistakes were made, "but there was an order from the Imam."

The 2009 Iran Human Rights Documentation Centre Report has a section devoted to "Planning the Massacre," but it too relies on the late 1987 classification interrogations and inferences from the transfers of prisoners between Evin and other prisons at this time, and on survivors' impressions of increasing tension between guards and *Mojahedin* as 1988 wore on. It also suggests that Montazeri lost his influence in 1987, when hardliners regained control of the prison system. [76] No direct evidence has emerged after twenty years, from prison officers or from the factions within the government (including Montazeri himself) to suggest that these developments were part of any long-brewing conspiracy to massacre prisoners, although there are indications that at least since 1983 the authorities had come to view MKO members and Marxists alike as a threat to the regime, and the Ministry of Intelligence surveillance and classification of prisoners was undoubtedly an ongoing classification exercise related to their eventual disposal, whether by release or continued incarceration or by some form of "final solution."

It must be remembered that the government was focused on fighting the war with

Drawing by a prisoner of her cell at Evin Prison.

From the book *Memories from Prison*, by Sudabeh Ardavan, published in 2003 by Trydells Tryckeri AB in Laholm, Sweden.

Iraq, which at this time had begun to go badly. After Iraq succeeded in re-capturing the Fao Peninsula, it had launched Scud missiles: more than two hundred of them fell on Tehran and Qom. Popular support for the war effort had begun to ebb; there were even demonstrations in favour of "forgiving" Saddam Hussein and the numbers volunteering for the front fell alarmingly.[77] For the first time, public figures were permitted to appear on television to urge the acceptance of a truce on terms that had been suggested in August 1987 by the UN Security Council in Resolution 598. In March 1988, the Budget and Planning Ministry concluded that severe cuts in public expenditure would be required were the war to continue.[78] The families who visited prisoners passed on reports that the regime was in difficulty, a fact that could be divined even from government-censored television and newspapers. Political prisoners were cheered by the news, not realising that if the war ended on unfavourable terms there might well be a reckoning with those among them who were perceived as traitors. The weakening position of their protector, Montazeri, was dangerous to them as well: they could well be sacrificed in a factional struggle to succeed the Supreme Leader, who was stricken by cancer. Members of his inner circle did not want Montazeri to inherit his virtually absolute power.

Meanwhile, Iran had succeeded in persuading the French authorities to expel Rajavi and his *Mojahedin* from Paris: they relocated in Iraq, formed an expatriate fighting force and stepped up their radio propaganda. These developments gave heart to the *Mojahedin* in Iranian prisons and at Evin they organised hunger strikes and other forms of disobedience, in which defiance they were joined by other political prisoners, asserting their right to be treated with a minimum of humanity. This may have been the real motive for dispersing many of them to Gohardasht and other prisons in late 1987 and early 1988. The pardon committee, announced in January, does not appear to have been a ruse: there is evidence that some prisoners were in fact pardoned and released several months later, although its activities necessarily helped the classification process. Montazeri remained in public a stalwart of the regime and continued to be referred to as Khomeini's appointed successor. He was widely quoted in government newspapers in June and early July 1988 giving "guidance" to Rafsanjani on the latter's appointment to head the armed forces. He expressed the nation's condolences to the Supreme Leader when, on 3 July 1988, the USS *Vincennes* mistakenly shot down an Iran Air passenger plane.[79]

But Montazeri in this period was having his role as conscience of the revolution undermined to an extent that would render him powerless to stop the prison massacres later in 1988. His emphasis on repentance had been criticised by Lajevardi, who took the view that a hypocrite's remorse was worthless, while other hardliners warned that released prisoners

might go over to the enemy and would certainly require supervision by Revolutionary Guards at a time when all loyal men of fighting age were required at the frontline. They were said to have encouraged Khomeini to warn Montazeri that "inappropriate freedom, conferred on a few hundred hypocrites by a soft-headed and trusting group, has resulted in an increase in the number of explosions from terrorist attacks and robberies."[80] He was criticised by the up and coming Ali Khamenei, a theologian of much less renown, as "a poor judge of character." Montazeri had no love for the *Mojahedin* (his son had been killed in the 28 June 1981 bombing) but his political clout was weakened by the arrest of his daughter's brother-in-law, Mehdi Hashemi, in 1987 for leaking details of the Iran-Contra affair and implicating Rafsanjani in it. (The Reagan administration had secretly supplied arms to Iran in breach of the UN embargo, in order to secure its support for the release of US hostages in Lebanon – the so-called "Irangate affair.") Montazeri was kept out of the loop that arranged Hashemi's torture, secret trial and execution, just as he would later be kept out of the discussion that produced the massacre *fatwa*. His faction seems to have made a dangerous enemy in Rafsanjani. It must have occurred to others in the circle around Khomeini that if Montazeri could not protect his daughter's brother-in-law, he certainly should not be permitted to protect those prisoners who were trying the patience of the nation – and that if he tried to do so, the Supreme Leader might not permit him to inherit the Supreme Leadership.

At this time, there was a clear focus on apostasy as a crime against the regime. Since 1981, those suspected of being enemies of the

A Ward in Qezel Hesar Prison

1) The ward entrance from the main hallway of the prison

2) The guards' room, used to punish prisoners

3) The office of the guard in charge of the ward

4) The exit to the yard, used for exercise breaks and outdoors activities

5) The prayer room

6) 8 cells, dimensions: 5 x 2.5 m (16' 5" x 8' 2")

7) 4 cells, dimensions: 5 x 4.5 m (16' 5" x 14' 9")

8) Bathroom sink

9) 12 toilets

10) Kitchen sink

11) 12 showers

Source: Iraj Mesdaghi, *Neither Life Nor Death, Volume 4: Till... The Dawn of Grapes*, Alfabet Maxima Publishing: 2006 (Stockholm, 2nd edition, 2006).

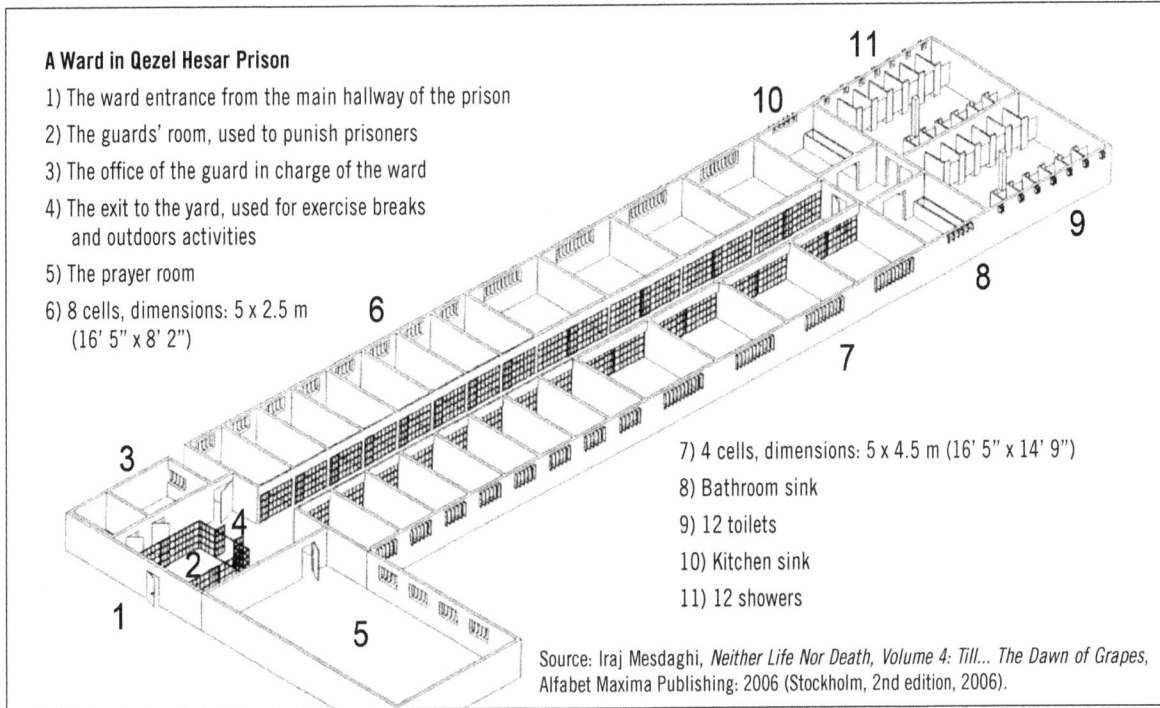

regime had been arrested for specific involvement in one or another of the "mini-groups" which had been banned by reference to its political ideology. Now, senior clerics across the country began to demand the arrests of "*moharebs*" (warriors against God) often without reference to their political grouping: they were out to eliminate any unbeliever whose unbelief they chose to perceive as an outward sign of political opposition. As the revolutionary prosecutor of Shiraz put it, "those who badly veil themselves, even unconsciously, are following the path of anti-revolutionists and monarchists... they are disrespecting the blood of the martyrs and will be dealt with radically, these boys and girls, and God's sentence will be enforced against them as corrupters and *moharebs*."[81] The more recent arrests had brought a new influx of "political" detainees into the

prisons and the authorities did not mix them with the old timers.[82]

The "repenters" were re-interviewed to see if they not only repented their previous political affiliations but were also willing to say their prayers. This explains why the 1987-88 interrogations and questionnaires directed to imprisoned leftists probed their religious views and their attitude to the *velayat-e faqih*, the Shia theory of Islamic government.[83] For *Mojahedin* prisoners whose former comrades were encamped in arms on the Iraqi border, questions were directed to whether they would denounce Rajavi and fight for their country.

The prison transfers and the classification procedures in late 1987 and early 1988 made the "final solution" much easier to carry out and although there is no compelling evidence that they were directly intended for that appalling purpose, survivors sincerely believe that they were straws in the wind. For example, one *Tudeh*-affiliated woman prisoner whose husband was a *mellikesh* (and later a victim of the mass killings) recalls that he and his followers were taken to Gohardasht in 1987 and badly beaten by guards "which shows that they had something bad planned for them."[84] Manuchehr Es'haqi, a former sympathizer of the MKO, said that he thought the killings were pre-planned because of the transfer of prisoners from Evin: "something like this had never happened before."[85] But he acknowledges that this movement could be explicable as a reaction to the hunger strikes at Evin. Shahab Shokuhi, from the Marxist-Leninist faction *Rah-e Kargar*, is clear that his transfer from Evin to Gohardasht with a large group of prisoners was "because the guards were concerned about how often we were going on strike to protest against the conditions. They decided to separate the prisoners in Evin to stop them from organising together."[86] This seems a more likely reason for the prison to transfer them than to set the stage for a massacre at some indefinite time in the future.

Other survivors firmly believe that the interrogations and questionnaires were a planned prelude to the massacres. Nima Parvaresh writes in his book[87] that "in February 1988 the prisoners in all the wards at Gohardasht went through a major interrogation. Later we realised that these interrogations were the start of the pre-planned massacre." But he admits that the questions asked "were not new and ever since 1985 the authorities had periodically asked such questions to assess the status of the prisoners." He accorded importance to this new round of questioning "because the way it

was carried out was new and distinguished it from previous ones and indicated its significance for those who asked questions," but in the month after the public announcement of a pardon process for political prisoners questioning would indeed have more significance. The questions were to some extent different to those later asked by the Death Committees. Both communist and *Mojahedin* prisoners were still in this period being invited to make televised confessions – no such invitation would be proffered later by the Death Committees.

The main source for the Iran Human Rights Documentation Centre (IHRDC) claim that the massacres were pre-planned was its interview with Mehdi Aslani in June 2009. A few weeks later, he was interviewed on my behalf and stated that the reason he told the IHRDC this was that questioning in the classification process was "more about ideas and not actions" (i.e. the probing of prisoners' religious views rather than the nature of their support for their group). But he accepted that at the time he was not suspicious because "the prisons had improved so much, the regime was weaker, the prisoners were stronger and more arrogant, the *mellikesh* were protesting – it is only later we realised that this had a particular significance."[88] Iraj Mesdaghi in his memoirs[89] says that Davoud Lashkari assigned colours – white to those who were broken and penitent, yellow to those no longer politically active and red to enemies of the regime. He also claims that on several occasions prison officials warned him "just wait until the Imam gives a *fatwa*, then you will be sorry for all you've done." But there remains doubt – which I explore further in Chapter 9 of this report ("Unanswered Questions") as to whether, prior to July 1988, the officials of the regime were determined to kill men and women they had corralled in their prisons for up to seven years since 1981 – torturing them, certainly, for information and to induce repentance, but not working them to death or overtly preparing a holocaust.

There is one curious story, from a chemical engineer whom I found an utterly reliable witness. An ex-FKO (Majority) member, he was being held in ward 13 of Gohardasht in June 1988 when a strange new group of guards appeared. They sealed the doors, turned on the overhead fans and circulated a gas which caused severe nausea and semi-asphyxiation. It was much worse than tear gas, and when the vapour escaped underneath the doors it made the guards sick as well. No-one died and the effects soon wore off, but it was suggested that this may have been an experiment – a trial run for gassing prisoners to death, the substance in this case proving insufficiently noxious. By this time, of course, Saddam was using poison gas on the battlefield, and the trial may well have been of a chemical weapon, which Iran certainly had the capacity to produce. When the killing time came, however, there is no evidence that it was accomplished other than by hangmen and firing squads.

Survivors have described to me the prison atmosphere and conditions in this period before the massacres, and the following quotations are representative:

In 1987 we held a hunger strike to protest against the conditions in Evin Prison, in particular about the lack of food. Two representatives of Montazeri came to meet us and interviewed us about our concerns, especially about overcrowding as we had about 50 people in each ward. Later the wards were opened up and we were able to move around the prison. This was a cause for great celebration initially but after a few months they began to separate us into different categories. I was separated because I refused to repent and in April 1988 I was moved to Gohardasht.

Affiliate of the FKO (Majority), not sentenced

1986 was the best year, but then Montazeri's people were removed from the administration of the prison and the conditions became much worse. In 1987 the conditions became so bad that the prisoners began striking all the time and fighting with the guards. Throughout that time I was in Evin Prison. However, in the fall of 1987 I was transferred with a large group of prisoners from Evin because the guards were concerned about how regularly we were going on strike in protest against the conditions.

Shahab Shokuhi, *Rah-e Kargar*, death sentence reduced to 15 years in prison

Shortly before the mass executions, around 150 (I cannot tell the exact figure) of different political tendencies were brought to the Jihad section (this section, meant to hold repenters, contained several workshops). It seems to me that Davud Lashkari, the deputy head of prison, had intentionally transferred those prisoners in order to prevent them from being executed. But also around that time, the conditions in the prison had changed. Prisoners had started to go on strike; they were bolder in expressing their demands. For example, those prisoners brought into the Jihad section refused to eat after they arrived. They asked why they were transferred to the Jihad section, because the Jihad section was known as the repenters sections, and they did not want to be considered repenters.

Hamid Ashtari, MKO, sentenced to 10 years in prison

In 1988 the atmosphere in society was changing. This affected the mood in the prison. Family members would tell prisoners during their visits that society was turning against the regime and that people were beginning to think it would end. Because of this, the prisoners became very self-confident and sometimes they would even attack the prison guards.

Shahab Shokuhi (see p. 35)

In 1986 Montazeri's delegates came to the prison and things improved. The insults and humiliation decreased. They even allowed us to obtain academic books from the library. At the beginning of 1988, prisoners in Gohardasht were more assertive, particularly the Mojahedin. They became more forceful in protesting against the conditions. They demanded the right to exercise together, for example. The Revolutionary Guards would still beat them but not as badly as before. They protested about the food, which had worms in it, and went on hunger strike. They were less scared than before. The MKO on the outside would send them messages that things were going well for them and that they would be victorious, and so their spirits were boosted. The leftists also felt happier that the Islamic Republic was weakening because of the war. One example of how the MKO was gaining courage was that they started using the name "The Organisation" as the group with which they would give their affiliation. Previously, under the regime of Lajevardi, they never dared to say that they were "Mojahedin." They had to use the word "Monafeqin" – i.e. that they were hypocrites – or else they would be very badly beaten until they said it. But by the beginning of 1988 they had plucked up enough courage to refuse to say the word for "hypocrite" – they said that they were members of "The Organisation." They were still beaten, but their spirits were much higher. Leftists, too, became bolder.

Akbar Sadeqi (pseudonym), FKO (Majority), sentenced to 6 years in prison

In the spring of 1988 before the executions, there was a period when the MKO prisoners were very active. There were a lot of discreet talks among the MKO prisoners. The news was that the Mojahedin would come into the country. One day some authorities that were higher in rank than the usual prison guards came to Ward 3. They asked the Mojahedin only about the organization they were affiliated with. As a leftist I was asked "Do you believe in God?" At the time, this was an important question for leftist prisoners. The new arrivals in the prison (I was arrested in 1985) were much more energetic about resisting the authorities' demands that they should pray. The older prisoners had become tired of being beaten and so had started to pray. I tried, but couldn't pray. Prisoners in our ward were steadfast and in constant conflict with the guards. One day a Revolutionary Guard said, "We are going to make sure your laughter stops."

Maryam Nuri, FKO (Minority), sentenced to four and a half years in prison

The Ministry of Intelligence conducted a full inspection of our ideas. They asked many questions and left us a questionnaire. It asked us whether we prayed and sought information about who in our family is praying and who does not. It took several hours to fill out. Later in that year there was a reclassification of prisoners. I was placed with the repenters.

Affiliate of the MKO, sentenced to 12 years in prison

In relation to the MKO, they were made stronger by the Mojahedin operations. The MKO troops

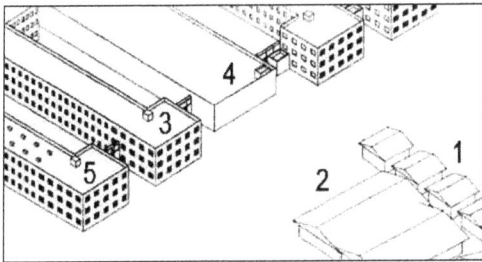

Gohardasht Prison

The execution location in Gohardasht on 30 and 31 July, 1988

1) Warehouses where prisoners were hanged

2) Room where the prison's generator was located

3) "Hosseinieh" of Hall number 2. [Hosseinieh is a hall, which used to be the gymnasium of the prison. Mourning ceremonies, speeches, and prisoners' "interviews" were held in this room. During the Monarchy, it was used as the canteen.] The illustrator remarks on this graph that he could see the Revolutionary Guards come and go, carrying ropes [used for hanging prisoners.]

4) Kitchen of the prison

5) Hall number 1. During the massacre, there were no prisoners here. They had been transferred to Ward One, next to the "jahad" section [where prisoners, mostly the repenters, worked for free in various construction and gardening projects.]

Source: Iraj Mesdaghi, *Neither Life Nor Death, Volume 4: Till... The Dawn of Grapes*, Alfabet Maxima Publishing: 2006 (Stockholm, 2nd edition, 2006).

not to retaliate against them. For example, when a PLO leader died, they observed silence and then chanted hymns. They refused to describe themselves as "hypocrites" and the guards would not punish them. At first they said they were members of "The Organisation" and sometimes they would push their luck and when asked their affiliation, they would say "The proud and respected Mojahedin Khalq *Organisation."*

Mehdi Aslani, FKO, sentenced to 5 years in prison

I remember the changes at Gohardasht in the spring of 1988: people were beginning to speak out on television against the war. The MKO demanded to meet their relatives in person and not behind the glass – they had confrontations with the Revolutionary Guards about this and about their right to exercise as a group. I was a ward leader and in this period I don't remember feeling that anything was going wrong. People were certainly being questioned about their positions but they were mainly prisoners that the regime wanted to release. A group of clerics came to see some prisoners about pardons although not me. I was an unrepentant Marxist.

Mehrdad Neshati Malekians, FKO (Minority), sentenced to 5 years in prison

These statements and many more in similar terms indicate that there was no premonition among the prisoners of the slaughter that was soon to come. Although beatings continued, conditions had improved and both *Mojahedin* and leftists in their (often separate) wards were in reasonable spirits, bolstered in the former case by Rajavi's little army and his radio station. They obviously had access to smuggled radios[90] and maintained group dis-

took up armed action inside Iran and took over a town for a few days in early 1988. During this period, there was the chemical bombing of Kurds and later the Iranian airbus that was hit by the Americans in the Gulf. The news of these events testified to the weakness of the regime on the war front. One example of the increased boldness of prisoners was the refusal of the leftists to fast during Ramadan. The guards, who would normally beat them for such an offence, provided them meals. The Mojahedin *prisoners would have rituals and the guards had orders* cipline, but they remained captive and were not by any stretch of the imagination acting as spies or enemy combatants. Nor were they rioting or planning a prison uprising: there were hunger strikes and they had regained a little of their dignity, sufficient to identify themselves as members of an "organisation" rather than to abase themselves by declaring they were "hypocrites" *(Monafeqin)*. There was no awareness on the part of the prisoners of their impending doom, and their guards (if they knew) gave nothing away.

5: July 1988: The Truce and the *Fatwa*

The crunch for Iran in its war with Iraq came in July 1988. It was a war that Saddam had begun opportunistically back in 1980, but after early reversals Iran had fought back with superior manpower and with missiles supplied by China and (secretly) by the Reagan administration. But public exposure of the Iran-Contra affair had forced a reversal of policy by Washington: it now supported Iraq and was pressuring Iran's other arms suppliers, including China, to desist, whilst Russia had been on Iraq's side throughout. The world looked the other way in 1988 when Saddam used chemical weapons: his victories multiplied and his long-range Scuds caused chaos in Tehran. Panic increased on 3 July when the shooting down by a US warship of an Iran Air passenger plane seemed to presage American aggression. UN Resolution 598, calling for a truce, had been on the table for a year, and suddenly appeared preferable to the prospect of an eventual surrender which would put the Islamic government in peril.

Rafsanjani convened a secret meeting of military, political and clerical leaders on 14 July 1988 which advised acceptance of the UN resolution and this advice was endorsed by cabinet and by the assembly of experts. Rafsanjani conveyed it to the Supreme Leader, who personally made the bitter, resented decision. "Accepting this [resolution] was more deadly for me than taking poison. I submit[ted] myself to God's will and drank this drink for His satisfaction" he told the nation in a rambling

"WE ARE WAGING A WAR OF IDEAS THAT IS NEITHER LIMITED BY GEOGRAPHY NOR BORDERS."

A speech by Khomeini in *Kayhan* newspaper, 21 July 1988. Special Issue, page 1.

90-minute broadcast on 20 July 1988. Three days earlier he had delegated the President, Ali Khamenei, to notify UN Secretary General Perez de Cuellar of Iran's consent to a ceasefire. "The fire of war…has gained unprecedented dimensions, bringing other countries into the war and even engulfing innocent civilians. The killing of 290 innocent human beings [in the Iranian airbus]…is a clear manifestation of this contention,"[91] wrote Khamenei. The President's letter was the clearest admission that the country was engaged in an international armed conflict, which meant that the Geneva Conventions applied to its prisoners, although this particular consequence was the last thing on the minds of its leaders who now had to justify the ceasefire to a people who had been whipped up by years of war propaganda to fight until death and who by now had suffered a half a million casualties.

"I know it is hard on you – but isn't it hard on your old father?" was the self-pitying note struck by the Supreme Leader as he told his people of the poison still coursing through his veins. He warned them against criticising officials who had advised acceptance of the truce for the sake of expediency, but warned that it was not yet a done deal – "we should be prepared for jihad to deflect possible aggression by the enemy." This was a prescient warning. UN Resolution 598 required a declaration of principle, but not a formal downing of arms until the parties agreed on certain conditions, so Saddam Hussein – ever the opportunist – saw an opportunity to bring down the hated Iranian regime with a final military push. Key to his misbegotten plan was Rajavi's armed *Mojahedin*, 7,000 strong, now grandly styled "The National Liberation Army of Iran" stationed on the Western border. Misled by fantasizing expatriates, Saddam thought that the people of Iran would welcome the *Mojahedin*

with open arms and strewn flowers, overthrow the tottering clerics and install "The People's Democratic Government" headed by Prime Minister Rajavi. So on 25 July "Operation Eternal Light" began with a Liberation Army advance, coordinated with Iraqi air forces.

The semi-trained *Mojahedin* entered Iran and set off along the highway which they thought would take them in triumph to Tehran. They captured a number of small border towns in the first two days, victories that even the state-controlled Iranian media, caught off guard, reported – to the massive excitement of all political prisoners, who imagined that liberation would soon be at hand. But when they reached the city of Bakhtaran, the Iranian forces rallied: in the absence of support or air cover by the Iraqi air force, Rajavi's troops (many of them women) were cut to pieces by Iranian fighters and helicopter gunships. On 29 July they beat a hasty retreat, leaving several thousand dead or else facing lynch mobs.[92] Many Iranian people, bemused by the ceasefire, were suddenly infused with patriotism and with an aversion towards a double-crossing enemy amongst whose ranks the *Mojahedin* could henceforth be counted. Saddam's opportunism, at the fag-end of this war, only served to prop-up Khomeini's regime. It was the trigger for his order to kill all *Mojahedin* prisoners.

It takes little imagination to understand the fury which must have inflamed the leaders of Iran in the last week of July, not so much at Saddam's predictable treachery but at the "treason" of those Iranians who tried to take advantage of it. Just who advised Khomeini to issue the fatal *fatwa* ordering the execution of all *Mojahedin* prisoners is unclear, although the acting Commander in Chief of the combined forces Rafsanjani and President Ali Khamenei, who had been centrally involved in the decision the previous week to accept the ceasefire, must have been key counsellors. His son Ahmad, to whom the *fatwa* was dictated – probably on 28 July,[93] was by his side. On that day, with *Mojahedin* victories ringing in his ears and the battle of Bakhtaran undecided, the Supreme Leader's anguish at this new dose of poison ran through a diseased body that his doctors had warned would shortly succumb to cancer. He and his advisors were Islamic jurists, custodians of a theology based on ancient battles in which enemies were killed without compunction, although they were also knowledgeable about the Geneva Conventions and the law of war (they had constantly accused Saddam of war crimes) and they would have been aware that international law has regarded the execution of surrendered or "quartered" prisoners as a war crime since the 16th century. There were more recent precedents: the Japanese generals who sent the allied prisoners on death marches at the end of the Second World War had been condemned to execution at the Tokyo Trials and the German soldiers who carried out Hitler's orders to execute the prisoners recaptured after their "Great Escape" from Stalagluft III were hunted down and condemned by Nuremberg tribunals. But the Supreme Leader and his acolytes deliberately disobeyed the law of nations. His *fatwa*, issued (ironically) *In the Name of God the Compassionate and the Merciful*, decreed:

> *Since the treacherous* Monafeqin *do not believe in Islam and whatever they say stems from their deception and hypocrisy, and since according to the claims of their leaders they have become renegades, and since they wage war on God*

and are engaging in classical warfare on the Western, Northern and Southern fronts with the collaboration of the Baathist Party of Iraq, and also their spying for Saddam against our Muslim nation, and since they are tied to the World Arrogance and have inflicted foul blows to the Islamic Republic since its inception, it is decreed that those who are in prisons throughout the country who remain steadfast in their support for the Monafeqin *are considered to be* Mohareb *(waging war on God) and are condemned to execution.*

The "treason" of Rajavi's army was by this decree imputed to the *Mojahedin* prisoners, most of whom had been in captivity since 1981. *Monafeqin* ("hypocrites") was the regime's official categorisation for the MKO. Although they did believe in Islam, it was the wrong kind of Islam as far as the state was concerned because its theology would accommodate democracy and human rights, and would not require total obeisance to its judge-guardians. So *Mojahedin* prisoners were deemed by this *fatwa* to be apostates: there would be no need to enquire whether they kept the faith, because their claim to do so would be the deception of the hypocrite. Since they wage war on the regime, they "wage war on God." The only question was whether they remained "steadfast" in their political affiliation before the death sentence, passed on all such persons by this *fatwa*, was carried out. It duly went on to establish the machinery for this life and death classification:

> *The task of implementing this decree in Tehran is entrusted to Mr Hojjatoleslam Nayyeri (the Religious Judge) and his Excellency Mr Eshraqi (Prosecutor of Tehran) and a Representative of the Intelligence Ministry. Even though unanimity is preferable, the view of a majority must*

prevail. Likewise, in prisons and provincial capitals, the majority views of the Religious Judge, the Revolutionary Prosecutor or the Assistant Prosecutor, and the Representative of the Intelligence Ministry, must be obeyed.

The Tehran "Death Committee" of Nayyeri, Eshraqi (sometimes replaced by his Deputy, Ebrahim Raisi) and an intelligence official (usually Pourmohammadi) went into immediate operation in both Evin and Gohardasht Prisons. There is evidence that its decisions

Fatwa issued by Ayatollah Khomeini in July 1988 ordering the execution of all *Mojahedin* prisoners.

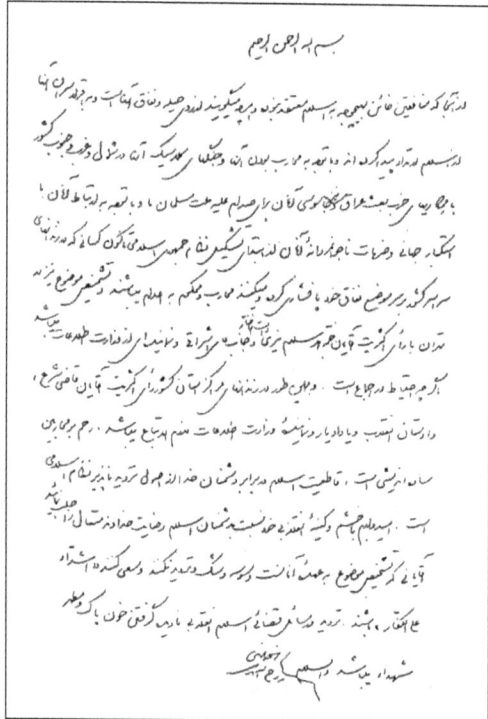

were sometimes taken by majority, with the intelligence official invariably holding out for execution. Eshraqi was, reportedly, the member who intervened favourably on behalf of

several prisoners from families descended from the prophet. It may not have been an altogether comfortable task for Tehran's Revolutionary Prosecutor, only a fortnight after he had been holding press conferences about the need to crack down on drug dealers and commenting that his office merely "continued to investigate" acts by the mini-groups.[94] Some religious judges appointed to Death Committees in the provinces had reservations, and contacted Ayatollah Montazeri for guidance – this was the first he knew about the *fatwa*, which concluded with this chilling exhortation to cruelty:

It is naive to show mercy to Mohbrebs ("those who wage war on God"). The decisiveness of Islam before the enemies of God is among the unquestionable tenets of the Islamic regime. I hope that you satisfy almighty God with your revolutionary rage and rancour against the enemies of Islam. The gentlemen who are responsible for making the decisions must not hesitate, nor show any doubt or concerns with detail. They must try to be "most ferocious against infidels." To hesitate in the judicial process of revolutionary Islam is to ignore the pure and holy blood of the martyrs.

This was an order from the highest authority, and its existence has not been denied, although the regime has not made any direct statement on the subject. During the 2009 election campaign Mir Hossein Mousavi replied to questions about his involvement in the massacres with a standard response that as he was the head of the civil administration he had nothing to do with them.[95] Another opposition figure, ex-President Khatami said that he and his fellow reformists should not have remained silent about this "tragedy" but was not forthcoming further. However, some corroboration was accidentally provided in 2004 by the Secretary of the Islamic Motalefeh Party, in an interview with a student newspaper about Lajevardi, the brutal prosecutor of Evin, who had been "martyred" (i.e. assassinated) on the 10th anniversary of the massacres by the *Mojahedin*. He admitted that Lajevardi's hardline conduct in the prisons had been opposed by Montazeri, but the former had been vindicated by the Supreme Leader: "With his decree regarding the *Monafeqin* prisoners after the *Mersad* operation the Imam demonstrated his displeasure at the lax attitude of the judiciary towards the *Monafeqin* and the pardon policy it was implementing... of course the content of this decree is of a sensitive nature and it cannot be discussed here..."[96]

On the day it was issued, it was communicated to senior figures who needed to be involved in its implementation, most notably to Ayatollah Mousavi Ardebili, Head of the High Judicial Council. This jurist was so concerned that he immediately telephoned the Imam's son Ahmad, seeking clarification and – so it would seem from his three questions – some limitation in its dragnet language and extra-legal operation. He asked:

1) Whether it was only for those *Mojahedin* in prison who had already been sentenced to death, but who had not yet been executed and were not repentant (on this interpretation, as so limited, it would not have been unlawful) or did it condemn to execution "those who have not yet been tried?"

2) Did it condemn to death the *Mojahedin* who had already been tried and given a specific jail sentence by a religious judge which they were currently serving?

3) In reviewing the status [i.e. the classification] of particular *Mojahedin* prisoners, was it necessary to refer their case files to the "independent judiciary" in provincial capitals or could the Death Committees act autonomously?

These questions were conveyed in writing to the Supreme Leader, who gave this chilling clarification:

In all the above cases, if the person at any stage or at any time maintains his position on supporting the Monafeqin, *the sentence is execution. Annihilate the enemies of Islam immediately. As regards the case files, use whichever criterion speeds up the implementation of the verdict.*

There could be no going back, and the very next day – 29 July – the implementation measures began. The prisons were put on lockdown, with all family visits cancelled and radios and televisions removed from wards. The Death Committee hearings commenced. Meanwhile in Qom, Ayatollah Montazeri heard of the *fatwa* from clerics distressed at the prospect of having to carry it out, and made a desperate attempt to have it reversed. He wrote a letter to Khomeini which pointed out that "it was in complete disregard for all judicial standards and rulings." Montazeri began by accepting that summary executions of the *Mojahedin* soldiers after the heat of the battle were inevitable, but then spelled out nine reasons why the cold-blooded killing of serving prisoners was distressing for religious judges and would be unconscionable, unlawful and counter-productive:

1) Under present circumstances it will be perceived as an act of vengeance and a vendetta.

2) It will distress and aggrieve many families, even those who are pious and revo-

lutionary, and they will turn their backs on the regime.

3) Many of the prisoners are really repentant but would not be treated as such by the by the more intransigent officials.

4) Due to the invasion, and pressures from Saddam and the hypocrites, we appear on the defensive and the international media and many international personalities have come to our support. It is not expedient for you or the regime to change this by an action that will encourage negative propaganda against us.

5) To execute people who have been sentenced by our courts to punishments short of execution, without any fresh court process, completely disregards all judicial standards and rulings and will not reflect well on the regime.

6) Our judicial officials, prosecutors and intelligence officials are not perfect and certainly not as learned as Chief Justice Ardebili: mistakes and decisions will be numerous. Under the *fatwa*, many people who are innocent or have committed only minor transgressions can be executed. In such an important matter, nothing should be left to chance.

7) So far we have not benefited from our own violence: it only increases enemy propaganda and increases the appeal of the hypocrites and anti-revolutionaries. So it is appropriate to use mercy and kindness for a while, as this will be attractive to many people.

8) If you will not reverse the *fatwa*, then at least issue a clarification that any decision should be based on consensus, and not on majority vote and that women

prisoners must be spared, especially those with children.

9) The executions of several thousand prisoners in a few days will not have a positive impact and will not be free of mistakes.

"It is far better for an Imam to err in clemency than to err in punishment" was Montazeri's final message, citing a holy text. But Khomeini was deaf to any appeal for mercy. The *fatwa* was not recalled, and the only effect of Montazeri's intervention was to set the seal on his own dismissal (Khomeini sacked him as successor a few months later, pointing out that "the responsibility [of the position] requires more endurance than you have shown"[97]). It does, however, seem to have persuaded the regime that the document should be kept a state secret. As if to provide cover – probably in order to provide cover – Mousavi Ardebili put the law courts on unscheduled vacation and announced in his sermon at the next Friday prayers (on 5 August):

> *The judiciary is under a lot of pressure from public opinion; the public is asking why we even put them [the* Mojahedin*] on trial and why we are not executing them.*[98]

By this time they were being executed, almost without exception. His public sermon alerted those who read between its lines: nobody was actually being put on trial, because "public opinion," as divined by the regime, was being respected. The families began to panic and Amnesty International issued its first Urgent Action a few weeks later.[99] The leftwing prisoners were permitted to hear the sermon over loudspeaker in their segregated wards and suddenly the strange actions and sounds they had noticed in their prisons over the previous week made a certain appalling sense

6: The First Wave

First they came for the *Mojahedin* to the wards in which they – the steadfast – had been segregated.[100] The prisoners were in a state of jubilation: their televisions had been confiscated before news of the defeat of Rajavi's army had come through, and they were still exalting at the ceasefire and the subsequent *Forugh Javidan* (i.e. "Eternal Light") invasion, which they had interpreted as heralding the regime's fall. They were at this point in no psychological state to renounce their political faith: they were flush with the possibility of victory. When they were taken out of their cells blindfolded, to answer questions from a delegation, some actually thought they were going before a pardon committee. It certainly was not a court, in any sense of that word. In most cases Nayyeri needed to ask only one question: "What is your affiliation?" The proud prisoners would reply "*Mojahedin*," scorning the regime's derisive appellation "*Monafeqin*" or even their own defensive euphemism, "The Organisation," which they had felt confident enough to use over the past few months. But those who gave the honest answer were immediately sent outside to join the queue that led to whatever makeshift gallows had been put in place.[101] In Gohardasht six nooses were dangling at the foot of the Hosseinieh auditorium stage, whilst at Evin they were despatched in a lecture hall or from nooses attached to the lowered – then raised – arm of a mobile crane. (Hanging in Iran is traditionally carried out by "stringing up" rather than "the drop" down a trap door:

strangulation takes more time and consciousness remains for longer.)

Any who gave the politically correct reply ("*Monafeqin*") survived while their files were checked and they were required to answer further questions. Would they be prepared to

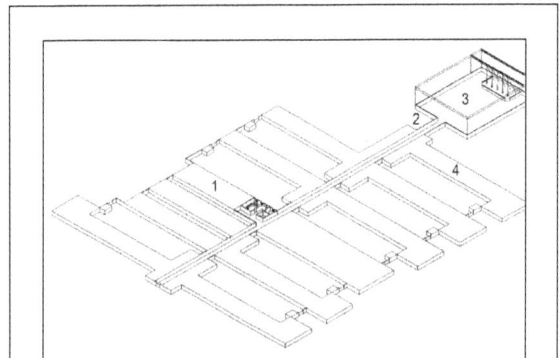

Ground Floor of Gohardasht Prison

1) Administrative Office where the trials took place
2) The hallway of death
3) The Hosseinieh were the executions took place
4) Cells where the prisoners were informed of their own execution verdict and were told to write down their wills

Source: Iraj Mesdaghi, *Neither Life Nor Death, Volume 4: Till... The Dawn of Grapes*, Alfabet Maxima Publishing: 2006 (Stockholm, 2nd edition, 2006).

inform on erstwhile prison comrades? To identify fake repenters? To go on television and renounce Rajavi? To fight against his liberation army? To form the advance guard that had to clear a path through Iraqi minefields? To hang a former comrade who remained steadfast? Those few who managed to answer in ways that discharged the heavy burden of proof laid

Mehrdad Ashtari

Affiliated with MKO, Mr Ashtari was arrested, without a warrant, by Revolutionary Guards in the Narmak neighbourhood of Tehran on 5 October 1981. In 1982, Mr Ashtari was sentenced to ten years in prison, but he was executed in Gohardasht Prison approximately eight years after being imprisoned on 6 August 1988 at the age of 28. The prison authorities did not disclose the location of his burial to his family, who later found out that he was buried in a mass grave at the Khavaran cemetery.

Translation of verdict

[Emblem of the Islamic Republic of Iran]
Islamic Republic of Iran
The Revolutionary Prosecution Office of Tehran Province

Date: 13 April 1982
No. 11360/9/2

Warden

Regarding prisoner: Mehrdad Ashtari, son of Nezam Ali

The abovementioned prisoner was sentenced, by Branch One of the Islamic Revolutionary Court of Tehran Province on 11 April 1982, to 10 years imprisonment, and his sentence will be completed on 28 September 1991. It is required that one day prior to his release, the prison administration office contact the archives in order for him to be released.
This copy is equivalent to that of the original document.

Assistant Prosecutor
Archives of the Prosecution Office of Tehran Province
[signature]

Two young activists were arrested at almost the same age and sentenced to similar prison terms. One was re-tried and executed (right); the other was never taken to court for a second trial and survived (below).

Seifollah Moni'eh

Arrested in Tehran around September 1981 at the age of 17, Mr Moni'eh was affiliated with MKO. He was sentence to 12 years imprisonment; 8 years to be served in prison and 4 years suspended imprisonment which meant he would be released but if he were involved in any political activities he would be rearrested. He was released in 1989, and left Iran in 1998.

Translation of verdict

[Emblem of the Islamic Republic of Iran]
Islamic Republic of Iran
The Revolutionary Prosecution Office of Tehran Province

Date: 2 February 1983
No. 11835/2/60

Warden

Regarding prisoner: Seifollah Moni'eh, son of Bayram

The abovementioned prisoner was sentenced, by Branch [number unknown] of the Islamic Revolutionary Court of Tehran Province on 14 January 1983, to 8 years imprisonment and 4 years suspended imprisonment, and his sentence will be completed on 12 October 1989. It is required that one day prior to his release, the prison administration office contact the archives in order for him to be released.

Assistant Prosecutor
Archives of the Prosecution Office of Tehran Province
[signature]

upon them by the *fatwa* were taken back to their wards. In ward 2 of Gohardasht only 70 out of 185 returned; the female ward at Evin had no returnees after 50 *Mojahedin* women were taken away for invigilation. Those who failed to satisfy the interlocutors, after this further questioning, that they had entirely re-nounced their former allegiance were directed to the execution queue, which was through the door of the tribunal at Evin and at Gohardasht on the left. ("Take them to the left" was Nayyeri's coded death sentence). In some prisons, they were ordered to make their wills and to dress in a white sheet that would serve as their shroud.

Few *Mojahedin* have survived to tell the tale of this first, atrocious wave of killings. Several managed to tap out Morse-code messages from their wards to other prisoners or to carve elliptical comments on the walls of their holding cells. On 15 August Montazeri estimated that between 2,800 and 3,800 *Mojahedin* prisoners had been executed in this first wave,[102] an estimate corroborated much later by the *Mojahedin* when it issued a list of 3,208 members identified as having been killed.[103] Other estimates by survivors are much higher, but these take the second wave of executions into account. Left-wing prisoners – alerted by Mousavi Ardebili's sermon – soon managed to deduce what was happening in the *Mojahedin* wards. Here are some of their recollections:

In late July 1988 we heard that Khomeini had accepted the UN Resolution for the ceasefire. We then heard about the Mojahedin *attack. All of a sudden the prison guards stopped providing us with newspapers and stopped broadcasting the radio news inside the prison. They cut off all communication between prisoners and the outside world. We tried to get news by communicating with each other using Morse code but no one had any news from the outside. But through this communication we soon learnt from prisoners in other wards that there was trouble inside the prison. We were told that the prison guards were coming into the wards each day with a list of names who would be taken away to a court. Prisoners in other wards told us, through Morse code messages, that people were being executed after their court hearing. We were told that people were being executed en masse by hanging them in the Hosseinieh auditorium, which was a large warehouse-like place normally used for prayer.*

Affiliate of FKO (Majority) (see p. 35)

In 1988 I was being held in Gohardasht Prison in the Jahad ward. I remember things changed in the summer of 1988. It was about the time we heard about the Mojahedin *attack. Some prisoners in my section were working in other sections of prison during the day, as mechanics or builders inside the prison. I worked as a carpenter within my own section. We realised something had changed when they were no longer taken out of their cell during the day to work. All of a sudden they changed all of the security procedures and the guards. All of the old guards that we knew were transferred somewhere else and new guards were brought in. There was also one case worth to be mentioned: One of the officers responsible for our ward, had told some of the prisoners that the situation was deteriorating badly and that executions were being carried out massively and that we had better not to antagonise the authorities. He also recommended that the prisoners should answer any questions in favour of the authorities.*

One day, during the mass executions, We were taken to the office of the section, wearing blindfolds and one by one. They asked me three questions:

Do you still agree with the Monafeqin?

Will you go on television and give a public confession?

Do you accept the validity of the Imam's orders and decrees?

I answered no to the first question and yes to the second and third questions. I was blindfolded the entire time and could not see the judges. I recognised the voice of Lashkari asking me questions.

Hamid Ashtari (see p. 35)

I was held in section 3 of Gohardasht, which was a mixed ward upstairs with about 120 Mojahedin and 80 leftists. We heard the news that the MKO had attacked Iran over the radio but then they stopped allowing us to listen. The executions began after we heard that the Mojahedin attack was crushed. We were taken out of the ward in groups of 20. We were blindfolded and brought a hallway where I had a confrontation with Lashkari. I was beaten and my blindfold fell off. I recognised Nayyeri, a judge I had seen during my 1981 interrogation and Naserian, a prison official and Eshraqi, who I recognised from newspaper photographs. They took me back to the ward and I was never taken to court. One official recognised me, because I had been in prison during the time of the Shah and so had he, and I had helped him then by getting messages from him to his friends outside of the prison. I was later told that he was able to return the favour by taking my name off the execution list. I was taken back to the ward past the line that was made up of people to be executed. This man who saved me, Ezzat Shahi, was present to advise the judges about the prisoners' behaviour. Shahi was a high ranking security official. He had also served as the head of the Central Revolutionary Committee

The people in my ward were taken for interrogation and execution in batches of 20. I heard that on 5 August, two of my sisters had been executed…I was told that because Nayyeri had killed my sisters, he spared my brother. Of the 200 people in my section, only 10 survived. I was taken to another ward, which overlooked the Hosseinieh amphitheatre and was next to the prison bakery. We could see what was happening by twisting a bar on the cell window. We could see that bodies had been placed in big black bags — I think they were construction trash bags rather than ordinary plastic bags. But because this was at some distance we could not see how many bodies there were. When the guards realised that we were watching they came in and beat us and put us in a different cell where we had no view. But we had seen large trucks that were moving the bodies, although we could not tell to where.

Ebrahim Mohammad-Rahimi, MKO, sentenced to 10 years in prison

They were very quickly killing everyone. To not miss anyone, they would come to our ward every night …and come into our room. They would look at our faces one by one and anyone they didn't like they would say "take your stuff and go." In those moments, one would feel like one is in the slave market and they were inspecting you as if they were inspecting and hand-picking their slaves. Some people were signed up for the infirmary and instead of being taken to the infirmary they were being taken back to the Court again. Nayyeri was there until lunch time and then in Gohardasht in the afternoon. The court started in the prosecution building; then moved to section 209; in the basement of section 209 was where they were enforcing sentences. Fathollah was one prisoner taken back to the court a second time and been asked to give an interview; he had three daughters and Nayyeri had told the Revolutionary Guard, "take him and show him." They took him to the place where the prisoners were being hanged. He saw five people hanging from the gallows. Then they took him back before Nayyeri and everyone in the courtroom was laughing at him saying, "Well now do you want to collaborate? Or do you want to go and be hanged?" They were asking the prisoners to write their names in large letters on their own hands before being hanged. The Afghans working in the prison were a channel of information for us. They were telling us that they were having to take several bags of slippers out of section 209 every night.

It was really hard to be taken out of the cells – each time a prisoner would be taken out he would be given two plastic bags: one for his belongings, and one for his will. The sound of plastic terrified us – if we heard it we thought it was a guard coming to take us out and tell us to pack our belongings

…

Zamani had played a key role for the Ministry of Intelligence in the killings…Zamani asked me for my views about the execution of my friends. I asked, "Why did you execute them? Even based on your own laws they all had sentences and many were about to be released." He replied, "These people had disrupted the order from within the prison and had endangered the security. Every day there was some fuss. If we didn't stand up and prevent it you would have gotten armed." I said, "Well, even if you are right, within the prisoners you executed some of them had been sick and had psychological problems and had never done anything wrong!" He replied, "Yes, I agree, in some places mistakes were made. This is normal when there is such a big action there are bound to be mistakes. But we try to minimise those mistakes." I then said, "But what you call rebellion were simple protests – it was a normal reaction to what had been done to us by Haj Davoud and Lajevardi." Zamani responded, "Yes, I have heard what they had done. But they are not our people. The stupid things that stupid people like Haj Davoud did hardened you against us. But they aren't here any more and they have no role. They were anti-revolutionary." Finally, I said, "but if they are not here any more, why did you kill all the people that were protesting these things?" He would not answer – he just said it was none of my business and that there was an order from the Imam. He said, "You go back and tell your friends: we will not accept any more protests. No

more noise about human rights against us – it has caused us a lot of problems. We want to release you, but we will follow you like a shadow and we will execute you on the spot if you do anything to reconnect with your organisation."

Reza Shemirani, MKO, sentenced to 10 years in prison (from the Didgah website)

We saw on the news that the Mojahedin had attacked the country. At that moment the guards came into the cells and took the televisions. They told us that there would be no visits, no television and no newspapers. All of our privileges were removed. We communicated with other wards in Morse code and heard that there was a court determining the fate of the prisoners. We also overheard the guards talking about it… they came into the cells in my section and told us to put on our blindfolds. Our section was mixed with both Mojahedin and leftist prisoners. When we were outside, the guards separated us and put all of the Mojahedin into a separate queue. The Revolutionary Guards said we would be asked some questions. They didn't tell us that we were going to the court; they told us we were meeting with an amnesty delegation. We did not understand the significance of this at the time. For those of us who were leftist, we were basically only asked two questions at this stage, whether we were Muslims and whether we prayed. However the Mojahedin were asked different questions. They were asked "Which group do you belong to?" if they answered Monafeqin (i.e. "hypocrites") then they might be saved. Those who answered Mojahedin were taken to the court to be executed later. We were only able to piece together these events afterwards. At the time we did not know how other prisoners were being treated.

In my section there were 72 prisoners and only

9 of us came back. The others were taken out to one side of the main corridor and were taken and were processed for execution.

Shahab Shokuhi (see p. 35)

This witness, a Marxist, underwent a different interrogation to the MKO members and was ordered to be flogged. He accidentally saw how the *Mojahedin* were executed:

The guards took me away to be flogged but they were not sure where to take me. One guard went to find out and then came back and took me to the amphitheatre. When the door was open he was surprised and asked himself 'why is it so dark and quiet?' He shouted at me "Stay here. Don't touch your blindfold until I come back." Of course, as soon as he left I took off my blindfold. It was really dark although you could see a little light on the stage. There was a huge pile of prison shoes lying at the foot of the stage as well as piles of clothes. I looked up and saw six ropes hanging across the stage. It was obvious that they were executing everyone. At this point the guard came back and yelled at me "What are you looking at?" I said it was too dark to see anything. Fortunately for me, it was now so late that the executions had stopped for the evening.

Shahab Shokuhi (see p. 35)

The following, incredibly harrowing account is from one who got away. Mr Ashough's story has particular credibility as he is identified by name in the Montazeri letters as the person who had escaped *en route* to the firing squad. He was held in Dezful Prison, formerly a UNESCO block (hence known as the UNESCO prison) and he lived to tell a tale that described the suffering and death of *Mojahedin* in one provincial prison near the war zone:

I was in my third year at university when I was arrested in 1981 after the big June demonstration by the Mojahedin. *I was in prison for two years and released ... I was rearrested in 1986 and I was sentenced to 10 years for being a* Mojahedin *sympathiser. I was taken to a prison that had formerly been a UNESCO office, so it was called the UNESCO prison. I was beaten severely by cables on my feet and went through various interrogations. They would start in the early hours of the morning and hit me on the head and on the feet. I was taken regularly before a religious judge, who, on being told I had not yet confessed, ordered me to be beaten until I did. This happened six times. They would begin the torture with* bastinado, *beating me on the soles of my feet but then move up and in between questions would beat me on my back.*

At the time when the Iran-Iraq War ended we were told that a delegation would come to the prison to decide about pardons. We had a television in the ward and a few days after the ceasefire it showed the Mojahedin *attacking and it seemed that the war was finished and the* Mojahedin *were coming into the country. Five days later, we were told that the pardon committee had arrived. They came and told us that all visits were stopped and ordered us to put on our blindfolds and line up. There were about 60 or 70 of us. These orders were confined to MKO sympathisers, and we were taken in groups of 8 to the main prison office. There was a religious judge called Ahmadi, an interrogator called Kazemi, and a prosecutor called Avai. Hardovaneh the Head of the UNESCO prison was also there, as was Kafshiri the Commander of the Revolutionary Guards. They asked me only one question: "would you fight the* Mojahedin *or not?" I tried to avoid giving a positive response by explaining that I'm not a fighter, I'm a nutritionist. But they kept pressing me: "would you go or would you stay?" At the end they discussed my case between themselves, and the judge asked me "would you walk through a minefield and be prepared to die for Islam?" I replied that I would die if it were necessary but I could not understand why it would be necessary to walk on a mine. There was then a discussion as to whether my name should go on a list. The Religious Judge did not think my name should be on the list but the prosecutor and the intelligence officer said that it should be put down. So I was put on the list; it was an execution list. Of the group of eight, two were exempted from execution – both of them had said that they would fight against the* Mojahedin. *That left six of us condemned to death.*

We six were then taken to join a line of about sixty others who had been placed on the list. We waited for an hour and then the guards came and told us to get our belongings as we were being taken to the city of Ahvaz. We got our belongings and took them to the prosecutor's office – a large room with a table in the centre. We were then told to write our wills and given ten minutes to do so. The interrogator, Kazemi, said "We are coming back in ten minutes and you must have written your will." They came back with ropes and tied our hands and blindfolded us and took us out into the courtyard of the prison where we were made to sit and wait. At about 1:00 a.m. some mini-buses arrived and we were placed in them. It was soon clear that the buses were not headed to Ahvaz but were going in the opposite direction, towards a military barracks. The buses stopped at the barracks and we were ordered to go and wash in a bathroom and to put on white clothes of the kind that they wrap around a dead body. The washing that we were asked to do is a religious form of washing that is done with dead bodies. There were lots of other Mojahedin *prisoners and there was a very tense and chaotic atmosphere. We could hear girls in the female bathrooms washing them-*

Foruzan Abdi Pirbazari, killed in 1988

Ms Abdi Pirbazari was the captain of the Women's National Volleyball Team and a MKO sympathiser. She was arrested in 1981, sentenced to five years imprisonment, and hanged in the summer of 1988 at age 31. Her cellmates remember Ms Abdi Pirbazari for her open-mindedness and tolerant attitude towards other political prisoners. She spent about a year and a half in solitary confinement in Gohardasht Prison (from the fall of 1983 to the winter of 1984). Authorities did not release her after her sentence term was completed because she did not denounce her belief in the MKO. She was executed in August 1988.

---

selves and screaming.

Kazemi was still in charge. I took a very quick shower and put my normal clothes back on – I was not prepared to wear the shroud. Several guards began to beat me severely. When I was on the ground Kazemi came up and said "take him and bury him as he is. Execute him as he is." So they took me to the mini-bus and told me to sit on the back seat. Everyone else who came into the bus was dressed in white and was blindfolded with their hands tied. I think that while I was being beaten up, my bonds had been loosened and I was able to free my hands. By this time it was still dark and everyone was tired including the Revolutionary Guards who themselves seemed terrified. Everyone was screaming. The prisoners were screaming insults about Khomeini. I was determined to take an opportunity to escape. The bus was going very slowly along a bad dirt road. There was a lot of dust because of the cars and buses and there was a lot of noise in the bus. I took off my shoes and squeezed myself out of the bus window. I then ran for my life and I collided with some barbed wire, so I was still within the precincts of the barracks. I climbed over the barbed wire, cutting myself badly in the process, and had run about 1km to the river when I heard the shots. They were machine gunning first and then there were individual shots. They came from an area in the distance, near the barracks, where there were lights. I had come from this area and had hunted in the nearby mountains, so I was able to make my escape.

> Mohammad Reza Ashough, MKO, sentenced to 10 years in prison

Mr Ashough's evidence that the Dezful prisoners were executed by firing squad after being ordered to dress in shrouds and make their wills indicates that local prison authorities had some discretion in how the massacres were carried out, and that Death Committees were sometimes split on whether an MKO "repenter" should die. It was Montazeri's complaint that death sentences were, as in Ashough's case, frequently passed by agreement between the Prosecution and the man from the Ministry, over the dissent of the religious judge. In another provincial prison, Shiraz, it would appear that those who disavowed the *Mojahedin* were sometimes put to a lethal test:

> *I was arrested in 1983 and given ten years imprisonment for being a member of the revolutionary Marxist group FKO (Minority). My trial took five minutes and came after I had been tortured by beatings on my feet and back to extract information. I was put in prison in Shiraz, where there were about 700 political prisoners, most of whom eventually declared themselves repenters in order to avoid beatings. In 1987 prison conditions improved when a representative of Ayatollah Montazeri came to the prison. Until then, praying was mandatory and you were beaten for not praying. This was*

ended when the representative came and his decisions upset the Revolutionary Guards, some of whom left.

It is my opinion that the killings happened hastily and that they were started by the Mojahedin invasion in July after the ceasefire agreement. That was when about 45 MKO sympathisers were called out and taken to the prison office to be interrogated. They were asked what they would do if they were released, and whether they believed in the Islamic Republic. They assumed that this was part of a process under which their release was being considered because the war was finished and the regime was less concerned. But then, these 45 people were taken away to what we later found was a detention centre run by Revolutionary Guards. Only one of them returned, my cellmate Abbas Mira'iyan. For five days he was so distressed that he wouldn't speak to anyone. Then we finally managed to get him to talk and he explained that all the others who had been taken away had been hanged. He had been warned not to tell us, but he thought that he had been brought back on purpose to see what our reaction would be to this news. He had answered questions about believing in the Islamic Republic and was asked "if the Mojahedin's attack Iran and we want to hang one of them, would you hang him?" And he had agreed. They had then taken him to an execution place and given him the rope to pull up and he had started to cry and say that he couldn't go through with it. Then they had brought him back but obviously he had failed the test. Two weeks after he talked to us, Abbas was taken away with another group and was executed. I believe that up to 250 of our prisoners were executed, most of them MKO.

> Jahangir Esma'ilpur (pseudonym), FKO (Majority), sentenced to 10 years in prison

Women MKO supporters were not spared,

although as a measure of what might in fanatical minds count as mercy, they were often shot rather than hanged. This was done by Revolutionary Guards who psyched themselves up by chanting "Death to the hypocrites." Fariba Sabet who was arrested in the spring of 1983 for her involvement with the *Rah-e Kargar* Organisation, was in Evin in 1988:

> *After I was arrested, I was taken to section 209 of Evin Prison. I was 26 years old, married with a baby daughter, and in the final year of an Agricultural Engineering course at the University of Shiraz. My daughter was taken from me and I was put in solitary confinement and given severe beatings with electric cables. Later my daughter was returned to me, and I was placed in a ward where female prisoners were allowed to keep their children with them. We had a loudspeaker in our ward and were able to listen to the radio news and we heard that the government had accepted the UN Resolution. But after the ceasefire the guards came and took the televisions and newspapers and books and we didn't get any more papers and the family visits stopped. Then they came and took four MKO girls from our ward. They guessed that they might be executed because they said frantic "goodbyes." One of them came back to the ward later and talked to other MKO prisoners who told us "they are killing everyone." At night we could hear chants of "God is Great" and "Death to the Monafeqin" and then we would hear shooting. They came and took more of the MKO women and they never came back. They would come each day and call a few more MKO so other prisoners would come and stand with them in the hallway to say goodbye. After a few days there was only one MKO prisoner left and then she was called and did not come back. We were in agonies during this period – we just walked round the ward and told stories to dis-tract ourselves. The MKO girls had all packed their bags to give to their families and we discussed how to keep the packages small in case big packages were not delivered.*

Fariba Sabet, *Rah-e Kargar*, sentenced to 10 years in prison

Communists and other leftists – often fierce critics of the MKO and not inclined to believe them – were at this stage mostly left alone by the authorities. Only gradually did the truth dawn about what was happening in the MKO wards. The following testimonies explain how sights and sounds, rumours and unguarded remarks by guards, and the writing on the cell walls, began to add up:

> *I was in the fourth year of my technology course at San'ati University in Tehran, and was an active although not armed sympathiser of the FKO guerrillas. I had been in prison under the Shah. I was arrested and tortured by beatings on the soles of my feet so that I would give information. After the revolution, the FKO divided into the*

Maryam Golzadeh Ghafuri, killed 1988

A mathematics student at Tehran University and a sympathiser of the MKO, Ms Golzadeh Ghafuri was arrested in 1982 and hanged in Evin Prison in Tehran in July 1988. Her husband, Mr Ali Reza Haj Samadi, was also executed that summer. Two of her brothers, Mohammad Sadeq and Mohammad Kazem, were executed in 1981. Ms Golzadeh Ghafuri is remembered as a "quiet, dignified young woman with a lovely smile." On 26 July 1988, she was the first prisoner whose name was called. She left the cell and never returned. She was 29.

majority group and the minority group. The latter thought they had to fight the Islamic Republic because they were against the people but the majority thought that because we approved of their anti-imperialism, we should have a critical alliance. I was a member of the FKO (Majority). I was arrested in October 1983. I was accused of collecting weapons for my group, and convicted after a trial which lasted about 10 to 15 minutes. I was sentenced to 6 years in prison and I ended up in Gohardasht.

On 29 July 1988 our televisions were taken away and newspapers were stopped. So were family visits. The guards would not let us out to have fresh air – we would keep knocking for them at the door but they would say "no outing today." We did not know what the problem was. We contacted other wards using Morse code and we discovered that they were not being allowed out either and their television had been taken. Each ward held about 120 people and had an assembly hall. There was a big one at the back of the yard behind our cells. There was a complete news blackout – the guards would not even take sick prisoners to the infirmary, although it was close to our ward and we had one prisoner who was really ill. But everything was hidden from us. One MKO ward contacted us to say that almost all its prisoners were taken out. Then there were only three prisoners left, who told us they had all replied to the question "Which organisation do you belong to?" with the answer "Monafeqin" (i.e. hypocrites). They said that 27 Mojahedin had been transferred or else executed – they did not know which. Because the MKO were notorious for exaggerating the news, we did not take their execution stories seriously. We figured that the absentees must have been transferred but we did not knw why the transfer took place at night.

We were in ward 3 and although it had no

windows we used hidden razors to cut holes in the blinds so we could look outside and had an excellent view of the assembly hall. Early one morning – about 2:00 am – we observed a big truck with its trailer negotiating its way into the yard with difficulty. We had never seen a vehicle like this in the prison before. We later realised that it was there to move out the dead bodies. The next day we saw Lashkari and Naserian wearing military gas masks, giving directions at the same place where we had seen the truck. They were organising the spraying of the place where the truck had been. It was as though they were using pesticide – it was like the process they used every year to get rid of scorpions, grasshoppers, and other bugs. The fact that Lashkari was doing this himself was unusual and it was doubly strange that it was being done in the garden.

> Akbar Sadeqi (pseudonym), FKO (Majority), sentenced to 6 years in prison

I was arrested in the mid-1980s for sympathising with the MKO. I was active in one of its resistance cells as a high school student and I was sentenced to eight years in prison. In July-August 1988 I was in Evin Prison, in a ward split half and half between us and the repenters.

Our ward was the only one which did not lose their television when the MKO attack came because it was separate from the other parts of the prison. Nonetheless, the first cellmate in our ward was called out on July 27, 1988 [two days after the "Eternal Light" attack] and executed. We were told that he was being taken to a different ward and that there was a pardon committee that had arrived to release some prisoners because the war had finished. Then they started to take other prisoners away – particularly ones who were visible and popular and to whom the guards were hostile. Then they took fifteen of us to section 209. By this time, we had begun to think that this was not a pardoning process. The guards had started to tease us by saying "you are all goners. This is the path of no return," in a sarcastic rather than amused way. We started to think that this was very serious although a few of the guys could not believe that we were being considered for execution. One of the guys turned to a guard and asked "What do they want from us?" And received the reply "They only want your lives."

There were a few prisoners who survived, at least for a time, because they had connections. For example, one person in our ward was the nephew of a judge and he wasn't executed until the autumn. The main way in which we received news of the executions was to talk to the ordinary, non-political prisoners, with whom we were able to mix in the workshop. That was where the discussions took place. They told us that the people being taken from our wards were not being transferred but were being executed. They had seen numerous buckets of slippers being taken out of the prison. There were some Revolutionary Guards who gave us information. One of them had been an ordinary criminal and was something of a simpleton: he would come and tell us about the execution scenes.

Affiliate of the MKO (see p. 36)

I was a member of a Marxist-Leninist group which had split from the Tudeh *Party and was connected with the FKO. I was arrested in 1985 in Tehran. By the summer of 1988 I was in Gohardasht Prison where the spirit of prisoners at this stage was very good. We were allowed to listen to the national news for half an hour twice a day and I remember hearing the message from the President that Iran would accept the UN resolution 598 to end the war, and then, two days later, the Imam's speech in which he said it was like drinking poison. The prison*

Mohammad Taqi Hadidi, killed 1988

Mr Hadidi was 17 years old when he was arrested in Esfahan on 31 August 1981 for reading and selling a newspaper published by the MKO. He was held in Dastgerd Prison and executed at age 24 in August 1988. In prison he was called "grandpa," ironically because of his young age and short height. According to his brother, a few months after his execution, a prison official called his house and asked his mother when their last visit was. She asked the official when the family should visit him. He replied, "Whenever you want." She inquired where she should go to visit him. She was told: "Rezvan cemetery, section 16."

exploded from happiness that day because, so far as all the political prisoners were concerned, our enemy had been humiliated and it was a sign of the regime's weakness. We were also happy at the end of the war.

But on Friday 29 July the guards took the televisions away, pretending that they needed to change them for colour television sets. We asked why the radio news was not being broadcast and we were told that the guards had forgotten to turn it on. This had happened before, but not for several days in a row! Neither morning nor evening newspapers were delivered and we were not allowed out for fresh air. On Sunday family visits would always be permitted, but not this Sunday. Again an excuse: "We are remodelling the visiting room." All this was quite exceptional. I was being held with other leftist prisoners in a block that was separate from the MKO prisoners and we had no means of communicating with them to learn what was happening. We did have sight of part of the prison yard and by moving a blind we could look out. We saw container trucks of the kind that are used for transporting refrigerated meat. This vantage point was in the kitchen at the end of the second level of the building and looked out on the parking area for the administrative building. The truck was close to the building and a number of guards were around it with masks on their faces. They were in the green uniform of the Revolutionary Guards. They seemed to be spraying disinfectant on the area. We were puzzled, but we did not yet associate this with executions.

Mehdi Aslani (see p. 37)

I was arrested for my involvement with the FKO (Minority) and placed initially in section 209 in Evin Prison and then moved to Gohardasht. We heard about the end of the war from the radio but then the visits were stopped and they took away all the televisions and newspapers. From then we didn't know what was going on – we were not allowed to leave the ward for usual exercise and our food, usually brought in by common criminals (Afghanis, always alone). These delivery boys were accompanied now by a Revolutionary Guard. We tried to communicate with other wards by Morse code but nobody had any clear information about what was happening. Sick prisoners were not allowed to go to the infirmary.

The first people who were taken had dual affiliation with both the MKO and the FKO. They never came back except for one of them who returned after a few hours. We learned that they were separating the prisoners. The guards had asked "what is your charge?" i.e. with which organisation that they had been charged or convicted of membership. This was nothing exceptional – it was a common question. Two days later, some of our FKO group were relocated to former MKO wards which were now

empty. Some of us noticed writing on the walls and on the architraves which said that a certain number had been taken to be executed today.

Mehrdad Neshati Malekians
(see p. 37)

I was a leftist prisoner in Zanjan prison in summer 1988. I recall the time when televisions and newspapers were banned from the ward and visiting privileges were cancelled. This was on 28 or 29 July. Then they took away some 25 prisoners on our ward whose names were on a list. They were not told where they were being taken and no prisoners at this point had any idea that they were going to the slaughter house. Some were MKO repenters who obviously thought they were off to a better prison or to be considered for a pardon. I remember one of them shouting happily "We are ready to go, come and take us." Later we sensed that something was terribly wrong and the air was heavy with fear and foreboding.

Rahmat Gholami, FKO (Minority),
sentenced to 15 years (from the Bidaran website)

I was arrested in connection with the FKO in Es-fahan in 1983. I had been condemned to prison for life. We heard about the end of the war from the radio – some of the Revolutionary Guards were crying... they gathered us in a hallway to listen to the television when the Head of the Revolutionary Guards talked about the Mojahedin attack and the operation against them. They took away the television. We were totally disconnected from the outside world. They gave us no more newspapers and visitations were prohibited. We had no idea what was going on. Then they took the Mojahedin prisoners in groups of two or three. It took them about twenty days to take all of them away, not only those who stood by their political positions but those who co-operated as well. We did not realise at the time that they were being taken for execution, we could not believe that the regime would permit such a massacre.

We had no news until family visits were allowed and we were told the truth. Many of the Mojahedin *who had been taken for execution were* mellikesh*, had completed their sentence. They* executed all the Mojahedin *in our section of the* prison, save for two, one of whom had a close family relationship with an interrogator. They told us that the questions were few: "Do you believe in the* Mojahedin?*" and "Do you believe in Rajavi or Khomeini?"

> Reza Saki, FKO, death sentence reduced to life imprisonment (from the Bidaran website)

The process of massacring the Gohardasht Prisoners began at 9:00 am on Saturday 30 July. The prisoners were taken by surprise and did not learn of their fate until it had been decided. From our section (number 2) nine Mojahedin *were taken out that day. The executions took place inside a silo, located outside of the prison building and behind the prison wall. We could see it from the Hosseinieh of the prison. That afternoon, one of us saw Lashkari with a wheelbarrow full of ropes. In the next few days we saw many Revolutionary Guards who were looking inside the silo. There was a lot of unusual movement around the area. The* Mojahedin *women were also executed. One of them, Zahra Khosravi, was taken to the execution section to write her will. She took advantage of this opportunity to contact the prisoners on the nearby ward by Morse code. After introducing herself, she informed them that she was condemned to death in a court that was headed by Nayyeri. On 6 August I heard that 800 were executed at Gohardasht and another 1200 at Evin.*

> Iraj Mesdaghi, MKO, sentenced to 10

Mr Shahram Shahbakhshi, killed 1988

Mr Shahbakhshi, an MKO sympathiser, was arrested on 2 July 1981. He was reportedly not tried until 1985, when he was condemned to three years imprisonment. His first visit with family took place about six months after this trial. At the age of 28, he was executed in August 1988 at Gohardasht Prison in Karaj. Officials told Mr Shahbakhshi's family of his burial location, on the condition that they would not hold memorial services for him.

years in prison (from his memoirs *Neither Life nor Death, Volume 3: Restless Raspberries*)

In our ward, we heard from a guard that Mojahedin *had apparently attacked Iran. It was hard for us to believe what he was saying especially as he was mocking and sarcastic. A short time later, wards 7 and 8 informed us, through the* mellikesh *ward, that they were seeing big trailers, equipped with refrigerators, loading many corpses from the amphitheatre area that was connected to those wards. This was occurring both night and day. Later we were informed through the prisoners on wards 7 and 8 that they were upset by the odour of decomposing corpses and had mentioned it to the ward guards. That night they saw guards spraying the corpses that were going to be loaded on the trailers.*

A few days later we noticed some new prisoners in a room adjacent to our ward and we succeeded in contacting them through a small window. One of them was a Mojahedin *prisoner who told us that there was a special court set up with Eshraqi and Nayyeri and that it was re-trying* the Mojahedin *prisoners. Those still affiliated to the organisation or those who refused to give a public confession condemning the* Mojahedin *attacks were hanged in the prison amphitheatre. It was difficult to believe this news, although it was consistent with what we had heard from wards 7 and 8. Some of us thought that the news was part of the self-aggrandisement of the* Mojahedin. *They had told us false and boastful accounts before. But I decided to communicate the information and on the next morning, August 27, I contacted the* mellikesh *ward to pass the news on. It spread like wildfire and I think this was the first day on which we started to realise what was happening and could strategise a defence. But nonetheless of about fifty to sixty prisoners who were called that day only a couple survived.*

Nima Parvaresh, *Peykar*, sentenced to 7 years in prison (from his memoirs *Unequal Battle*)

About ninety percent of the MKO prisoners from our section left and did not come back. I had known that people were being executed – at night I would hear the Revolutionary Guards marching in the garden chanting "Death to Monafeqin, *death to communists." That is when I would hear single shots – and then the sound of marches in the courtyard. I overheard one particularly unpleasant Revolutionary Guard, telling her friends how tightly the* Mojahedin *women had gripped each other while they were waiting to be executed and how they had peed themselves in fear. She thought this was a great joke.*

Maryam Nuri (see p. 36)

A comrade overheard a conversation between the religious judge Nayyeri and one of the executioners. The executioner told Nayyeri "ten minutes is not enough. When we lower the hook

after ten minutes some of them are still alive. Please allow more time for the job." Nayyeri responded "We don't have additional time. Ten minutes is enough." The executioner asked "Why don't we execute them by firing squad, it will be much quicker?" Nayyeri responded "Here (i.e. in Gohardasht) we do not have many resources. When the hearses carrying the corpses go through the street they would leave a trail of blood. Do you want the whole world to know what we are doing here?"

Reza Ghaffari, *Rah-e Kargar*, sentenced to 10 years in prison (from his memoirs *An Eye Witness Report of the Islamic Regime's Prisons in Iran*)

The above statements comprise a small selection of the recollections from survivors, most of whom we interviewed and consider reasonably reliable and whose request in some cases for anonymity I considered reasonable. These accounts from members of different political factions in different prisons are remarkably consistent and emphasize the systematic and widespread nature of the killings during the first wave. There were many more testimonies to much the same effect and there are other published accounts of the first wave of massacres, mainly from survivors at Gohardasht but also from Evin and from over twenty provincial prisons. The *modus operandi* was much the same in each prison, although in the larger ones the *Mojahedin* occupied their own wards whilst in some prisons they were mixed in wards with leftists. Files containing records of their charge and their previous interrogations and questionnaires were available to the Death Committees and made it easy to identify those who were candidates for the gallows. It mattered not whether they were *Mojahedin* who had completed their sentence or had partly served it, and those who had been classified as *Mojahedin* "repenters" were unprotected from re-classification by the Death Committees if they refused to fight the MKO or run through mine-fields or hang fellow prisoners.

The prison officials favoured a few prisoners and saved a few individual lives and there was such haste and confusion in hanging hundreds a day that, just as Montazeri predicted, mistakes were made. Some leftists who shared "mixed" wards were executed as well in this first period. The Death Committee hearings were short and the victims had little or no idea that the answer to the first question – what is your affiliation? – might save their life or cost their life. In the early days, many thought they were attending a post-war pardoning procedure. Identification of themselves as *Mojahedin* was enough to have them despatched to the execution queue and the follow-up questioning of those who admitted hypocrisy was designed in every case to provide the committee with a basis for classifying them as "steadfast," despite their denial. Executions in Evin and Gohardasht were by hanging, although for women in provincial prisons (especially those near the battle zones) firing squads were used (as Mr Ashough, the only MKO member who escaped from a death convoy, so dramatically recounts).

There were complaints – immediately – to Montazeri. A Revolutionary Prosecutor from Fars came to tell him about a young girl: "I opposed her execution but they outnumbered me 2-1 so they executed her." One of his prison representatives told him of seven pious brothers who had genuinely left the *Mojahedin*, but were reluctant to look dishonour-

able by agreeing to recant on television. The authorities said this meant they must still be "steadfast" and executed six of them. A judge from Qom complained about the blood-thirstiness of the Intelligence Ministry representative who had said "let us kill them as quickly as we can…The Imam has delivered the verdict. All we have to do is check that the prisoner is still holding [onto] his views." That question – do you still support your group? – was asked, and when the unsuspecting prisoner answered "Yes" he would be marched to the gallows.[104] One religious judge from Khouzestan Province, who had been appointed a member of a Death Committee, had contacted Montazeri as early as 1 August: "They are executing them with great speed. They conjure up a majority vote from the three member panel. They are angry about the *Monafeqin* operation (Eternal Light) but are venting their rage on the prisoners."

This particular judge, Mohammad Hossein Ahmadi, had copied to Montazeri a letter he had the courage to send direct to Khomeini, pointing out that the "*fatwa* question" namely whether a *Monafeqin* prisoner remained steadfast in his belief, was subject to different interpretations. He gave the example of four prisoners from Dezful (the "UNESCO" prison from which Mr Ashough escaped) who had been prepared to recant on television but had wavered when asked to fight at the frontier. Since many loyal Iranians were not prepared to fight for the regime by joining the army, he pointed out that this could not be an answer that implied a steadfast commitment to the enemy, yet the intelligence ministry representative and the prosecutor joined in a majority vote that sent all four of them for execution. (He remarked that one of these four prisoners, whom he named as Ashough, escaped on the way to the execution site: this corroborates Mr Ashough's statement which is set out above.) Montazeri took up the complaint in his own letter to Khomeini on 4 August, when he pointed out how unfair it was to hold against a *Monafeqin* who had recently repented his views, a reluctance to walk over minefields and how unsatisfactory it was that intelligence ministry officials, who had great influence in the Death Committees, were making crucial decisions "about the lives of thousands of prisoners." There was no reply from the Supreme Leader, and the executions continued until all the "steadfast" MKO prisoners were exterminated.

Ayatollah Montazeri then hit upon a religious reason for halting – or at least suspending – the first wave of executions. On 15 August 1988 he summoned the Tehran Death Committee in person: Judge Nayyeri, Prosecutor Eshraqi (and his deputy Ebrahim Raisi) and the powerful man from the intelligence ministry, Mr Pourmohammadi, and told them it was untraditional to spill blood in the calendar month of Moharram, which was about to begin. "At least halt the executions during this month." Nayyeri replied that they had already executed 750 prisoners in Tehran and had only 200 to go. "Once we finish off this lot you can order as you wish…" Montazeri was dismayed by this admission and read the four of them the lecture which two days later he summed up in a memorandum. He began by pointing out that he had more reason than anyone else to want revenge on the *Mojahedin* as his son had been killed by them in the 28 June 1981 bombing. But in the interests of the revolution "I am worried about the judgment that posterity and history will pass upon us." The world

would condemn them for massacring helpless prisoners without trial. Many of the *Monafeqin* had only held on to their beliefs because of the cruel way they had been treated in prison. Besides, a person's beliefs, *per se,* were not sufficient grounds to declare him *Mohareb* (waging war on God). The death penalty should only be passed in an unemotional environment and instead they were taking out their upset with the *Mojahedin* incursion on the *Mojahedin* prisoners who had nothing to do with it. Besides, executing them when they had not committed fresh crimes after their sentence cast doubt on the legitimacy of the trial judges who had sentenced them in the first place. How can it be just to execute a prisoner who has already been given a lesser sentence?

Of course it never could be just, but Nayyeri and Eshraqi lacked the integrity to admit it. So did Ayatollah Mousavi Ardebili, the head of the Supreme Judicial Council, when Montazeri upbraided him for making his telephone inquiry to the Imam's son: "You should have gone to the Imam in person; you should have told him that if someone had been in jail for some time and had been sentenced to five years, and had no idea about the *Mojahedin's* operation, how could we execute him?"[105] The Chief Justice and the Death Committee members seem to have had no moral or legal qualms about carrying out the *fatwa,* which by necessary implication annulled the decisions of dozens of religious judges, sitting as representatives of God on earth, rendered on prisoners over the past eight years. Executing prisoners for an invasion to which they had not been party was not only illogical, cruel and unjust, but violative of the country's constitutional order.

7: The Second Wave

Prison survivors all speak of a lull in interrogations and executions for a ten to fourteen day period which began in mid-August 1988. This may have been due to the beginning of the holy month of Moharram and its taboo against punitive bloodshed – a taboo that Montazeri had drawn to the attention of the Tehran Death Committee when he met them on 15 August 1988. But it may have been due to the simple fact that there were no more *Mojahedin* prisoners to execute: Montazeri estimated that up to 3,800 had been slain by that time. The lull may also be connected with the end of the war: the UN ceasefire had taken effect, finally, on 20 August 1988. The real question is why the Death Committees reconvened, on about 26 August, and in the succeeding weeks turned themselves into courts that proceeded to try, for the crime of apostasy, all the left wing prisoners and the odd liberal, and sentenced them either to execution, or to persistent torture until they agreed to bow down towards Mecca and say their prayers.

The *fatwa* of 28 July had very clearly targeted "the treacherous *Monafeqin*" – the "hypocrites" in league with the Baathist party of Iraq. Everyone understood this as a specific description of the *Mojahedin,* to be distinguished from all the other left-wing prisoners who were not hypocritical (they made no secret of their disbelief in Islam, or any other God) and they did not have an army in Iraq, fighting for Saddam. The distinction was insisted upon by the political prisoners themselves, who demanded

Mojtaba Mohseni, killed 1988

Mr Mojtaba Mohseni, an Arak-born agriculture student at Karaj University, was a sympathiser of the FKO. He was arrested in Esfahan in 1984 and executed in the same town in December 1988 at the age of 31. His family was only informed of his burial location.

separate wards and declined associations with each other when placed in the same ward (although accounts of life in women's wards suggest that there was less insistence upon ideological divides).

The *fatwa*, in short, cannot be interpreted as an order for the death and torture sentences inflicted on the leftists – referred to by the government as members of the "mini-groups." It is possible that there was a second, secret *fatwa*, withheld this time from Montazeri and the other religious judges who had complained about the edict of 28 July, which has never been revealed. Montazeri himself suggests that this was indeed the case, and that by the end of August a secret decree was issued to the Death Committees by the Supreme Leader.[106] Alternatively, the Death Committees may simply have been tasked to investigate and apply to all remaining political prisoners the fundamentalist Islamic law which decreed death for unrepentant male apostates, and torture for female apostates and for men who could establish that they had not been born into Muslim families. On any view, the second wave was designed to break the spirit of potentially dangerous or difficult prisoners who would have to be released after the war, so that the Islamic Republic could settle back into a reign less marked than previously by ideological division. This must of course have been a factor in the thinking behind the first *fatwa*: MKO members, whether

---

Qorban Ali Shokri, killed 1988

Mr Shokri, a member of the *Ettehadieh Komonistha* (Union of Communists), was born in Arasbaran (in the East Azarbaijan province). He was arrested in August 1985, along with his wife and son, who remained imprisoned for more than four years. Mr Shokri was tried in Evin Prison and sentenced in the winter of 1986 to five years imprisonment. He was hanged during the mass execution of political prisoners in August 1988. Years later, when his death certificate was given to his family members, it stated "natural death" as the cause and August 1988 as the date of death. He was 38 years old.

---

or not they repented the political and military actions of their organisation, who were "steadfast" in their blasphemous version of Islam and their opposition to theocracy, would remain a post-war problem unless eliminated.

The evidence – our own interviews with leftist prisoners and the numerous accounts that have been published by others – establish what happened in the second stage of the massacre period. Leftist prisoners were summoned

before the Death Committee for a religious inquisition, during which they were asked whether they were Muslim, whether they believed in God, whether and how often they prayed and whether they were prepared to start praying again. This time the committee more resembled a court, and sessions lasted somewhat longer, as its members had to consult the prisoners' files, probe their family backgrounds and discuss among themselves when a defendant's answers raised a fine point of theology. Most of the prisoners were Marxists and had no idea of the theological significance of their responses. For example, one communist woman who had been a high ranking *Tudeh* Party official was subject to an interrogation over whether she had ever heard her father pray, and found that her denial was supported by Eshraqi, who happened to know him. She subsequently commented: "I did not understand the consequence these answers would have for me: I did not realise the response 'my father did not pray' would help reduce my sentence."[107]

For women, the wrong response would entail a torture sentence – whippings (5 lashes) administered during each of the five prayer periods in the Muslim day, until they undertook to pray regularly, or died. Only during menstruation was the torture suspended – because of the primitive belief that the duty to inflict violence on women's bodies was then suspended if those bodies were "unclean." Many second wave prisoners who received these beatings told us that they were very different and much more painful than the *tazir* beatings on the soles of their feet that they had received during earlier interrogations. The cables now drew blood, and this time they were lashed all over their body. In the case of male leftists, the inquisition would lead to a death sentence if the prisoner was judged to be an "innate" apostate (i.e. one born into a Muslim family) and who either maintained his refusal to pray or was thought to be insincere in offering to do so. There were some questions about political party membership, but these appear to have been asked in the context of establishing a commitment to atheism – to the godlessness, rather than the class-based politics, of Marxist-Leninist thought. A number of prisoners were brought back three times to the committee before they were condemned to death – the proof of apostasy must be clear, which it is if God is repudiated thrice.[108]

In this phase the proceedings took longer: hearings occupied more time and some prisoners were called back for further hearings by the committee. In due course they came to understand what was in store for them, and recollections of this period are clearer and more numerous than accounts of the first wave. Ruses for evasion and delay were discussed in, and by Morse code between, the wards. One which appears to have confounded the committee in Tehran was for the prisoner to excuse his failure to pray by saying, hand on heart, that it was impossible to pray in the presence of unbelieving fellow prisoners, because their spiritual rankness invalidated a true Muslim's prayers. This argument seems to have been accepted by Nayyeri, until he was reminded by Eshraqi that they had heard it many times before.[109] There are accounts of the Tehran Death Committee members arguing between themselves about the religious significance of details volunteered by prisoner "defendants" (although prisoners were never charged or formally told that they were on trial for any offence). There were com-

paratively few questions about whether the prisoner was willing to confess on television or to fight against enemies (the war had ended when the ceasefire became unconditional on 20 August) and although their stance towards the Islamic Republic remained relevant, it was now religious rather than political loyalty that was being tested. Membership of a godless "mini-group" did not merely manifest seditious intent – it was taken as evidence of blasphemy.

This new emphasis on conformity in religious belief was apparent in the public pronouncements by the regime's leaders. At the end of August 1988, Ayatollah Mousavi Ardebili opened the High Judicial Council, after its one month vacation, with a diatribe against the "mini-groups" and a demand that judges and prosecutors act with resolve in confronting them and be "ruthless to the unbelievers [Koran 48:29]."[110] This is exactly the approach that the Death Committees took during the second wave. The Chief Justice explained that these groups had demonstrated "opposition to Islam" as well as opposition to the "brave people" of Iran by associating with foreign enemies (which included the Soviet Union, a backer of Iraq). He criticised the UN for failing to condemn the Iraqi war crime of using chemical weapons, without of course making any reference to the Iranian war crime of slaughtering prisoners.

On 4 September 1988 the Supreme Leader announced that he relinquished his emergency prerogative to punish, which was henceforth bestowed on the Expediency Council and its President (Ali Khamenei) who would have responsibility for determining punishments for crimes against religion and for crimes against the state.[111] The date of this announcement supports Montazeri's claim that a secret *fatwa* was issued the day before – on 3 September – to deal with leftist prisoners, and to spare the President and Council the inconvenience (and illegality) of using their powers to overturn sentences passed by religious judges years before. Ali Khamenei and Rafsanjani may nonetheless be held responsible for the actions of the "Death Committees," inquisitorial courts allowed to investigate, try and punish by death and by torture. On 23 September, a message was sent to the provinces by the Vice-Minister of Information, exhorting all parents to prevent their children falling prey to propaganda: "the danger from the hypocrites has not been completely removed." In addition, it was made clear that there was a need to battle blasphemy and to "fight our mini-group opponents as well as hypocrites."[112] While the mini-group opponents were in prison being hanged and flogged, the regime was telling people that they deserved to be treated like the *Mojahedin*, who by this time were in mass graves.

Before long, reports of the first wave of executions reached the Western press from anguished families, and on 10 December Chief Justice Mousavi Ardebili made the first attempt to construct a public justification.[113] "We are not a secular state," he explained, so irreligion and blasphemy was not allowed in Iran (an implicit conclusion that the MKO were viewed as blasphemous). He said the regime was ready to answer the allegations by providing documents at a conference (which was never convened) on mini-group terrorism. These documents would prove that those executed had all received death sentences at their trials but execution had been delayed to give

them an opportunity to repent. Unfortunately these people not only refused to conform, but they began stirring up trouble inside the prisons, which reached a peak after the *Mersad* operation. "These convicts who had already been sentenced to death…even started to beat up prison guards…thus proving their hostility to the regime.." This was a thoroughly dishonest example of the tactic of confession and avoidance, i.e. acknowledging executions in passing but falsely blaming prisoners for their failure to take the opportunity to reform and falsely accusing them of committing additional crimes and so forfeiting any prospect of mercy.

These statements can be interpreted as an indication that the highest levels of the regime were aware that proceedings were being taken against "mini-group" prisoners on account of their refusal to accept the state – or any – religion, but there was no public announcement to this effect and no such inquisition was ever inflicted upon ordinary prisoners, or upon civilians generally. It was a continuation of the terror unleashed in the prisons by the *fatwa* of 28 July, using the same legal machinery and involving the same group of executioners: the Death Committee members, prison governors and prison guards (some statements suggest that battle-hardened Revolutionary Guards were brought in to do the actual killings). It continued through September and into October and although there are a few reports of later executions it was in November that the "tidying up" operation began: the final phase of notifying families of the deaths of their children, returning belongings, refusing to identify burial places and banning all forms of mourning. By this time, the country's political prisoners had either been executed or else flogged into submission by a regime which would think it safe to release them over the next few years. The second wave had been more bureaucratic than the first, with more scope for leniency and for mistake, and it did not directly take the lives of women (although there are reports that some died as a result of beatings or from suicide after beatings).

The Genocide Convention of 1948, to which Iran has been a party since 1949,[114] applies to killings of, or causing serious mental or physical harm to, members of a racial or religious group as such, with intent to destroy that group in whole or in part. The "religious group" that the Iranian regime intended to destroy in the second wave were those in its prisons who had been born Muslim but who had later renounced Islam. Whether or not atheists should count as a "religious group" for the purposes of the Convention, it is clear that persons who are born into a particular faith that they later renounce can be so categorised. This is a feature of the second wave of killings and is one reason why they must, in international law, engage continuing attention. And it must never be forgotten that the first wave of killings, although triggered by fury at the "Eternal Light" incursion, was based on the conclusion that the MKO version of Islam was a blasphemy. Both the MKO and the leftists were condemned as *mohareb*s, warriors against God, whose divinely ordained punishment was to be enforced by the state.

There are many harrowing accounts of the "trials," and of the death and torture sentences inflicted during the second phase. Prison security officials such as Lashkari and Naserian were prominent in bundling the blindfolded prisoners in and out of the tribunal room and

> **Rahmat Fathi, killed 1988**
>
> Kind and compassionate, Mr Fathi was and loved by family and friends. He was affiliated with the FKO (Minority), and was arrested on 4 November 1985. He was condemned that same year to 10 years' imprisonment in Evin Prison in Tehran. He was executed in August or September 1988 at the age of 28. Evin Prison officials later told his mother: "If you write [a testimony] that your son committed suicide in prison, we will show you his grave location and give you his wedding ring."

making prejudicial statements about them to the judges. The following examples are from left-wing survivors of Evin and Gohardasht.

A group of us were taken from the cell blindfolded and made to queue in a large hall. When it was my turn, I was taken into the court room and my blindfold was removed. I recognised Nayyeri, who presided – he was a very well-known cleric whom I had seen on television. He did most of the questioning and was clearly the most senior. Eshraqi I also recognised as he had prosecuted me. I confirmed my name and was asked whether I accepted the Islamic Republic and I said I did not. I was asked whether I believed in my organisation, the FKO and its ideas, and I confirmed that I did. I denied any belief in God – I denied that I had ever believed in God for a second, even during my childhood. I was then asked about my mother and father and whether they prayed. I said they did not. "Why didn't they pray?" I explained they were Kurds from Khoramshahr and were members of the Ahl-e Haq cult, a mystic group which does not believe in prayer. Nayyeri eventually seemed to accept that I had always been a non-believer.

He ordered that I should go to the left. There were many people in the corridor on the left by that stage – I counted 142 – and we whispered to each other trying to figure out what was going to happen – the guards brought a trolley with bread and cheese and we jokingly called it "the last supper." We said goodbye to each other because we thought we were going to be executed because we had heard so many stories about the Mojahedin *killings*.

The prison guards called names out from a long list. All of the 142 people were called, except for me and three others who were all "non-believers" who had never been Muslim. They

Reza Esmati, killed 1988

A political prisoner of the previous regime, Mr Esmati was a husband and a father, who was arrested in Tehran on 8 September 1981. He was affiliated with the *Komalah* organisation. His first trial was held at Evin three months after his arrest. He had no access to his case's files and was denied the right to an attorney. He was condemned to death during the first trial and later to 20 years' imprisonment during a second trial. Mr Esmati was executed at Evin Prison on either 29 or 30 August 1988, at the age of 38.

were from communist families and they had never been Muslim or considered to be Muslim. Other than us, the other 138 people were taken to the Hosseinieh, the assembly hall that we knew had been used for hanging prisoners. We never saw our friends again. I believe they were taken away and hanged. Later during my torture period I was held in prison holding cells, where some of them had written on the walls whilst awaiting their execution. Because there were limited ropes, and hanging took some

time, those who could not be executed immediately were left in cells where they were able to open their blindfolds and scratch messages on the walls. I remember one said "we are not blindfolded and we can see what is going on." Another was signed by a friend of mine, Kasra Akbari Kordestani, and he wrote on the wall – his message causes me grief to this day – "I offer my small heart to all the workers of Iran." After discussion with the other survivors and information from other groups we concluded that those transferred to the right of the corridor were those who admitted to being Muslims and had promised to pray. Those of us on the left had refused to pray, and the four survivors of that queue had been confirmed as non-Muslims and so had been saved. None of us were asked any questions about our political views – the interrogation was all about our belief in God and our willingness to pray.

Although I survived execution they determined to torture us in order to make us become Muslims. The procedure was to use torture five times a day at each call to prayer. They flogged us on the soles of our feet, telling us that we had to become Muslim. We were beaten with electrical cables after being tied down to a metal bed. At each call to prayer I was given 15 lashes. This went on for some weeks and eventually I decided to give up and commit suicide. This was on 1 December 1988 when I was unable to endure the floggings for refusing to pray, and I slit my wrists. Since suicide is forbidden in Islam, my cellmates did not report my attempted suicide to prison authorities. Instead, one of my cellmates, who was a doctor, took good care of me and even gave me antibiotics.

Affiliate of the FKO (Majority)
(see p. 35)

I was in a section which had held both Mojahedin and leftists. Sometime towards the end of August I was called out for interrogation. I was taken to a queue in a corridor and kept for several hours before it was my turn to go into the courtroom. I was permitted to remove my blindfold but I only recognised Nayyeri and Eshraqi. I was asked whether I was a Muslim and when I replied that I was not, I was asked, since when had I not been a Muslim, and I responded that I could never remember having prayed or even having said "God." I was asked whether my parents were Muslims and when I agreed that they were, I was asked how it was possible for my parents to be Muslim but for me to be non-Muslim. I was aware that this was a trap and that if I had admitted being a Muslim at any point in my life they would have convicted me as an apostate and executed me. So I replied that the Mullahs of my neighbourhood drink alcohol and dance on Friday. This really annoyed Nayyeri who shouted "take him away and give him lashes until he becomes Muslim."

I was taken away for flogging and the next morning I was taken back to court. Nayyeri asked me what would I do if I were released because Iran is an Islamic country and I am not a Muslim. I said that I was just going to live my life and he asked me further questions about the prophet of Islam and the fundamental principles of the religion. I knew what the five principles were but I was not going to allow them to trick me into admitting that I had once been a believer and so now was an apostate. Eshraqi was trying to be fair and actually said to Nayyeri "Look, it is obvious that he has never been a Muslim." But Nayyeri kept up the questioning and at some point was so frustrated he shouted "Take him away." But Eshraqi intervened and said "Please Mr Haji, let me ask him one more question" and turned to me: "If you go into an Islamic society will you abide by the laws of that society?" I replied firmly "Yes." Eshraqi turned to Nayyeri and said "Look, Mr Haji, he is willing to abide by our laws." Nayyeri then agreed, finally, that I was a non-believer but not an apostate. He sentenced me to be flogged for three days and said "we will give you three days to become a Muslim. Take him away."

I was taken back to a cell with other surviving leftists and assaulted with great brutality by Revolutionary Guards. I had my ribs broken and I saw a young kid whose head was cut open and who subsequently died. One guard jumped on my back whilst I was writhing on the floor in agony and badly injured me – I had to have a back operation when I was released. After a particularly brutal beating, we were taken to a room where a cleric came in and said "now are you ready to pray?" One of our cellmates said to the cleric "We are all bleeding and so we are unclean and cannot pray in this state." The guards left us alone for some time. That evening we decided to pretend to pray although several prisoners thought that suicide would be preferable. The next day the guards came back and asked whether we were ready to pray. Our leader said "We cannot pray in this state. Look at us! We are covered in blood and dirt." The cleric who then came in accepted this excuse and said to us "That's fine, I will tell the guards that you have agreed to pray and they will not give you any more problems." We were later taken into a section with twelve other survivors and we were excited to see them again. But then it dawned on us that we were the only ones left in the prison. As the magnitude of the killings sunk in, we went into a state of shock and depression.

Shahab Shokuhi (see p. 35)

When I came into the room they asked me to remove my blindfold. There was a big table with Nayyeri and Eshraqi whom I recognised, and another whose name I am not sure about. They told me that they were a delegation examining the prison situation. They asked whether I was still holding onto my views as a member of the FKO (Majority) and I said that I was in prison and therefore uninformed about the policies of the FKO. I was then asked whether I prayed and I said that I did not. I was asked whether I was a Muslim. I said I was like my parents, a Muslim. I tried to avoid straight answers. Suddenly Nayyeri said "Stop. He is an apostate." He called me Mortad *[apostate]. Eshraqi intervened and said "No, he said he was a Muslim." At this point I realised that the circumstances were serious. For these clerics, flogging or interviews are less of an issue than Islam. Then Eshraqi turned to me and said "You have a wife and kids. Just sign this." He showed me a paper, which said "I believe in the three foundations of Islam. I don't believe in Socialism or Marxism and Leninism." I said that this was all very confusing – "I am a Muslim." Naserian then came up and hit me on the head with his pen and said to the court "Didn't I tell you he is evil?" But he did not put me on the right or the left of the hallway because they had not made a clear decision. Naserian took me away to a new ward. There were Revolutionary Guards in charge of it and they had new torture weapons such as chains. They beat us up badly – there were about twenty of us – and they beat everyone who refused to pray.*

Akbar Sadeqi (pseudonym)
(see p. 36)

I remember the killing of the Mojahedin. *A friend of mine was in a building near the amphitheatre and told me that he would hear the noise of the trucks and the sound of bodies being thrown into them. They would count – 20, 25 a day. He said how the first bodies falling on the floor of an empty truck would make noise but later they did not make so much noise because they must have landed on other bodies. This continued until mid-August and then for a couple of weeks the prison was calm. Then the killings began again – this time of leftists. There were eighty in our ward and we were not prepared for what was to happen. We were taken to the hallway and then into the committee. We were asked whether we prayed, whether we were Muslim, whether we had changed our group. From those eighty leftists of different groups, only about seventeen were sent back to the ward. The others were never seen again.*

Mehdi Aslani (see p. 37)

About a month after they took the television sets away they took the leftists out of the ward. Naserian came in and picked some of the people he knew and took them downstairs. I went into the room and took my blindfold off. Nayyeri was sitting beside the desk, with his turban on and next to him was Eshraqi. A third person was sitting with a bunch of folders. I was brought in by Naserian – because I was a ward representative I had a lot of encounters with Naserian. He said to the judge "This is a mellikesh. *He is one of those organisers who have been causing problems in here." I explained to the judge that Naserian was lying – I was not a* mellikesh *because my sentence had not finished. Nayyeri said "What were you charged with?" and asked my organisation. He asked me then whether I was a Muslim and I didn't respond. He looked at my file and asked me whether I was Armenian and I explained that my family is Armenian although my mother is a Muslim. I thought it best to keep some element of doubt in the situation and so I denied that my family was Muslim but I also denied that I was a Christian. Eshraqi asked me about my family and my children and told me because I have a Muslim family I have to pray. I refused and he told me that "we are trying to separate prisoners" and said that I had to pray. He told the guards to take me outside and they gave me a piece of paper and asked me to sign it.*

We were taken back upstairs in a conga line, blindfolded, prisoners with their hands on each others' shoulders. I was put in solitary and collected by Naserian at 8:00 a.m. He told me that I had to pray. I said that I was Armenian and that I would not pray. I was left in a room with four other people including Akbar Shalguni from the Rah-e Kargar *Organisation, one person from the FKO Minority, and others from the* Tudeh *Party. Akbar told me that many from his party had already been executed and we then knew that the stakes were high. We talked together and decided that we would not pray. Our experience in prison is that you give the authorities a little bit and they want a great deal more, and so it was better to deny them, notwithstanding the risk. Naserian opened the door and said "Who is not praying?" Two of our comrades immediately changed their minds and said that they would pray. The rest of us – the remaining three – said that we would not. The three of us were put on a bed one by one, and each given ten lashes on the soles of our feet, which were incredibly hard. Then they made us run in the hallway. They asked, "Are you going to pray now?" Akbar and I refused, so they gave us both ten more lashes, which broke the skin of our feet.*

I had never been beaten like this before. It was as if we were being beaten in order to be killed. Your brain really wanted to explode – it was shocking. Then they put me and Akbar in the same cell and we decided that we would pray because it would allow us to be taken back to the

ward and warn the others. But later that night Naserian came back and after establishing that we were praying he simply closed the door and

---

"THEIR [THE *TUDEH* PARTY] NATURE IS VERY CLEAR."

"There is nothing to be proud of in their past. They opposed the previous regime with their own tenets. Even if their struggle has been beneficial in the past, the nature of this party is not good at all. They are against religion. The only thing that we fight for, and will continue to fight for, is Islam."

Hojatoleslam Ali Akbar Hashemi Rafsanjani on the *Tudeh* Party, quoted from an interview with *Ayandesazan* magazine, 29 November 1981

Anusheh Taheri, killed 1988

Mr Taheri was expelled from the Science and Technology University during the "cultural revolution." A member of the *Tudeh* Party, he was arrested on 27 April 1983, tried, and condemned to 8 years' imprisonment. Mr Taheri was hanged in September 1988 during the mass killings of political prisoners at Gohardasht Prison. He was 30 years old.

---

left. Later we met others when we were taken to the Hosseinieh – it was an assembly hall in the prison that served as a mosque – and everyone pretended to pray before we were sent back to our rooms. Here we were able to assess just how many had been executed.

Mehrdad Neshati Malekians
(see p. 37)

Eleven days passed and there was no sign of any further massacre at Gohardasht. But when Moharram's mourning period ended, we expected developments... it is said that Mohammad Yazdi accompanied by Ahmad Pournejati, an as-

sociate of Reyshahri, the Minister of Intelligence and Javad Mansouri (a founder of the Revolutionary Guards) had gone to Khomeini and had persuaded him that massacring the Mojahedin whilst keeping the remaining Marxist prisoners alive would not be satisfactory for some of Qom's clerics. They had argued that it was better to take advantage of the opportunity at hand to do away with the Marxists as well.

Iraj Mesdaghi (see p. 59)

At 9:00 p.m. on 30 August 1988 we received information from the mellikesh *ward that one of their prisoners had returned and said that any prisoner who declared that he was not a Muslim and would not pray was taken to court, and if he insisted upon rejecting Islam he would be executed. This information was that most of the prisoners taken out of the leftist wards were executed on the same day. He had declared himself a Muslim and therefore was not executed. This person was a trusted and militant prisoner whose information could not be doubted. We then heard that supporters of the pro-Soviet Tu-deh* party who were mellikesh *had said that they would not defend their political views if taken to court. Two prisoners from the* Peykar *organisation, however, declared that they would defend their political view as Marxists and that was their personal decision.*

The next morning on 31 August, Naserian and the guards opened the doors to the wards, ordered us to blindfold ourselves and leave to line up in the hallway. We were taken one by one to an adjacent room to be questioned about whether we were a Muslim or not. Those who declared that they were not Muslims and would not pray were ordered to sit on the left side of the hall. Those who declared that they were Muslims were seated on the right. They were then asked to perform an Islamic prayer and if they refused they were taken away and whipped. The

prisoners on the left were taken to a court, where I recognised Eshraqi. The court asked them the same questions and if they denied that they were Muslims they were ordered to sit on the left side of the door outside of the courtroom. They were then taken to the prison amphitheatre where they were hanged.

I waited my turn outside the court. One prisoner ahead of me was brought out of the court swearing loudly at Islam and its brutality. The guards dragged him off to the amphitheatre and he was executed that day. However the next two persons ahead of me had declared themselves Muslims and were taken out of court and seated on the right. Naserian pushed me into the court room and there Eshraqi started questioning me. He asked if I were a Muslim and I answered "If you're intending to execute me then I am a Muslim, if you don't intend to execute me I will give a different answer." In the end I was taken to the right side of the hallway although Naserian beat me and said "we should execute all of you."

We were taken to ward 8 and those of us who refused to pray were lain on the bed and flogged five times a day... after numerous beatings I told my co-prisoners that I was going to agree to pray and they told me that they were going to do the same. After we made the declaration we were sent back to ward 8 where we met some of our friends who had also survived. We hugged and we cried and we remembered those who were not with us anymore. Out of about 500 leftist prisoners in the five wards with which I was familiar, about half had been executed.

Nima Parvaresh (see p. 60)

Women apostates were spared execution, but were ordered to be beaten five times a day, although in some cases with five strokes rather than the fifteen inflicted on the men. The following testimonies are typical:

I sat in front of the head judge of the court... Nayyeri asked: "Ms. Mahiar, what are you accused of?" I said: "I am a member of the Tudeh *Party." He asked: "Are you still a member?"...I said: "I have been in prison during the past five years and have had no connection with them. I don't know what their position on current issues is. For this reason, I cannot say whether I am or am not a member." He said: "She is still a* Tudeh *supporter. Are you a Muslim?" I responded: "This information is personal." He again asked: "Do you pray?" I responded: "This information is also personal." He then asked: "What about your father and mother?" I said: "My mother and father are Shia and I was born in a Shia family." He said: "She does not pray. She is* mortad *[apostate]." He added: "[Particular verses] of the Quran state that an apostate man must be executed. An apostate woman must be whipped until she accepts to say that she is a Muslim or dies. Take her out, brother." The guard came and took the corner of my chador as though he were touching something dirty. They blindfolded me and let me out...[the guard] began reciting the call to prayer. Then he began whipping me as he recited verses of the Quran related to treatment of apostate women. Around 4 p.m. or 5 p.m., the guard came back and asked if I would pray again. Again, I said no. And again, he beat me...They summoned us during pray hours: at 12 a.m., 4 a.m., 2 p.m., and 4 p.m. The last round was sometime in the evening. These intervals did not allow me any time to sleep.*

Witness statement of Ms. Mahiar Maki in the Iran Human Rights Documentation Center's report, *Speaking for the Dead: Survivor Accounts of Iran's 1988 Massacre*

Trial and execution location of prisoners in 1988, Evin Prison, Tehran

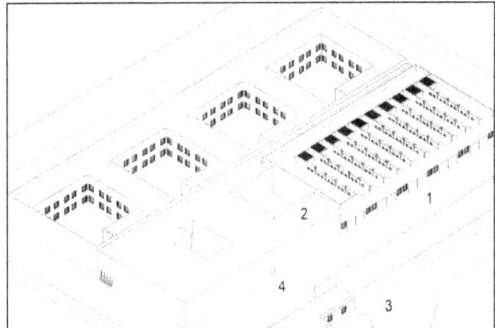

1) Section 209. Those prisoners who were "in the process" of execution, were transferred to the cells in this section
2) The basement of Section 209. A few days after the beginning of the massacre, prisoners' trial and execution took place here
3) Vehicle entrance to this building
4) Entrance to the basement of Section 209

Source: Iraj Mesdaghi, *Neither Life Nor Death, Volume 4: Till... The Dawn of Grapes*, Alfabet Maxima Publishing: 2006 (Stockholm, 2nd edition, 2006).

When the Mojahedin *prisoners had gone from the women's ward, they started to call the leftists. Unlike for the* Mojahedin*, they did not ask us to pack our bags and hand over our belongings before we left for interrogation. They started with the* Tudeh *and the FKO members. When they came back they told us that they had been asked whether they believed in the Republic, whether they prayed and whether they were willing to repent and to pray. If they refused to pray they would get a sentence of being flogged five times with five lashes each time. It was explained to them that woman apostates were not to be killed but were to be beaten until they prayed. The reason they started with the* Tudeh *party and FKO was that they were moving from right to left – for them the* Tudeh *and then the FKO were considered the more moderate of the leftist parties.*

The beatings started before the morning call to prayer. Everyone could hear our screams. It was bastinado, repeatedly flogging the same area, which made it difficult. The beatings and interrogations happened over twenty-two days and all but two gave in and started to pray. This was in September. Those two who came back were in very bad shape. They were very weak and had lost a lot of weight and were tense and nervous. Their bodies were full of lesions. After such beatings they were disoriented.

Fariba Sabet (see p. 55)

The whipping sessions seemed endless. They woke us up in the morning, tied us to a bed and lashed us over and over again. They would repeat this every day at 2:00 p.m., 4:00 p.m., 6:00 p.m. and 9:00 p.m. We spent most of our time in anticipation of the next round of lashes. It was not only the physical pain that tormented the prisoners, but the anxiety, sleeplessness and the dreadful waiting. Sleep deprivation caused many of us to break.

> Witness statement of Ms. Shahla Azad (pseudonym), in the Iran Human Rights Documentation Center's report, *Speaking for the Dead: Survivor Accounts of Iran's 1988 Massacre*

In August we got a newspaper clipping that read that the spokesman for the Supreme Judicial Council, after much cursing at the "discredited" communists, had asked for the "maximum penalty" for them. He had said that "after the hypocrites (Monafeqin) it is the turn of the non-believers." The words were clear and needed no analysis. On the second week in September, the whipping of the leftist women began. With the

first light at 4:00 a.m., at the sound of the Muezzin's call to prayer, the cell door was opened, the prisoner was taken out, was laid on a bed in the middle of a corridor and was whipped. Five lashes. The cell door is then locked and another door opened and the second prisoner is laid on the bed. The third, the fourth and so on – takes about an hour. The next turn is with the midday call to prayer, the third about 4:00 p.m. the fourth at nightfall and the last before midnight. Twenty-five lashes in all, five occasions... The old prisoners, who had been in for several years, sent us news that they had agreed to pray – they regarded themselves as defeated. They had been told in their trial that the punishment for non-believing women is death under the lash or else repentance. They wished they had been given a death sentence rather than a slow death. They saw no hope for an end to whippings. The guards took away seven or eight of us. They were taken to court and asked "Are you a Muslim, do you pray?" They had all answered in the negative. The religious judge had given out a verdict of death under the whip, or repentance. They announced that they would go on a hunger strike in protest. They were all prisoners who had been arrested in relation to the Tudeh *party and the FKO (Majority).*

> Monireh Baradaran, *Rah-e Kargar,* sentenced to 10 years in prison (from her memoirs *The Plain Truth*)

The sentences imposed on apostate men depended on the religiosity of their families, and specifically on that of their fathers. As Amnesty International reports:

At the end of August 1988 the "Death Commission" turned its attention to the prisoners from leftist groups held in Gohardasht Prison... [Prisoners [were] asked if they were prepared to make public statements criticizing the political organization with which they had been associated. The leftist prisoners were also asked about their religious faith. They were asked such questions as: Do you pray? Do you read the Qur'an? Did your father read the Qur'an?

One eye-witness of an interrogation in Gohardasht Prison described how he was taken before the "Death Commission" with five other prisoners. The six were asked if they prayed or read the Qur'an: they replied that they did not. They were then asked whether their fathers had read the Qur'an. Four of them answered "yes" and two of them "no". After some discussion between members of the commission, it was decided that those who had not been brought up in a religious family were not as guilty as those whose parents were religious, because the former group had not been brought up as believers. Consequently, the two men whose fathers had not prayed were spared, but the four others were executed.

These testimonies all confirm that the second wave executions and torture orders were based on judgments about the prisoners' attitude to Islam: their political beliefs were relevant only to the extent that their organisational affiliation placed them under suspicion of atheism. We spoke to many who had been beaten into prayer, and who had given undertakings to abide by the laws and the religion of the Islamic Republic as a condition of their release over the following years. In every case, they suffered discrimination in employment and education (university re-enrolment was not permitted) and constant surveillance. Their lapse from religious orthodoxy was never forgiven, no matter how genuinely most abandoned their youthful left-wing politics. As the man from the Ministry of Intelligence, Mr Zamani, said to one of our witnesses after the massacres, "we will follow you like a shadow and we will execute you on the spot if you do anything to harm us or the regime."[115]

8: The Aftermath: Mourning Forbidden

Most studies of Iranian society remark on the centrality to it, culturally and spiritually, of mourning. Every Friday the nation's cemeteries are attended by families putting flowers on the graves of their deceased relatives: in the martyrs' section will be found the mothers grieving at the gravestones of their sons killed by fighting in the Iran-Iraq War. It is a matter of some poignancy that the mothers whose children were killed by the state at the end of that war have nowhere to mourn, because the state denied them the right to bury their dead, and suppresses to this day displays of grief at the sites identified as their mass graves. Those sites have been located in sections of major cemeteries that are usually reserved for the corpses of criminals and atheists. They have become places of pilgrimage for the victims' families: in August 2008, the 20th anniversary commemoration of the massacres at a cemetery in Tehran was forcibly broken up by police, with seventeen arrests.[116] In January 2009 Amnesty International condemned the Iranian government for bulldozing the mass grave at Khavaran, and stated that it was an attempt to destroy evidence of its crime against humanity.[117] That the government refuses to answer questions about the massacres and has conducted no investigation into them is a breach of the "right to life" provisions of the International Covenant on Civil and Political Rights. That it still denies to families information as to where it buried their loved ones is a further breach, inflicting punishment on the parents for the purported sins of the children. As we shall see, the continuing denial has further legal significance, in fixing the present regime with a continuing responsibility for crimes committed in its name and by its order.

By November 1988 the potential threat to the regime posed by thousands of young atheists and oppositionists had been removed by taking their lives. There are no definite fatality statistics, but credible reports suggest that several hundred were killed in each of more than twenty prisons throughout the country, with up to 1,000 victims at Evin and many more in Gohardasht. Only the state knows how many lives it took, and it is not telling. Rafsanjani's claim that "less than one thousand were executed in July to September"[118] is a serious underestimate, but remains the only official admission. Embarrassment at the monstrosity of its crime doubtless caused the regime to postpone its duty to notify families of those who had been executed. All prison visits had been cancelled at the end of July, and some desperate families, hearing rumours of the killings, had rushed to Qom to complain to Montazeri, but he was unable to help: he was shunned by the regime after his protest in August, and removed as Supreme Leader-in-waiting a few months later.

So relatives besieged the prisons. Visits resumed in November 1988 and some family members were then presented with plastic bags containing the belongings of their dead child

> **"Sentences don't matter. A day or more, as long as you don't become who they want, they keep you."**
>
> *- Abbas Ali Monshi Rudsari, killed 1988*

Mr Monshi Rudsari was a member of the FKO (Majority). Mr Monshi Rudsari was expelled from medical school at Esfahan University during the "cultural revolution." After the universities were closed, Mr Monshi Rudsari was in charge of the publication section of the FKO in Esfahan, and later in Tehran. Mr Monshi Rudsari was arrested in his home in July or August of 1986, along with his wife and two children.

During the nearly two years of imprisonment in Tehran's Evin Prison, Mr Monshi Rudsari wrote letters from prison, and had visits with his family, the last of which took place on 17 July 1988. In one letter, he wrote, "Sentences don't matter. A day or more, as long as you don't become who they want, they keep you." His wife believes that his first trial took place in February or March of 1988, which condemned her husband to 6 months' imprisonment. He was taken to a three-member committee during the summer of 1988, and executed sometime in late August or early September. Prison officials returned Mr Monshi Rudsari's belongings to his family, which consisted of his clothes and pictures of his children. In his trousers, he had hidden his wedding ring and some pieces of paper on which he had written poetry.

death. They were informed that belongings could be collected in plastic bags if they attended by appointment at the prison, and families of *Mojahedin* victims would be permitted to collect the wills that their children had hastily made before being rushed to the gallows or put before a firing squad. Condemned leftists, however, had not been given the opportunity to make new wills because Marxists were assumed to have no interest in life after death. As one woman was told, when she asked about her husband's will and burial site:

> Your husband was a communist. He did not have a will. He was an atheist so he does not have a burial spot... what do these people know about the importance of burial? It means nothing to them.[119]

No information was provided to any relative about burial sites and all were ordered, when notified of the death or given belongings, that they must not hold memorials or funeral services or attempt to locate the grave. Of course rumours abounded and cemetery workers let out secrets and designated "places of the damned" were obvious candidates. There are horrific stories of mothers, desperate to find the remains of their children, digging at mounds of fresh earth in these places in an attempt to identify a corpse. Amnesty International describes how one woman "dug up the corpse of an executed man with her bare hands as she searched for her husband's body in Jadeh Khavaran cemetery in Tehran in August 1988 in a part of the cemetery known colloquially as *Lanatabad* (The Place of the Damned)." She said "Groups of bodies, some clothed, some in shrouds, had been buried in unmarked shallow graves in the section of the cemetery re-

or spouse. This callous way of breaking the news provoked these families to demonstrate, in their grief and anger, outside the prison, and so a new notification process had to be adopted. Thereafter, families received telephone calls from the prison, usually telling them to attend at a nearby Revolutionary Guard committee office to receive news of their prisoner relative. Eventually (after a bureaucratic run-around) and inevitably, it turned out to be news of their served for executed leftist political prisoners. The stench of the corpses was appalling but I started digging with my hands because it was important for me and my two little children that I locate my husband's grave." Amnesty reported that "She unearthed a body with its face covered in blood but when she cleaned it off she saw that it was not her husband. Other relatives visiting the graveyard discovered her husband's grave some days later."

Khavaran cemetery in south-east Tehran has now become a place of pilgrimage for relatives. Each year they meet on the first Friday of the month of September, the date that the second wave of massacres commenced in 1988. In 1996, a construction company excavating in the area came across a huge mass grave, believed to contain the remains of hundreds of executed prisoners. Family members soon besieged the area, but security forces dispersed them by firing in the air, and then arrested company employees whom they accused of spreading state secrets. In 2001, the National Council of Resistance of Iran claimed to have identified twenty-one mass grave sites where its *Mojahedin* members lay.[120]

The first burial place to be identified was at Behesht-e Zahra cemetery in Tehran. The UN Special Rapporteur on Human Rights in Iran reported that he had been reliably informed that 860 bodies had been taken there between 14 and 16 August 1988. Although Iran denied this claim, the number may have given Rafsanjani the notion that it would be credible to admit to "not more than one thousand" executions. In December Ali Khamenei, who was about to replace Montazeri as the successor to the Supreme Leader, admit-

> **"I see life as a beautiful thing."**
> *"I speak of the bad and the ugly only when I have to. I love life. I love the beauties of life and I see the beauty of life in you. I love you...."*

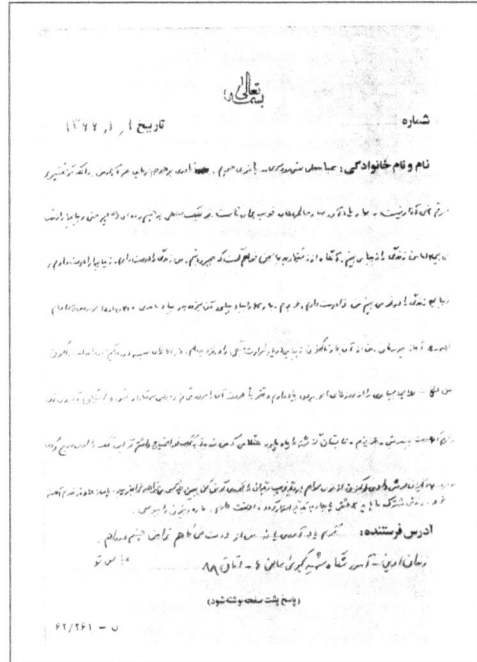

Letter from Abbas Ali Monshi Rudsari, Evin Prison, Kachu'i Amuzeshgah, Hall 6, Cell 88, to his wife, dated 29 March 1987

ted in one of Iran's conservative newspapers to executing some *Mojahedin* in prison who had been found guilty (or so he claimed) of being in communication with the Rajavi forces when they launched their "Eternal Light" attack.

Did we ever say we had abandoned executions? In the Islamic Republic we have capital punishment for those who deserve to be executed... do you think we should hand out sweets to an individual who, from inside prison, is in contact and plotting with the *Monafeqin* who launched an armed attack within the borders of the Islamic Republic …? If his contacts with such a traitorous organisation have been established, what should we do about him? He would be sentenced to death and we will certainly execute him. This is not an action that we would hide. Of course, when I say "we" I am referring to our regime: I am not in charge of the judiciary system.[121]

This was a deliberate lie, as was Mousavi's interview in the same month with Austrian television[122] and the claim made in December by Chief Justice Mousavi Ardebili that they had been executed for attacking prison guards. Although the *Mojahedin* in some wards had access to smuggled transistor radios which they could tune to the Iraq radio stations, this was not "contact" of a sort that could ever justify execution. Nor is there evidence of anyone being charged with espionage or communicating with the enemy, or even a suggestion that anyone was interrogated about any such offence.

Accounts by family members of cruelty they suffered in obtaining information about the deaths of husbands and wives, and sons and daughters, are consistent and credible. For example:

The families gathered at Khavaran every Friday. I went to Khavaran the Friday after the authorities gave me my husband's belongings. Khavaran is essentially a deserted field. Next to Khavaran is the burial place for the Baha'is. On the other side, many of the political prisoners who had been executed during the early 1980s are buried. Before carrying out the 1988 massacres, the government had dug two large canals at Khavaran.

When we arrived there, both canals had been filled. The ground was left uneven and rippled. You could still see pieces of clothes, slippers and combs on the ground. We were not allowed to touch the dirt or sit down on the soil. There were lots of families there and all were ordered to stand on their feet. Security forces were everywhere and I could see several Revolutionary Guard vehicles parked outside. We could smell the stench of the dead...

[T]he families visited Khavaran every Friday. The women intentionally wore colorful scarves and tried not to wear black. We wanted to let them know they could not break us. We also took lots of colorful flowers and picture frames containing images of our children, spouses and siblings. During the course of the ceremonies the authorities often destroyed or confiscated the picture frames. Uniformed or plainclothes security agents were always present during these visits, and often threatened people to leave the premises.

> Witness statement of Ms. Sepideh (pseudonym), in the Iran Human Rights Documentation Center's report, *Speaking for the Dead: Survivor Accounts of Iran's 1988 Massacre*

After three months the doors were opened and we were allowed visitations with our families. My mother was crying and told me that my husband was on the list of executed people. Before the executions began, the Revolutionary Guards had said "we are going to make sure your laughter stops." The laughter certainly had stopped. We still had no idea of the scope of the executions but each time we had more visits from our families we found out that more and more people had been killed. The environment was really very sad. I cried when I saw my husband's mother. She asked the prison authorities for my husband's wedding ring and asked where he was buried. The prison governor refused to tell, but offered to sign a paper saying that he had committed suicide. Later, my family got a telephone call to come to the prison: it wasn't for a visit but they just got back a bag of his possessions, three sweaters which I had knitted for him and a book.

After I was released from prison I went with my mother-in-law to Khavaran cemetery. It was very important for us to go there. I needed to see what we had heard was his grave even though it was a common grave. We were always supervised at the gravesite by Revolutionary Guards who screamed at us and would trample the flowers that we tried to plant and would arrest some of us and usually try to disperse us.

Maryam Nuri (see p. 36)

The authorities kept denying the massacres of prisoners for nearly two months. Many families thought that their imprisoned relatives had simply been transferred to a different site. Finally the prison authorities let the families learn the truth by delivering to them a plastic bag containing their relative's belongings and saying that their executed relatives had been traitors and enemies of the revolution. They further instructed the families not to make the news public and to refrain from holding memorial services. The bodies of the executed were buried at night. They were buried in a mass grave in the corner of Shiraz cemetery called "The Place of the Damned." Some of the victims however were buried in the city's common cemetery, with only their names and dates of birth engraved on the tomb stone.

Jahangir Esma'ilpur (pseudonym)
(see p. 55, from the Bidaran website)

I was told to go to the large gates of Luna Park

"I found a stone in the courtyard and, for one year, I rubbed it on the ground for hours."

Stone carved by a survivor of the 1988 prison massacre. She told the story of the carving in an interview conducted in November 2009:

"There was no life in the ward. Nothing felt real. It was as if we came back from the dead. One day, they moved us to another ward... the room looked like a war zone. Bags, clothes, slippers and personal belongings were scattered around the ward as if prisoners had been attacked or pushed out in haste with no time to pack or change... I found a letter on the floor. It was a letter a prisoner had written to his wife... the letter ended with a small drawing of a man and a woman looking at the mountains... I found a stone in the courtyard and, for one year, I rubbed it on the ground for hours during our time in the courtyard to make it small and smooth. Preserving the image was all I could think of. I had a needle and I used it to carve the letter's drawing on the stone."

for news of my husband who had been, even before the Revolution, a member of an underground group for the Tudeh Party. He was a factory manager until his arrest in May 1983 and was a mellikesh at the time he was killed. There they told me of his death and I asked "Why did you kill him?" The official said that he was an apostate, I said "Can I have his will?" And he said "Apostates don't have a will, the will is only for Muslims." I asked "Where is he buried?" They said they would let us know later but even though we came back time and again *they would never, for twenty-one years, give us an honest answer. We went with other families to Khavaran cemetery and saw that some of the holes were so shallow that you could see parts of the clothing on the corpses and bloody blankets that had been thrown down. They were grey-ish coloured prison blankets that I recognised. I discovered one blanket near a wall, covered in dried blood but we couldn't touch it – it made us feel sick. But the families became one big family, emotionally very close to each other and always commemorated the anniversary together. I have been arrested on two occasions at these commemorations. One time they said "Why is it you make so much fuss about this?" I said, "You killed my husband even though he had a two-year sentence."*

Rezvan Moghaddam, *Tudeh*, sentenced to 2 years in prison

A few months later, the family members of prisoners were called to come to the prison. It was hard to breathe, everyone wanted to find out what happened to their loved ones. They were upset, worried, waiting for a glimmer of hope whilst staring at the mouths of the prison authorities to tell the news. A few names were called. The family members of the main prisoners were asked to stand together. Everyone's eyes were watery. Those family members looked at the others whose loved ones' names had not been called. Nobody knew if the named group comprised the victims or the survivors. The air became heavier and heavier. Then the voice of the head of the prison called other names, the family members of whom were told to come forward to pick up a piece of paper. The piece of paper was a dated receipt for their relative's belongings. Suddenly people started to sob as the catastrophe became obvious. After years visiting the prisons, a piece of paper was the only thing remaining for griev-ing mothers and fathers, spouses who had just

learnt of their widowhood and restless children.

Ahmad Mousavi, FKO (Minority), sentenced to 10 years in prison (from his memoirs *Goodnight Comrade*)

In Mashhad, as far as I know, they didn't no-tify anybody. The families were waiting for their children outside the prison or the prosecution office for weeks and months. No-one wanted to believe that his or her loved one had been executed. For months they would tell the fam-ilies that the children had been "sent off." To where, it was not clear. My brother-in-law was among the executed and for months they told my sister that he was not executed, only sent off to somewhere. The father of one of my friends, both of whose children were executed, was an employee of the Mashhad Municipality. The head of the Behesht-e Reza cemetery morgue, who knew him, had apparently contacted him from the morgue and said "we have two kids here both of whom have your last name." They were both later buried in "The Cursed Land" a section of the cemetery designated for those who had been executed. This father was among the first to learn about the tragedy and little by little the news spread to other families. They did not disclose the place of burial to any of the families but "The Cursed Land" is probably where most of the kids were buried. It is the only place the families know to go to cry for their children and loved ones, imagining that it is where they once rested their heads on the chest of the cold earth.

Reza Fani Yazdi, *Tudeh*, sentenced to 20 years in prison, (from the Bidaran website)

The release of the survivors – female left-ists, reformed apostates, some fortunate MKO repenters – took place over the next few years, beginning in February 1989 with an amnesty to celebrate the 10th anniversary of the revolution. Broken, fearful and subjected to intense surveillance, some managed to leave Iran and their stories are beginning to be told, although candour is still tempered by fear; there is concern about reprisals against families back home and the threat from government assassins abroad. Khomeini's willing executioners were promoted to high positions in politics and the judiciary, where many remain today. Most are engaged in tackling a new generation of dissidents though a few (like Mousavi) are leading that generation. One notable absentee is Lajevardi, "The Butcher of Evin," said to have forced MKO virgins to "marry" Revolutionary Guards so that they could be raped in order to resolve theological difficulties that stand in the way of executing virgins.[123] He went back to his pre-revolution day job, and was assassinated outside his tailor's shop in Tehran's bazaar by a *Mojahedin* hit squad during the 10th anniversary of the 1988 massacres.[124]

9: Unanswered Questions

There are two questions of some legal significance, relating to the intentions of the perpetrators of the massacre, which cannot be clearly answered by the facts established in the preceding chapters. The first is whether the prison killings were planned long before the *Forugh Javidan* ("Eternal Light") attack, which was plainly the immediate occasion for embarking upon the extermination of MKO members, and the second is whether the dominant purpose of the killings was to eliminate political enemies or was rather to destroy religious dissidents – those who opposed, for one reason or another, the state version of Islam. These appear to be separate questions, although the answer to both may lie in the nature of the theocratic government established by Khomeini and promulgated by Rafsanjani and other powerful clerics – *velayat-e faqih*, the rule of Shia jurists.

It must be said that there is an instinctive revulsion against imputing to any government a preconceived plan to commit a crime as vile as massacring thousands of its prisoners, a great majority of whom were arrested as idealistic students rather than as armed revolutionaries, especially if that crime was committed for no better reason than to eliminate those who do not share the state's religious beliefs. An alternative explanation, though barbaric, is at least comprehensible: the *fatwa* was a furious reprisal for the Saddam-backed MKO invasion, but the temptation to continue the killings after the war, to apply Islamic penalties for apostasy to left-wingers and communists who might otherwise subvert the peace, became too great a temptation for Iran's dying Supreme Leader to withstand. This alternative explanation fits the bare facts, and gains from the absence of any clear proof of preparations for killing undertaken prior to the *fatwa* on 28 July 1988.

> "[After being released] it felt the same: dead. I was not happy. There was no meaning to freedom. Before, I liked to be out... After 1988, there was no joy. I felt dead, wherever I was. It was very hard... After the killings, I was like someone who doesn't know anything, doesn't know where she is. [I was] more than numb, almost dead."
>
> -Testimony of a survivor of the 1988 massacre, who was arrested on June 10, 1981 at the age of 17 and held in Gohardasht and Gezehl Hessar Prisons.

The survivors whom we interviewed believed, with hindsight, that the classifications, interviews and questionnaires over the previous year, and some movements of prisoners, were preparations for a "final solution." For example:

A few months before the killings the prison guards distributed a typed form to everyone. There were questions about our charges, our case, and our sentence as well as questions requiring personal information. We had to sign it. For us to write our charge was more complicated. The Fadaiyan *could say* Fadaiyan *and didn't have that problem. We had to write "organization" or "hypocrites" or "Mojahedin." Our responses would clarify our positions. So I didn't write anything.*

During the same period, they called a few people out as if they had signed-up for the infirmary. They did this in order to not attract other people's attention. Perhaps three days after, I was called to go to the infirmary. I had not asked for being taken to the infirmary so I was surprised. This was about 5 months before the killing.

There was one interrogator: Zamani. At the time, he was the head of intelligence at Evin. He took me to a room with a desk and a chair and started to talk about politics. He asked me, how is the organization within the prison? How do we decide and communicate policies?

"[When the visitation started], my mother came to visit. She was terrified. She said. 'I came several times but they didn't let me in. They were handing out bags or plastic bags to people and telling them 'This belonged to your child. Go now.' They have killed many people. Many are missing."

-Testimony of Seifollah Moni'eh, who was arrested in Tehran in September of 1981, at the age of 17 and sentenced to 12 years.

I knew that this was an evil discussion and no doubt had unstated goals. He wanted to know more about what was happening in the ward. I kept telling him that I didn't know anything about an organization within the prison, that I didn't know what prisoners' political views were. I was just silent. He would then start again and say "you are in Amuzeshgah [learning center] 5. Tell me about the organization. What role do you play in it?" He said he wanted to under-

stand the organization and I, as someone within the organization, should tell him about it and say where I am in the hierarchy, who is above me and who is below me. He would say, "you people are weak, we will break your will. There is nothing left of the Mojahedin organization."

This man always smelled of cologne. You could see that he was clean and well-ironed. Unlike the people from the prosecution offices who were not well-dressed or cleaned. He would call me every day or every other day for interrogation. The second day, he was not into a mood for dialogue. He brought out several cables from his drawer and started to beat me. He beat me when I was standing. With the cable on my head and my body. If I sat down, he would stand above me and continue to beat me. Then he would stop and talk. I could also hear a tape recorder that he used. He talked generally about the organization. I didn't have any indication regarding what this accusation was based on and the beatings also were general. It was a slow torture. Small but regular dose of beating that would open your wounds but not deepen them. This daily routine was destroying my mind slowly. They first told me that I am part of an organization inside prison. Then they said that I have organizational contacts outside the prison. He would bring the recordings of other prisoners who had confessed. I was confused. Was organizing in prison a crime? Did he want me to say that there is an organization? Really, there was no such thing and I had no organizational relationship with anyone. But we had solidarity to defend our interests. If we ate at the same time, or refused to repent in numbers they would say you are resisting and you have an organization. If we were all hungry, this meant we had an organization. If we cleaned the room together, this was organized behaviour. But we only had a common interest: we wanted to live.

At the end, after seven weeks of interrogation and beatings, Zamani asked me to give a televised interview. I refused. I was beaten with the cable for one more week. I didn't confess to anything so he wrote himself on a piece of paper and asked me to read. He said that I had to say that I have organizational contacts with the outside and I am in charge of the prisoners' contact with the outside. I had to say that I did this through the visits. How could this have been true? No one but my mother came to visit. And she opposed the Mojahedin.

Seifollah Moni'eh, MKO, sentenced to 8 years in prison[125]

One day Masoumi [a prison visitor who attempted to persuade inmates to accept the regime] came to our ward and 7 or 8 people, including myself, went and sat with him. He talked to us and told us that "our problem was to evaluate prisoners and we have come to the conclusion that there are three different types of prisoners. The first type have abandoned their political views and are cooperating with prison officials. These are what you [prisoners] call 'repenters.' The second type have abandoned their political views but are not with us and just want to get out and resume a normal life. The third type are those that are not only maintaining their political ties but are still actively

against the regime. We want to identify these three types and deal with everyone accordingly. The repenters would be freed. I think that those who really intend to get on with their lives and not be involved in politics but are not with us should also be released. But for the third type, we want to deal with them in a way that is appropriate to them." These are his exact sentences. It was maybe June or July. The weather was warm. This discussion came about after Masoumi tried to get people to discuss politics, for example about the Mojahedin *going to Iraq and their alliance to Saddam.*

Throughout 1986-1987 [for about one year] prisoners would periodically be blindfolded and taken to interrogations. My turn came in the spring of 1987. It was probably after the Iranian New Year [April 1987]. A number of us were called and we were taken to the interrogation blindfolded... We sat and waited to be called in one by one. The questions were political and ideological. "What do you think about the Islamic Republic? What do you think about the US? What do you think about a certain policy of the Islamic Republic? What do you think about Islam? What do you think about the Islamic Republic's policy on the war?" I think it was three pages. There was a blank space between each question for us to write down our answers. There were no questions about family or relatives. There were no personal questions. There were no questions about the charges against us and they didn't ask what we thought about our own political group. We had to write and sign the form. I wrote that I refuse to respond because these are inquisitorial questions. He didn't say any-thing. He just told me to get-up and leave. When we refused to answer these questions on account of "inquisition" we were not beaten or hurt physically. Amongst ourselves we thought that maybe it was even possible the regime was becoming compassionate be-cause of their lack of response. This was very surprising to us.

Hossein Maleki, *Forqan*, sentenced to 8 years in prison

They called me and they took me to a room where the death delegation was sitting. Go-ing in the main door, there was a large, long hallway. At the end of this hall there was a room. I was told to take my blindfold off. Nayyeri, Eshraqi, and a cleric in a white robe were sitting. Two people in ordinary clothes were also there. I think they were from the Ministry of Intelligence. I sat in front of Nayyeri and Eshraqi. When I said 'Monafeqin' very quickly he said to the per-son in civilian clothes, 'Give him a [piece of] paper so he writes it down'. He [the man in civilian clothes] kept saying, 'Ask him about what he was doing [and] how he was acting in prison'. Nayyeri was not listening [and said], 'We do not have time – give him the paper'. This paper was for us [to write that we reject] our group and to [write] that the Mojahedin were terrorists and had killed Ayatollah Baheshti and some Friday sermon clerics, and that they have rebelled against the Muslim people. When I came out, the person in civilian clothes followed me. I realised that he was from the Ministry of Intelligence and was aware of my interro-gations in 1987 and 1988. He was pushing me hard to say the things that I had refused to say before.

Reza Shemirani (see p. 51)

They wanted to know about the organisa-tion within the prison. All I wrote was the list of prisoners in every room and said, "I don't know who gives these ideas. I am not in every room." The torture and beating were so harsh. I resisted as long as I could. In the winter every day I was taken at 6:00 or 7:00 a.m. to the tazir *room and I would go back to my cell at the end of the day with swollen feet. I really was giving up. I had to sign the forms. They wrote the questions and I had to respond and sign. It was all about the organisation in the prison. I was worried that I would give in. When in No-vember I finally told the interrogator that I would give the information, I went back to my cell and into the bathroom and ate depilation cream to try to kill myself. But I threw it up. I tried to eat it again but they heard the noise and came in and took me to the infirmary. It burned all of my insides. I was in a critical condition for ten days. The interrogator came to visit me and asked me why I did this. I told him I had nothing to say and could not take the beating anymore. So they left me alone.*

Reza Shemirani (from the author's interview)

However, no evidence has emerged from prison guards or officials to support the theory that the "final solution" had been pre-planned for over a year, and Montazeri in his memoirs gives it no support – although it is quite likely, given his losing battle with the hardliners in 1987-8, that he would not have been privy to it. (He recalls that "some people decided, once and for all, to get rid of the *Mojahedin* and so they obtained a letter from the Imam." He died without identifying "the people," or the time at which they lobbied for the *fatwa*.)

Undoubtedly the classification records assisted the Death Committees in identifying "steadfast" MKO members – the hearings took only a few minutes – and in the examination of left wing apostates, but these records were routinely maintained for years and could have served less lethal purposes. Some witnesses report elliptical threats from guards and officials in the months before the massacres, but no rehearsals and no clear warnings. On the other hand, the theory that the MKO massacre was caused by an explosion of righteous anger has difficulty explaining why its machinery of death, after a brief suspension, ground into action against the leftists, unless this was part of some preconceived plan to eradicate problem prisoners.

The truth may lie in the answer to the second question, namely the regime's motivation in destroying both groups, and by examining its attitude towards them from the early days of the revolution. It is plain from the declarations of Ayatollah Khomeini, the Friday sermons of Rafsanjani and the announcements by the judicial authorities and the Ministry of Intelligence, that the *Mojahedin* and the leftists were condemned, not merely because they engaged in terrorist attacks, but because they denied the revolutionary state's idea of God. The *Mojahedin* were believers, but in a God who directed them to class warfare, equality and (so they later claimed) even towards democracy. The Marxists were non-believers. Neither group was prepared to obey the God installed

by the revolution, whose orders were divined and declared by Khomeini. So both opposition groups were "corrupters of the earth" and thus guilty of the Koranic crime of "waging war on God" (Koran 5:33). As Rafsanjani and other political clerics constantly stressed in the early and mid 1980s, God's punishment for *moharebs* was death.

This analysis invites the thought that the massacres were not an unpredictable and unprincipled deviation from Islamic governance, but a consequence – almost a logical consequence – of the theocratic state constructed by Khomeini after his helpers and Revolutionary Guards had seen off the three Bs (Bakhtiar, Bazargan and Banisadr) and the clergy's erstwhile liberal and secularist allies. There was no magic about that state's progressive elimination of political opponents – a task facilitated

> "We used to buy figs from the prison shop. When we would buy [dry] figs, we would clean them and wash them first, and we would keep them. This way we always had some figs ready for use. After the mass executions, we bought some figs from the prison shops. When they brought us the figs, we realized that they were already washed and cleaned. I later found out that those figs belonged to prisoners who had been executed. They had taken the figs from their cells after they were executed, and they had resold them to us."
>
> -Testimony of Hossein Maleki, who was arrested on September 27, 1980 in Tehran at the age of 19 and sentenced to life imprisonment, which was later reduced to 8 years.

by the war against Saddam, which galvanised national loyalty and made it easier to justify harsh action against fifth columnists. The consolidation of power through one party rule, intolerance and despotism is not at all uncommon; what was unusual about this revolution's progress was that it came to treat as subversive different approaches towards Islam, as well as disbelief in general – and to regard its extirpation as a duty ordained by God.

In practical terms, this meant that "corrupters" – whether atheists or *Mojahedin* – could not be allowed back into society to spread their heretical doctrines amongst the people, and especially the youth (the regime constantly laments not taking earlier action to stop their propaganda successes amongst students). For "steadfast" prisoners, doctrinally there was, literally, no way out – which is precisely why those

> "But I knew that as long as I was in Iran, I was still really in their claws. In prison they can directly swallow you – but in Iran they can still grab you. You never feel safe. You feel that you are always controlled. It was only when I came out of Iran that I felt free."
>
> -Testimony of a survivor of the 1988 massacre, who was arrested in January 1985 at the age of 16 and sentenced to 8 years imprisonment.

who completed their sentence were not let out. They were *mellikesh*, too dangerous to release. This policy was announced by the Ministry of Intelligence in 1985: "Henceforth, no prisoners will be released unless it is proven that they have repented and are willing to conform."[126] Hence the problem: would the non-reformed be kept in prison indefinitely, long after their sentences expired, or was there some other solution? This must have been a question posed by the authorities – particularly within the Ministry of Intelligence – once it became clear that many of the left-wing and MKO prisoners were incapable of genuine repentance. The well-known (if behind the scenes) struggle between

Montazeri's supporters, and Lajevardi and the hard liners reflected this debate: the latter's victory towards the end of 1987 coincides with escalating attempts within the prisons to classify detainees according to their stance towards the Iranian theocracy. In February 1988, the new amnesty provisions were announced: members of "counter revolutionary movements" would not be entitled to pardon unless their repentance had been proved before the public prosecutor, the Sharia judge and the Intelligence Ministry – the very people who, six months later, formed the Death Committees. The logical – and more compassionate – corollary was also spelled out: "If they are rehabilitated and do not prove a risk to society they will be pardoned, even if they have not finished their sentence."[127] It is significant that these policies were being debated and adopted after the UN's resolution for a truce was put on the table (in July 1987) and an end to the long war with Iraq had at last become foreseeable. It is likely that, throughout this period, the issue of what to do with political prisoners was under discussion, and the classification process was undertaken to assist whatever course the Supreme Leader and his senior advisers might decide ultimately to adopt. (Several prisoners have said that they were aware of "colour coding" in Gohardasht – white for those who are truly repentant, yellow for the politically passive and red for enemies of the regime: a categorisation that could, of course, serve a number of purposes, not all of which would involve the execution of red prisoners.)

It seems to me most likely that the purpose of the classifications and re-groupings was to assist whatever policy was eventually adopted towards the political prisoners, and that a debate over that policy was ongoing, based on the premise that the non-repentant could in no circumstances be released to rejoin a society that they would try to corrupt. One option – supported undoubtedly by the hard-line Lajevardi faction – was to execute the un-repentant. It would have been obvious to them that this could only be achieved by sidelining Montazeri, the more compassionate heir ap-parent, whose fall was designed by a group led by Rafsanjani and Ali Khamenei, all the more urgently once they realised Khomeini was dy-ing of cancer. In any event, executions on this scale would require a *fatwa* from the Supreme Leader, since that would be necessary to over-rule retrospectively the sentencing decisions of the original Sharia judges and to replace them by the sentence of death. No such *fatwa* was forthcoming until the *Mersad* operation, which so enraged the Supreme Leader that he brought it down as a reprisal against the MKO rather than (as "final solution" supporters had envis-aged) against all the unrepentant counter revo-lutionaries. This final act of the "final" solution was probably effected by a second *fatwa*, issued clandestinely late in August or early in Septem-ber 1988, its issuance influenced by how easy and how satisfying it had been to annihilate several thousand *Mojahedin*.

This is speculation, of course, but in the absence of evidence from high level perpetra-tors it accords with the facts and with a reason-able interpretation of statements made by the regime at the time and afterwards. The decision to go with the massacre option may have been a direct consequence of fury over the MKO in-vasion, but it also reflected the genuine views of men who shared Lajevardi's belief that "we execute because we care for humanity"; of true believers, who thought that they were paving their path to paradise by sending God's enemies to accursed corners of cemeteries across Iran.

That raises another question in its turn: what was their dominant purpose in canvassing and then carrying out the death option? The pri-mary intention was clearly not to rid the coun-try of communists or Marxist-influenced *Mo-jahedin*, but rather to carry out the Islamic sen-tence on those who, by their non-belief or their perverse beliefs, were deemed to have "waged war on God." This comes across in the wording of the *fatwa*: the *Monafeqin* "do not believe in Islam" asserts Khomeini, and their claim to do so is a hypocritical deception: "those who are in prisons throughout the country who remain steadfast in their support for the *Monafeqin* are considered to be *Mohareb*s and are condemned to execution." They are to be killed without trial because of their religious beliefs, quite apart from the MKO's alliance with the enemy. The leftists, similarly, are to die because of their re-ligious unbeliefs, their godless atheism (if their apostasy is voluntary) and not because of their political ideology. The distinction may be im-portant for legal reasons, since destroying a re-ligious group carries more serious consequences than eliminating a political group, although this distinction is questionable in logic and in any event is otiose in a theocratic state like Iran.

10: International Legal Consequences

The executions and tortures described in the preceding chapters were ordered by the leaders of the state of Iran. I am not concerned with their compliance with national law, though it is worth observing that Grand Ayatollah Montazeri and other highly respected theologians regarded the *fatwa* as evincing "a complete disregard for all judicial standards and rulings." I also understand that Sharia jurisprudence guarantees certain rights to people facing criminal penalties, including the right to a trial and the right not to be subjected to torture; if this is correct, then the Sharia itself must have been violated in 1988. These are questions that Iran's courts should resolve, but since the men who enforced the *fatwa* in 1988 today still occupy high position in those courts, it is unlikely that the subject will be raised any time soon. But all states, and their leaders and their agents, are subject to international law and may be subjected to international legal process. That higher law is made up of treaties which the state has ratified, and what is called "customary" law which has been accepted over the years by states and jurists as universally binding, and which may be enforced by prosecution or civil action in other states, or in tribunals established by the UN.

It is a fundamental feature of international law that states are bound by obligations they have undertaken to the international community: governments come and go, regimes may fall and revolutions sometimes happen, but the state itself endures as an entity which must abide by its treaties. So those ratified by Iran during the time of the Shah – most importantly the Genocide Convention of 1948, the Geneva Conventions of 1949 and the International Covenant of Civil and Political Rights of 1966 – bound Iran in 1988, notwithstanding its revolutionary change to an Islamic Republic.[128] In any event, the basic rules of these treaties, which outlaw genocide, arbitrary executions and torture, are now (and were by 1988) a special part of international human rights law, that part which is enforceable universally as *jus cogens* – crimes that all states have a duty to prohibit and punish, and whose perpetrators might, subject to certain immunities, be prosecuted in the courts of other states, or at international tribunals established by the UN.

Although international criminal law began in 1946 with the judgment at Nuremberg, there had for many centuries been a special regime of humanitarian law to protect unarmed prisoners in times of war, because of their utter vulnerability to sudden or summary execution or to torture by their captors. By the time of the English civil war in the 1640s, the obligation to give "quarter" – to spare an enemy who yields – was a firm rule of all three belligerents: the King's army, the Parliamentary army and the army of the Kingdom of Scotland. Any soldier or officer guilty of slaying an unarmed prisoner in his custody was himself liable to execution.[129] At the first war crimes trial of a head of state, in 1649, the most telling evidence against Charles I was that he had supervised the torture of prisoners of war.[130] From this time onwards, a prohibition against torture and killing captives can be found in the ordinances of most European armies. For some time it was subject to a special tit-for-tat defence of reprisal (Shakespeare, to justify Henry V's notorious Agincourt order to slay his French prisoners, had to invent a French war crime – killing the boys in the baggage train –which would give the King the right to retaliate).[131] It was Grotius who first challenged the legality of the reprisal defence, arguing that "collective responsibility" was unjust: "nature does not sanction retaliation except against those who have done wrong. It is not sufficient that by a sort of fiction the enemy may be conceived as forming a single body."[132]

Francis Lieber was appointed by President Lincoln to draft his code for the US Army (which remains the basis of customary international war law) and he accepted that:

> *The law of war does not allow proclaiming either an individual belonging to a hostile army, or a citizen, or a subject of the hostile government, an outlaw who may be slain without trial by any captor, any more than the modern law of peace allows such intentional outlawry; on the contrary it abhors such outrage. The sternest retaliation should follow the murder committed in consequence of such proclamation, made by whatever authority. Civilised nations look with horror upon offers of rewards for the assassination of enemies as relapses into barbarism.[133]*

Article 13 of Geneva Convention III now prohibits any defence of reprisal: killing captive prisoners of war constitutes "one of the most obvious and absolute war crimes."[134]

Reprisal is precisely the description I would give to the issuance of the *fatwa* of 28 July 1988. It declared that all "steadfast" *Mo-*

jahedin captives were enemies in league with Iraq – which would make them prisoners of war – and condemned them to death in retaliation for the "Eternal Light" invasion, coordinated with the Iraqi Air Force, which was still underway. No doubt like most reprisals it was conceived in hot fury, a week after Khomeini had drunk the bitter cup of poison and agreed to the UN ceasefire. Since the *Mojahedin* were an identifiable Iranian group that had joined the "treacherous" Saddam, those members of that group held in his prisons were deemed collectively responsible for Rajavi's "treason." At this simple and visceral level, the murder of the *Mojahedin* was as monstrous and indefensible a crime as the Japanese death marches of POWs in retaliation for Allied victories, or the German reprisal killings of whole villages after partisan assassinations of Nazi officials in Czechoslovakia and Italy, or Saddam Hussein's malicious executions and destruction at Dujail after an attempt on his own life. Comparisons are odious, especially between atrocities, but the Iranian prison slaughter strikes me as the worst of all. Its calculation makes it more vicious than the killings at Srebrenica or the Nazi reprisal killings. There were more victims that there were at the Sandakan death marches in Borneo, where only 6 of the 1,300 allied prisoners survived.[135] If, as the *fatwa* assumed, the *Mojahedin* were prisoners of war, then killing them was the gravest of breaches of Geneva Convention III and thus a war crime that all state parties to that Convention would have a duty to prosecute by tracking down suspected perpetrators and putting them on trial. This duty applies to "grave breaches" committed in an international armed conflict (which the Iran-Iraq War most certainly was), and which had not ended at the time of the massacre: the ceasefire did not come into effect until 20 August 1988.

The problem with this analysis is that the *Mojahedin* victims were not, under this or any other definition, "prisoners of war." They were prisoners during a war, certainly, but they had been arrested (a few before the war even started) for minor acts of complicity with an underground movement opposed to the Islamic Republic but not at that stage in league with Iraq. Most of them had been arrested in or after June 1981 for demonstrating or distributing newspapers or merely for being 'sympathisers' – any who were taken in arms were shot on the spot or executed. In any event, although it might be said that they were members of an "organised resistance movement" they did not belong to Iraq and did not satisfy the other conditions in Article 4 of Covenant III, namely that they carried arms openly and wore uniforms or emblems that distinguished them as combatants. The 1949 Geneva Conventions were drafted to protect regular soldiers who fell into enemy hands. Convention III had been influenced by the execution and torture visited upon allied prisoners in the custody of Axis powers, notoriously of Japan. Members of urban guerrilla movements fighting a civil war against their own government, even if their government was also fighting a wider war against a foreign foe, could not claim protection if they fell into their government's hands, at least in the absence of some formal link with the forces of its enemy.

Tempting though it is to take the *fatwa* at its word and treat the *Mojahedin* prisoners as an active Iraqi-aligned force, to accord them retrospectively POW status is too much

of a stretch, despite the presumption that all persons should enjoy Convention III protection until their status has otherwise been determined by a competent tribunal. What is, however, important evidentially, is that the government of Iran was well aware of the Geneva Convention provisions: the state had ratified them and the government complied with them in respect of its large number of Iraqi war prisoners. It looked upon its *Mojahedin* prisoners as if they were members of an Iraqi-aligned militia, who would have had the same status of prisoners of war, yet it killed them without the process due to such prisoners. So there can be no doubt that those who carried out the *fatwa* knew well that it was an incitement for them to commit an act that was unlawful as a matter of international humanitarian law.

If the *Mojahedin* were not prisoners of war, then the leftists were even less so: whilst some of their organisations engaged in guerrilla violence against the regime, none had any obvious links with Iraq. Their status – and "every person in enemy hands must have some status in international law"[136] was that of civilians.[137] This gives them protection under Geneva Convention IV – relating to the protection of civilian persons in time of war – although the legal position requires some explanation. In 1949, UN members were not prepared to allow international law to intrude upon their sovereignty when it came to putting down insurgencies and other internal revolts by their own nationals, so Article 4 of Geneva Convention IV limits its protection to persons who "find themselves, in a case of conflict or occupation, in the hands of a party to the conflict or occupying power of which they are not nationals." So although the Geneva Conventions impose certain important duties on states in relation to internal conflicts by Article 3, which is common to all four Geneva Conventions and requires them to treat detainees humanely (i.e. without violence to life or person, without torture and without execution except after a fair trial), this does not come within the Convention "grave breaches" enforcement machinery.

It is, of course, possible to analyse the armed conflict between the Islamic Republic and the leftists – those it termed the "minigroups" – as a conflict quite separate and distinct from its ongoing war with Iraq and the *Mojahedin*, and as such a "non-international" armed conflict in which Iran was bound to comply with Common Article 3. This analysis probably reflects the facts of the case, at least in terms of the intentions of the perpetrators: in the first wave, initiated by the *fatwa* of 28 July 1988, the regime's intention was to kill suspected collaborators, but the second wave of killings was designed to eliminate religious dissidents who might threaten the Islamic regime's survival in the aftermath of the fragile peace with Iraq. Whether it is realistic to superimpose such an analytical distinction on the frenzied decisions taken in the murderous atmosphere of August 1988 would be a headache for any international prosecutor. This is one reason why reliance on an international humanitarian law crafted in the immediate aftermath of World War II has been supplemented by less technical rules of customary international law and of human rights law, binding on all states whether in war or peace and whether in time of international or internal armed conflict. The International Court of Justice has held that Common Article 3 constitutes just such customary rule and is therefore binding on all nations as a set of minimum standards in any armed conflict. So too is Article 75 of the First Protocol to the Geneva Conventions, a separate treaty promulgated in 1977, which defines minimum standards of humane treatment and the basic standards for fair trial – what are termed the "elementary considerations of humanity," breach of which may entail both state liability and individual criminal liability.[138]

Article 75 of *Geneva Protocol I* sets out the fundamental guarantees:

> *...persons who are in the power of a party to the conflict... shall be treated humanely in all circumstances and shall enjoy, as a minimum, the protection provided by this article without any adverse distinction based upon race, colour, sex, language, religion or belief, political or other opinion, national or social origin, wealth, birth or on any other similar criteria. Each party shall respect the person, honour, convictions and religious practices of all such persons.*
>
> 2. *The following acts are and shall remain prohibited at any time and in any place whatsoever, whether committed by civilian or by military agents:*
>
> a) *violence to the life, health or physical or mental well-being of persons, in particular:*
>
>   i) *Murder;*
>
>   ii) *Torture of all kinds, whether physical or mental;*
>
>   iii) *Corporal Punishment; and*
>
>   iv) *Mutilation;*
>
> b) *Outrages upon personal dignity, in particular humiliating and degrading treatment...*
>
> d) *collective punishments;*

e) threats to commit any of the foregoing acts...

These fundamental guarantees, which Iran blatantly breached in 1988 in respect of its political prisoners, are supplemented by due process guarantees which provide the definition of what counts as a fair trial. The following were obviously breached in respect of the *Mojahedin* (who had no trial at all) and in respect of the leftists who had unfair trials:

4. No sentence may be passed and no penalty may be executed on a person found guilty of a penal offence related to the armed conflict except pursuant to a conviction pronounced by an impartial and regularly constituted court respecting a generally recognised principle of regular judicial procedure, which include the following:

a) The procedure shall provide for an accused to be informed without delay of the particulars of the offence alleged against him and shall afford the accused before and during his trial all necessary rights and means of defence;

b) No-one shall be convicted of an offence except on the basis of individual penal responsibility...

f) No-one shall be compelled to testify against himself or to confess guilt;

h) No-one shall be prosecuted or punished by the same party for an offence in respect of which final judgment acquitting or convicting that person has previously been pronounced under the same law and judicial procedure.

i) Anyone prosecuted for an offence shall have the right to have the judgment pronounced publicly;

j) ...persons who are arrested, detained or interned for reasons related to the armed conflict shall enjoy the protection provided by this article until their final release, repatriation or re-establishment, even after the end of the armed conflict.

These elementary considerations of humanity were breached routinely in the course of the 1988 massacres. Prisoners were arbitrarily executed without fair or (in the case of the *Mojahedin*) any, trial; they were tortured and viciously beaten after proceedings of which they were given no notice and in which they were given no rights of defence. A technical distinction may be made on the basis that although the *fatwa* which sentenced the *Mojahedin* prisoners to death avowedly found them "guilty of a penal offence related to the armed conflict," the leftists were tortured and killed for apostasy. Article 75 of Geneva Protocol I has a treaty application only to international armed conflicts, but it reflects the position that customary international law had reached by 1988 and it informs the modern content and interpretation of human rights law in war time.[139] The basic prohibitions – against arbitrary execution, torture and unfair trials – are all *jus cogens* rules of international law – i.e. principles so fundamental that no nation may breach or opt out of them. They are endorsed and amplified by the provisions of the International Covenant on Civil and Political Rights (the ICCPR) which Iran ratified and which applied in 1988 notwithstanding the 1979 change in government. The ICCPR lays down that the death penalty is only permissible after a proper trial and appeal with defence rights guaranteed; it forbids torture and requires public trial without double jeopardy; it guarantees freedom of expression and of religion. All these rights, recognised as part of customary international law, were grossly and indefensibly violated by the government of Iran.

There is a further right which has in my opinion developed to the *jus cogens* stage and that is what Article 32 of the 1977 First Geneva Protocol refers to as "the right of families to know the fate of their relatives." It imposes a correlative duty on the state to identify the graves of those it has executed and to permit families to mourn in peace at burial sites. This collection of rights has been recognised by the Inter-American Court of Human Rights as derived from the right to life,[140] although more logically the Human Rights Committee has treated the refusal of a government to notify the family of an executed convict of the location of his body as a violation of the prohibition on inhuman and degrading treatment,[141] and the European Court of Human Rights has taken the same approach.[142] The anguish caused by the arbitrary denial of an opportunity to mourn the dead has been recognised at least since Sophocles dramatised the mental frenzy of Antigone, forbidden by Creon to bury her brother's body. I understand that the right to bury the dead is of fundamental importance to Muslims, and that the Shia have taken a particularly firm line in this regard ever since Hossein, grandson of the prophet Mohammad, was left unburied on the battlefield at Karbala in the year 680. On this basis, the behaviour of the regime is not only calculated to inflict psychological torture, but would be an especially cruel kind of hypocrisy.

The obligations that Iran undertook by ratifying the ICCPR are not directly enforceable, other than by way of petition to the Human Rights Committee under an optional protocol that Iran, like most other parties, has not ratified. So there is little practical point in dwelling on the breaches of this particular Covenant, unless they provide evidence of an offence, or at least a civil wrong, which can be the subject of an action in courts or tribunals outside Iran, either of other nations or set up specially by the UN. To the extent Iran has breached its treaty obligations or rules of customary international law, then state responsibility arises and it could be subject to International Court of Justice determination if referred there by the General Assembly or certain other UN organs. But to have any prospect of world court adjudication, other states need to take up the cause.

There are, of course, non-legal mechanisms available at the United Nations – it has "Special Rapporteurs" on extra judicial killings and on torture who might be prevailed upon to pick up the baton dropped by Professor Pohl and to conduct a proper investigation. Iran might be required to co-operate by the Human Rights Council, which purports to guard the ICCPR and has replaced the Human Rights Commission which so dismally failed to call Iran to account in 1988. It has to be said that the UN human rights mechanisms are highly politicised as well as being underfunded, and tend to be reserved for inquiries into recent atrocities (for example, the Alston Inquiry into the Kenyan election violence and the Goldstone Inquiry into the Gaza war).

But in my view there are a number of features of the 1988 massacres which justify a UN inquiry. Firstly, the nature of the atrocity: there has been no comparable act of state slaughter of so many prisoners since the Japanese death-marched their POWs at the end of World War II. (Unless the massacre of Muslim men and boys at Srebrenica is counted, although those victims were briefly taken hostage and were not serving prisoners.) Secondly, the embarrassing fact (for the UN) that Professor Pohl's investigation was stymied, partly because of lies and lack of co-operation from Iran (although he found out enough to put the General Assembly on notice of the crime, if not of its full magnitude). Thirdly, despite the passage of time, many of the men responsible for the massacres are (with the notable exception of Khomeini) still mainly in place or in higher place: there are survivors who remain alive and neutral witnesses available. Grand Ayatollah Montazeri died in Qom on 20 December 2009 and so he cannot give the evidence he wanted to give to Professor Pohl. Member states whose concerns have been much focused on Iran's nuclear pretensions and potential may wish to investigate the human rights record of a regime which asks to be trusted in respect of current undertakings to the international community and to consider how trustworthy have been the words of its leaders and diplomats in the past. If ever Iran harbours pretensions to sit on the Human Rights Council of the UN: in view of its failure to repent or even to admit the conduct revealed in this report, its election would make a mockery of the Human Rights Council (as its predecessor, the Human Rights Commission, was mocked when it was chaired by Libya). Whether its leaders – including its opposition leader Mir Hossein Mousavi – can be trusted to comply with international law is a question that will have to be pondered in light of their conduct in mid 1988.

I am not greatly optimistic about UN action, although the factors outlined above may make it more likely than in the past: this is an appropriate time for the Human Rights Council to examine the *bona fides* of the Iranian leadership and a "Special Rapporteur" would today have the benefit of evidence from witnesses who in the past were too terrified of Iranian reprisals to speak: there are many who have come into the open in the past few years. I would expect such an investigation to confirm my findings in this report, but what then? The UN Security Council could establish an *ad hoc* war crimes court, as it has for the Cambodian genocide ordered by the late Pol Pot back in 1979, although that court was established with the support of the Cambodian government – the leaders of the present regime in Iran would certainly not support a criminal court that might put some of them in the dock. At least, a Human Rights Council investigation would put pressure on Iran fully to identify those who had been killed and to provide details to relatives of their burial locations and to permit public mourning. It is unlikely to do more, unless placed under pressure or in return for the relaxation of UN sanctions – the circumstances that produced a trial of the Lockerbie bombing and Libya's payment of compensation to the relatives of its victims.

As a matter of international law developed by the Inter-American Court, Iran has a duty to provide "adequate compensation" to victims' families and survivors, and especially to victims' children.[143] In *Aloeboetoe v Suriname*, the Inter-American Commission found the defendant state responsible for its soldiers, who arrested and tortured a group of fishermen and ordered them to dig their own graves before shooting them. It was ordered to pay US$500,000 for the benefit of each of the victims' children and relatives.[144] These reparations were made up of actual damage (compensation for the trauma of having a close relative assassinated) and moral damage (compensation for the terror suffered by the victims in the hours before their death, the right to which becomes enforceable by their heirs). This latter head of damage is particularly appropriate in the case of the Iranian massacres, where the right to life was extinguished after torture and terror. The difficulty, however, is in finding a forum – other than a special UN tribunal – where such a claim would be adjudicated. In the following sections I consider the possible heads of criminal and civil liability.

Crimes Against Humanity

The International Criminal Court only has jurisdiction to deal with offences committed since July 2002 and unless there is regime change in Iran it is unlikely that the Security Council would set up an *ad hoc* tribunal to try the perpetrators of the 1988 massacres. The world court (the International Court of Justice) could rule on issues of law, but since Iran does not accept its jurisdiction this could only happen if a UN organ like the General Assembly asked the ICJ for an advisory opinion. There nonetheless remains the possibility that one or more of the perpetrators of the 1988 massacres will venture abroad, to countries where they may be prosecuted (or else extradited to countries that will prosecute them) for torture or genocide (crimes which are subject to universal jurisdiction) or for a broader category, "Crimes Against Humanity."

The crime against humanity entered international law by way of Article 6(c) of the Nuremberg Statute, which spelt out an offence of which Nazi leaders were convicted on 30

September 1946. The Statute provided a law against:

> *Murder, extermination, enslavement, deportation and other inhumane acts committed against any civilian population, before or during the war, or persecutions on political, racial or religious grounds in execution of or in connection with any crime, within the jurisdiction of the tribunal, whether or not in violation of the domestic law of the country where perpetrated. Leaders, organisers, instigators and accomplices participating in the formulation or execution of a common plan or conspiracy to commit any of the foregoing crimes are responsible for all acts performed by any person in the execution of such plans.*

This definition would plainly cover the extermination of the *Mojahedin* and the inhumane actions committed against the leftists, at the end and in the aftermath of the Iran-Iraq War, which actions in any event amounted to persecution on politico-religious grounds (in respect of the *Mojahedin*) and on religious grounds (in respect of the leftists) whether or not the *fatwa* was constitutional or the floggings were in compliance with Sharia law. Article 6(c) was the basis for convictions of Nazi government officials for the killing and torturing of their own nationals in concentration camps (German Jews and homosexuals were not "prisoners of war," for reasons given above) and the judgment in the main trial provides an authoritative basis for holding individuals at all levels, whether Revolutionary Guards, prison governors or political leaders or powerful theologians, liable for crimes against humanity. Torturers cannot rely on the defence of "superior orders" any more than commanders can rely on the privileges and immunities of the states they serve. Article 8 of the Nuremberg Charter provided:

The fact that the defendant acted pursuant to the order of his government or of a superior shall not free him from responsibility, but may be considered in mitigation of punishment...

The true test, the Nuremberg judgement decided, was "whether moral choice is in fact possible" for a soldier or official ordered to kill or torture in defiance of international law.[145] This leaves the proven perpetrator of a crime against humanity only two avenues of exculpation if the action was taken under orders: either that he did not appreciate its unlawfulness, or that he acted under a duress so threatening to himself or his family that it left him no reasonable option but to comply. In the follow-up Nuremberg trials, duress usually failed as a defence for officers and soldiers and guards who feared disciplinary sanctions or minor punishments, in no way comparable to the gravity of the harm they inflicted by choosing to obey the lethal order.[146] The evidence suggests that prison governors like Naserian were extremely enthusiastic in their compliance with orders that they should have known were unlawful, and there has been no suggestion that Revolutionary Guards who refused to join the hanging or firing squads would have been punished by deprivation of their own lives, although no doubt disobedience would have entailed some disciplinary sanction. There is some evidence that hardened Revolutionary Guards were brought into some prisons to do the killings, probably because of concerns that ordinary prison guards might be reluctant to hang or shoot the people who had been in their custody for some years.

In one respect, important to international jurisdiction to try any persons charged

with killing leftists after the end of the Iran-Iraq war, international law had moved on, by 1988, from the terms of Article 6(c). That statute provided that crimes against humanity were only committed "in execution of or in connection with any crime within the jurisdiction of the tribunal." This suggested (ambiguously since the absence of a prefatory comma could indicate that this was a requirement only for charges of "persecution on political, racial or religious grounds") that any prosecution would have to prove a nexus with other crimes over which a tribunal had jurisdiction e.g. war crimes or the crime of aggression. The Nuremberg Tribunal itself adopted this approach and declined to convict any defendant for the persecution of German Jews before war was declared. But this nexus was to disappear as a customary international law requirement over the following decades, as treaties (beginning with the Genocide Convention in 1948) and the draft Criminal Codes promulgated by the International Law Commission contained no such limitation. A few years after the 1988 massacres, the statutes for the Rwanda tribunal and the ICTY excluded any linkage requirement, and the ICTY decision in *Tadic* stated that it had withered away as an element of the defence.[147] Crimes against humanity may therefore be committed in peacetime, and irrespective of any need to prove that international armed conflict was continuing. The only linkage required in the conduct charged as such a crime is with an exercise of the power of the state. As one Nazi War Crimes Tribunal explained, "crimes against humanity... can only come within the purview of this basic code of humanity because the state involved, owing to indifference, impotency or complicity, has been unable or has refused to halt the crimes and punish the criminals."[148]

Liability for crimes against humanity not only extends downwards to underlings who do the killing and torturing (subject to any defence of duress) but upwards to the leaders who gave the orders and who will not be permitted to claim diplomatic or sovereign immunity in UN courts (although they may do so in national courts if they are functioning as ministers of a foreign state at the time of their indictment).[149] Those in leadership positions may be accused as accomplices under the doctrine of "Command Responsibility" fashioned by the US Supreme Court to convict General Yamashita for the lawlessness of his troops:

> A person in a position of superior authority should be held individually responsible for giving the unlawful order to commit a crime, and he should also be held responsible for failure to deter the unlawful behaviour of subordinates if he knew they had committed or were about to commit crimes yet failed to take the necessary and reasonable steps to prevent their commission or to punish those who had committed them.[150]

This may be important in deciding whether Mousavi is indictable for the massacres which occurred on his watch as Prime Minister. He must have known of the *fatwa* and his office had responsibility for the administration of prisons: did he take any steps to stop or even mitigate the killings and later to end the torture? His interview with Austrian television in December 1988 suggests that, on the contrary, he was trying to cover them up. There is no evidence of his direct involvement,

but his position as Prime Minister makes him a suspect: he has to explain what he knew, when he knew it and what he did about it. These questions were asked repeatedly during the electoral campaign between May and June 2009 and his standard answer was that he had no jurisdiction over judicial matters.

The most authoritative contemporary definition of crimes against humanity is provided by Article 7 of the Rome Statute of the International Criminal Court. Such crimes include:

> *...any of the following acts when committed as part of a widespread or systematic attack directed against any civilian population, with knowledge of the attack*
>
> *a) Murder*
>
> *b) Extermination...*
>
> *e) Imprisonment or other severe deprivation of physical liberty and violation of fundamental laws of international law*
>
> *f) Torture...*
>
> *h) Persecution against any identifiable group or collectivity on political, racial, national, ethnic, cultural, religious, gender... grounds that are universally recognised as impermissible under international law, in connection with any act referred to in this paragraph or any crime within the jurisdiction of the court...*
>
> *k) Other inhumane acts of a similar character intentionally causing great suffering or serious injury to body or to mental or physical health.*

In my view, the government policy towards the *Mojahedin* and the leftists in 1988 plainly satisfies this definition. They were not prisoners of war, as I have explained, but were part of the civilian population, albeit serving (or in the case of the *mellikesh*, having served) prison sentences for the most part unconnected with the war. The acts of murder and torture suffered by individuals were indubitably "part of a widespread or systematic attack": they occurred almost simultaneously in at least twenty prisons throughout the country and they were organised and synchronised in the days after 28 July by the cancellation of prison visits, the denial of access to the media, the questioning of the *Mojahedin* and then of the leftists, the hangings or shootings and alternatively the beatings five times a day to force prisoners to pray. Although *murder* may seem an inapt way to describe any judicially-sanctioned killing, the crime of *extermination* fits the facts, implying "by its very nature" both a "direction against a group of individuals" and "the element of mass destruction."[151] *Persecution* on political and religious grounds is also an accurate description of the fate inflicted upon the *Mojahedin* and the leftists.

There has been some confusion because Article 7(2)(a) goes on to say that the attack must be "pursuant to, or in furtherance of, a state or organisational policy to commit such attack." This does not mean that proof of some pre-conceived or pre-planned state policy to commit such crimes is a necessary element of the offence[152] – a mistake that has encouraged some commentators to look for evidence that the massacres were planned much earlier – e.g. when the questionnaires were distributed and interrogations for classification took place back in 1987. There is little doubt that the issue of what to do with the "unislamic" prison population was a constant issue for the Ministry of Intelligence since the 1981 arrests, and

that files were being kept on MKO and leftists alike, containing their interrogation notes, sentences, questionnaire answers and, in some cases, information received from repenters and prison stool-pigeons. The issue would urgently have crystallised after the very reluctant acceptance of the ceasefire and was galvanised by the "Eternal Light" invasion. But as a matter of law, it simply does not matter whether the murderous plans were made on 28 July 1988 or a year before. The state had the organisation in place through which the *fatwa* was delivered to the judges and to the prison governors, and implementation began almost immediately. All prisons that I have studied observed a lull in interrogations and executions in the middle of August, and then began again with a purge of leftist prisoners who were judged apostate. While there was some chaos and overlap in the course of the implementation process, as could only be expected from its speed, the over-arching impression is that of a policy to destroy or neutralise any religious dissenter who would pose a political problem for the Islamic regime after the war, and that this was implemented in two separate waves. This must have taken a great deal of expeditious organisation, building upon the information analysis that had accrued over previous years and the ward separation of the *Mojahedin*, repenters, *mellikesh* and leftists that had taken place in the larger prisons such as Evin and Gohardasht. But whether pre-planned in 1988 or hastily conceived and put into operation in July and August 1988, the massacres were without doubt "pursuant to a state or organisational policy to commit such an attack." They constituted a crime against humanity, contrary to international law.

Genocide

One Convention which must be considered for applicability to the 1988 massacres is the Genocide Convention, which places an obligation on states to investigate and punish cases of killing or inflicting severe bodily or mental harm on members of a "national, ethnical, racial or religious group as such" with the intent to destroy it, in whole or in part.[153] It will be appreciated that political groups have been expressly excluded from this definition, so the threshold question is whether the *Mojahedin* were a political group, or a group defined by their different approach to Islam – because if the latter, it was clearly the intention of the *fatwa* to have the entire group eliminated. The confinement of the crime of genocide to religious, ethnic and national groups has been much criticised, and some academics have tried to find a broader definition of genocide in customary international law, although in my view the Convention was intended to "cover the field" and so political groups are indisputably excluded.[154] But in the Iranian theocracy, the MKO was objectionable essentially because it was a group which had adopted a different version of Islam – albeit a difference influenced by its Marxist politics.

The question is whether the MKO satisfies the definition of a "religious group," since there is no doubt from the terms of the *fatwa* that the regime had the intention of destroying it as such, or at least as it existed as a group in prisons throughout Iran (it was not permitted to exist outside prison: its members were subject to arrest on sight). This is not an altogether straightforward question. The Convention excludes political and social groups because they are mobile and a matter of individual choice, unlike race or ethnicity. But a "religious group" need not be one that denies its members the right to leave. At the drafting stage of the Convention, the UK opposed the inclusion of "religious group" precisely because people were free to join and leave them, and its objection was overruled.[155] The International Criminal Tribunal for Rwanda has confirmed that "a religious group includes... a group sharing common beliefs" which is stable and permanent:[156] the MKO as a group has been relatively stable and certainly permanent, with headquarters in Paris and since 1986 in Iraq. Its members venerate the Koran and admire the interpretation of Islam developed by Ayatollah Taleqani. It has had much in common with a cult, but this is no reason to deny it protection; even Scientology can count as a "religion" (and not only for the purpose of tax deductions).[157]

The MKO were treated as a religious group by their persecutors: those who did not repent their "hypocrisy" and repudiate their deviation were for that reason killed – for being "steadfast in their adherence to a corrupt version of Islam." The Khmer Rouge defendants who now face justice in Cambodia have been accused of genocide by executing Buddhist leaders and "unrepentant" Buddhist monks: Iranian leaders may be similarly accused for killing all of the *Mojahedin* on whom they could lay their hands for refusing to accept the state religion.

Almost all of the victims of the second wave – the male political prisoner apostates – were executed or died from torture. This would satisfy the requirement for destroying "part" of a group, namely atheists detained in Iranian prisons. The ICJ has ruled that although genocide was not committed generally in Bosnia, the killing of 7,000 men and boys in Srebrenica amounted to that crime,[158] and Radovan Karadzic is currently on trial charged with command responsibility for this particular genocide. The ICTY in the case of *Krstic* examined the requirement that there must be an intention to destroy a group "in whole or in part" and concluded that the intent to eradicate a group within a limited geographical area, such as a region of a country or even a municipality, could be characterised as genocide.[159] It follows that a group whose members have the status of political prisoners, held in a state's jails, would amount to a "group" for the purposes of the convention. The more difficult question is whether these prisoners – Marxists who do not believe in God – constitute a religious group or a political group. The common-sense answer is that they constitute both, but the law is not always sensible and in the case of genocide, this somewhat artificial distinction must be applied by deciding whether apostates can constitute a religious group.

The answer may hinge on the intention of the perpetrator of the killing and torture. Was the intention genocidal? We have no *fatwa* (and there may have been none issued to launch the second wave) but we do have ample evidence of the conduct and questioning that went on in these prison courtrooms. From that evidence it is plain that the judges had little or no interest in the defendants' politics: they were wholly or predominantly concerned with their attitude to God and to Islam and whether they were born into Muslim families with parents who prayed and whether they were prepared to abandon their atheist beliefs by saying their prayers. The decision that sentenced them to

death or (in the case of women) to potentially lethal torture was whether they were apostates, upon criteria determined by religious texts and not political treatises. Hence, the distinction between "innate" and "voluntary" apostates, the difference between the treatment accorded to men and women, and the life-or-death significance attached to repentance: all principles which were drawn directly from long established Sharia jurisprudence. Although it may seem paradoxical to refer to atheists as a "religious group," there is some authority for the proposition that "religious groups encompass both theistic, non-theistic and atheistic communities which are united by a single spiritual ideal." Judge Balthazar Garzon has ruled, in relation to an application alleging genocide in Argentina, that

> to destroy a group because of its atheism or its common non-acceptance of the Christian religious ideology is... the destruction of a religious group, in as much as, in addition, the group to be destroyed also technically behaves as the object of identification of the motivation or subjective element of the genocidal conduct. It seems, in effect, that the genocidal conduct can be defined both in a positive manner, vis-a-vis the identity of the group to be destroyed (Muslims, for example) as in a negative manner, and indeed, of greater genocidal pretensions (all non-Christians, or all atheists, for example)[160]

Although the fact that most were Marxists gives those groups a political complexion, apostasy and the waging of war against God are entirely religious concepts, defined by theological texts and tests according to principles that took shape among Muslim jurists more than a thousand years ago. There was no investigation of whether the defendants' atheism sprang from their politics, or vice-versa: the inquiry was simply whether they were born Muslim, whether they had lapsed from Islam, and whether they were ready to re-embrace the faith after being thrashed with an electric cable. It can be argued that this was genocide, because it involved the extermination of a substantial part of a group, whose membership was defined in the eyes of the exterminators by their attitude to religion. The motivation of the exterminators may have been political, namely to extinguish opposition to their theocratic state, but their intention was also genocidal in that they sought to eliminate those "religious groups" most likely to challenge their theology – the *Mojahedin* who promoted a different version of Islam, and the committed atheists who were of militant disbelief. The religious underpinning of the offence for which they were convicted is clear, for the crime of "waging a war on God on earth" is the only offence which must be punished by execution according to the Koran (Koran 5 33-4). Its genocidal aspect arises out of political realities rather than sacred texts however: namely, the fact that the Iranian government considered itself to be "God on Earth," a theocracy which could not suffer impenitent apostates to remain in its prisons, awaiting release into the community. Religion was uniquely suffused by politics in Iran, but the genocidal purpose underlying the policy was clear.

Insofar as there is any doubt on this point, there is a strong argument in principle for resolving that doubt in favour of the victimised groups. The Genocide Convention is, in some ways, the international equivalent of a domestic statute prohibiting religiously aggravated violence. In the latter context, it would be entirely wrong to exempt perpetrators from liability merely because they were 'lucky' enough to target victims who disagreed with the religious characterisation being placed upon them. A person who assaulted or killed someone for being a Jew or a Muslim (say) would quite properly not be able to claim lack of piety in the victim as a mitigating factor. In the same way, it would not be right to exempt Iran from liability on the basis that its victims did not share the religious outlook that was inspiring their torture and execution.

Assuming this analysis to be correct, the international community, or at least the 140 states which are party to this Convention – including the US – would be obliged to accept that the Genocide Convention is engaged in respect of both the annihilation of the *Mojahedin* and the evisceration of the left-wing groups. According to Article 1 of that Convention, *"genocide, whether committed in time of peace or time of war is a crime under international law."* The treaty has been ratified by so many states that it is now considered *jus cogens,* i.e. binding on all states (whether they have ratified the convention or not) and requiring them to investigate and prosecute. As the ICJ explained in its decision in the *Reservation to the Convention of Genocide Case,* the origins of the Convention show that it was the intention of the UN to condemn and punish genocide as "a crime under international law... involving a denial of the right of existence of entire human groups, a denial that shocks the conscience of mankind and results in great losses to humanity, and which is contrary to moral law and the spirit and aims of the UN."[161]

The law of state responsibility engages the liability of Iran because the orders were given and implemented by *de jure* organs of the state – i.e. by ministers and government officials, police and Revolutionary Guards. The state of Iran employed the executioners and gave the orders and co-ordinated the general planning of the executions. Its judges passed the sentences and its Revolutionary Guards carried them out.[162] Although the UN would be unlikely to establish a special court, as it did to deal with genocide in the former Yugoslavia and Rwanda and Cambodia, any state could refer the issue to the ICJ for decision as to whether Iran was required to compensate victims and their families and to prosecute those who gave and carried out the commands. The court could also rule on the question if it were referred by the General Assembly or by certain organs of the United Nations. Iran would doubtless refuse to accept the court's jurisdiction, just as Israel refused to defend the case brought in the world court on a General Assembly reference over the legality of its wall, but that will not prevent the court from reaching a decision. Genocide could be added as a count to any indictment against a perpetrator of the prison massacres who happened to fall into the hands of another state, and the same facts would of course amount to a crime against humanity, without the need for the prosecutor to prove genocidal intent.

Defences

Could Iran, or any individual official involved in the massacres, advance a credible defence to a charge of committing a crime against humanity? The death penalty *per se* is not contrary to international law and many other states, Islamic and secular, have penalties that include caning and whipping. But before any defence of "lawful execution" could be sustained, it would have to be demonstrated that the death penalty was carried out in accordance with international law – after a fair trial process for a serious offence. And in the case of corporal punishment, it would have to be shown that the beatings did not exceed the severity threshold that amounts to torture, inhuman or degrading treatment or punishment.

So far as the *Mojahedin* executions are concerned, no defence of lawful execution could possibly be advanced. There was no "trial," but merely a classification process by which all who were identified as adherents were immediately and arbitrarily killed. The *fatwa* imposed the capital sentence for all who still evinced support for this ideological group, irrespective of whether they had ever used violence to further its cause. Many were available for execution because they were serving uncompleted fixed-term sentences for their minor acts of adherence or support in 1981: the *fatwa* simply annulled those sentences and replaced them with the sentence of death. The rest – the *mellikesh* – were in prison despite having completed their sentence for minor offences: the *fatwa* sentenced them anew, for no crime other than irreligion or disfavoured religious and political views, to death without trial. Under Article 6(2) of the ICCPR and the UN Economic and Social Council standards, capital punishment must be reserved for serious crimes with lethal or exceptionally serious consequences: the Human Rights Commission has consistently held that they cannot be imposed merely for political or religious allegiance[163] nor can capital punishment be imposed for crimes committed when the individual was aged under 18 – and

many of these victims had been arrested for offences committed when they were high school
students. Nor can women with children suffer death – although this was not regarded as a
bar to the execution of *Mojahedin* mothers. As
for the *mellikesh*, of course, they had already
served their sentences and were simply available to be classified as "steadfast," i.e. within
the *fatwa*, and then killed.

There was a complete and utter disregard
of all international law safeguards: the "defendants" were not charged and, at the beginning,
MKO members were unaware that their appearance before the committee might involve a
death sentence (many thought that this was the
long-awaited "pardon committee") and they
had no right to defend themselves, to be defended by a lawyer, to call evidence or to testify
on their own behalf or to appeal. These denials
of fair trial rights were very much more extensive than in *Ocalan v Turkey*, where the Kurdis-
tan Workers' Party (PKK) leader's death sentence for the gravest terrorist crimes was held
to have been vitiated by failure to provide him
with adequate time and facilities to prepare a
defence or allow him access to a lawyer.[164] The
hearings lasted for no more than a few minutes
during which the *Mojahedin* prisoners were
merely identified as persons subject to a man-
datory death sentence by *fatwa*, imposed as a
measure of collective responsibility. The hearings were in secret and the sentence was not
pronounced publicly. Every safeguard required
by international human rights law for the in-
fliction of capital punishment was absent.

The "second wave" death sentences on
the apostates were also indefensible, and for
similar reasons. Although there appears to
have been in most cases a very short "trial,"

in the sense of questioning by the panel to establish whether the defendant was a practising
Muslim or not, there was no charge or indictment and most defendants were unaware that
they were on trial (after the lull which followed
the *Mojahedin* executions, many thought they
were involved in a pardon procedure) and they
had no idea of the significance of their answers
in respect of the theology being applied by
the judges. They were given no time or facil-
ity to take legal or religious advice and many
were not given the opportunity to "commute"
their death sentences by starting to pray. It was
not made clear what this commutation would
mean: those who agreed to pray were still kept
in prison for an indeterminate time, whether
they were already *mellikesh* or serving a fixed
sentence. Again, the complete absence of any
fair trial guarantees essential for the imposition of capital punishment in international law
negatives any defence of "lawful execution,"
quite apart from the fact that the sentence
was imposed for a crime – apostasy – which
is not in the category of "exceptionally grave
offences" for which the death penalty must be
reserved. The Human Rights Committee has
specifically held that international law does
not permit capital punishment for apostasy – a
"thought crime" which directly contradicts the
right to change religion that is guaranteed by
all human rights Conventions and by the Universal Declaration.[165] It follows that the second
wave of apostate executions, as well as the first
wave of MKO executions, cannot be justified
or defended: they were crimes against humanity, involving the arbitrary deprivation of life
contrary to Article 3 of the Universal Declaration and Article 6(1) of the ICCPR as well
as war crimes involving "violence to life and

person, in particular murder" under Common Article 3.

There is an interesting precedent afforded by the decision of the Iraqi High Tribunal in the *Dujail* case. That town – a haven for oppositionists – was the site of the attempted assassination of Saddam Hussein in 1982. Although attempted by only a few men, Saddam's officials rounded up 148 citizens: they were tortured and then executed without proper trial by a revolutionary tribunal. Saddam (who confirmed the sentences), the judge who imposed them, and officials who organised the torture and executions were all convicted of crimes against humanity. The Court rejected the defence of necessity, i.e. that the prisoners were terrorists aligned with Iran, the war-time enemy, because their deaths were "not necessary to stop an immediate and imminent danger" and the executions were disproportionate to any actual threat. It also rejected the argument that crimes against humanity were not part of Iraqi law: murder and torture were both local crimes and committing them on a large scale contravened both local and international criminal law. The revolutionary judge who conducted the sham trial argued that he was under a legal obligation to do so, but the tribunal ruled that he had no justification for enthusiastically "following the whims and moods of those that outranked him in power." Like the Nazi judges convicted in the *Altstoetter* case, "the dagger of the assassin was concealed beneath the robe of a jurist."[166] Although the Iraqi High Tribunal was not an international court, and its bias and vulnerability to political manipulation undermines the authority of its actual verdicts,[167] there is a general consensus among commentators that it was correct to reject the defences of 'necessity' and 'superior orders' preferred by the judge and the security officials.

Torture

Those leftist prisoners who were excepted from the second wave apostasy executions were subjected to *bastinado* – severe beatings by electrical cable on the soles of their feet, five times a day until they agreed to pray or else died from the ill-treatment or committed suicide in pain and despair. Was their undoubted suffering capable of a justification defence based on a proviso to the 1984 UN Torture Convention, which excuses suffering "arising only from, inherent in or incidental to, lawful sanctions"?

No sanction can be lawful, at least in international law, if it arises from torture, which is absolutely prohibited and was defined in 1975 by the UN's Declaration Against Torture as:

> *Any act by which severe pain or suffering, whether physical or mental, is intentionally inflicted by or at the instigation of a public official on a person for such purposes as obtaining from him or a third person information or confession, punishing him for an act he has committed or is suspected of having committed, or intimidating him or other persons.*

In my opinion, the evidence shows that the punishments inflicted on all female apostates, and on men who were either given an opportunity to re-acquire their Muslim religion by prayer and penitence or who were classified as non-Muslim, undoubtedly reached the severity threshold that constitutes torture. This is not a judgment that is made on individual cases in isolation: as the ICTY Appeal Court has ruled in relation to the Omarska Concentration Camp, punishments inflicted in a prison "where detainees were kept in inhuman conditions and an atmosphere of extreme mental and physical violence pervaded the camp" (an apt description of the wards in Iranian prisons where political detainees were kept in August and September 1988) must be taken into account.[168] Whippings and beatings in this environment produce an intensity of suffering that is absent from the routine administration of corporal punishment in some other countries. Moreover, as early as 1969, in the landmark *Greek Case* brought against that government by other European states, the European Commission found that the use of *falange* (involving beating on the soles of the feet which is excruciating and causes swelling but leaves no other physical trace), amounted to torture and ill-treatment.[169] In a series of cases from Turkey, where this technique is known as *falaka,* the European Court of Human Rights had no hesitation in treating it as torture.[170]

In 1978 the European court in *Ireland v UK* ruled that torture, as distinct from ill-treatment, required a severity threshold so as to "attach a special stigma to deliberate inhuman treatment causing very serious and cruel suffering."[171] This strikes me as an appropriate description of the beatings to which the female apostates were subjected, and the men were subjected to much harsher whippings: in both cases, far beyond the requirements of *tazir* punishment. It may be pointed out that the jurisprudence on the definition of torture widened somewhat in the years after 1988, but this does not alter the fact that the treatment of the second wave of prisoners amounted to "torture" as it was well understood at that time. It would, of course, satisfy the current definition which takes account of whether the

acts were "such as to arouse in the applicant feelings of fear, anguish and inferiority capable of humiliating and debasing him and possibly breaking his physical and moral resistance."[172] This was exactly the purpose of the beatings – to break principled moral resistance to the religion of the state and to require five manifestations each day of grovelling obeisance to it.

It may be objected that the sufferings of those ill-treated during the second wave were little different, in kind, to the sufferings of Guantanamo Bay prisoners as a result of water-boarding and other techniques approved by the Bush administration. This I doubt – (*bastinado* was not inflicted at all by the CIA, let alone five times a day) but if extreme pain was caused by Guantanamo techniques, then they too amounted to torture ("water-boarding" being a prime example). The defendant's attempt to rely on the poorly reasoned arguments in memoranda written by White House Counsel was forcefully rejected by ICTY Appeal Chamber in *Prosecutor v Brdanin*, which re-iterated that "the purpose and seriousness of the attack upon the victim sets torture apart from other forms of mistreatment."[173] The purpose, of course, was the illegitimate one of forcing a prisoner to abandon conscientious convictions incompatible with the religion of the state. It cannot be argued that the thrashings administered to this end were analogous to permissible corporal punishment: the European Court of Human Rights, the Inter-American Court of Human Rights and the African Commission on Human and Peoples Rights have all rejected arguments that severe violence may be inflicted as punishment upon convicts.[174] These cases all involved canings or whippings in conformity with the laws enforced in the particular country. The principle upheld by all these decisions was stated in the *Tyrer* case: "There is no right for individuals, and particularly the government of a country, to apply physical violence to individuals for offences" and that "such a right would be tantamount to sanctioning state sponsored torture under the Charter and contrary to the very nature of this human rights treaty." This is an application of the Nuremberg principle that obedience to national law is not necessarily a defence to a charge of committing crime under international law.[175]

It is clear that torture is an international crime that attracts universal jurisdiction. As the leading judgment in the *Pinochet* case put it:

> *The jus cogens nature of the international crime of torture justifies states in taking universal jurisdiction over torture wherever committed. International law provides that offences jus cogens may be punished by any state because the offenders are "common enemies of all mankind and all nations have an equal interest in their apprehension and prosecution."*[176]

This is all very well and good, but whether torturing states and torturers will ever be punished or required to pay compensation depends more on happenstance than international law. States that are sued in the courts of other nations can usually rely upon sovereign immunity to avoid civil liability.[177] Such immunity would not prevail for individuals prosecuted in an international court established by the UN Security Council, but the ICJ has held that in foreign domestic courts, incumbent government ministers cannot be made the subject of any legal process.[178] This ruling covers only those with diplomatic immunity:

it would not extend to protect judges or prison officials. Individual torturers may, of course, stray into jurisdictions prepared to put them on trial or to extradite them to countries that will put them on trial, but this depends not only upon the travel plans of the torturer but upon whether he still holds an office which is protected by an immunity. Those Death Committee members who now rank amongst Iran's most senior judges would not be protected by state or diplomatic immunity were they to travel to London for medical treatment, as did General Pinochet, but Supreme Leader Ali Khamenei has Head of State immunity wherever in the world he chooses to go. It is very doubtful whether ex-Prime Minister Mousavi would have any immunity, however – and even if he did, he is probably the only suspect from whom President Ahmadinejad would be prepared to withdraw it.

Civil Actions

Since perpetrators of this crime against humanity cannot realistically be prosecuted or sued for damages in Iranian courts, a secondary duty may devolve upon other states to bring or permit proceedings should any of the perpetrators come within its jurisdiction, on the principle that crimes against international law "may be punished by any state which obtains custody of persons suspected of responsibility."[179] It follows that civil actions can be brought as well, certainly when the damage flowed from an act of genocide or torture or other breach of a *jus cogens* rule (i.e. a rule defined by Article 53 of the Vienna Convention on the Law of Treaties as one "accepted and recognised by the international community of states as a whole from which no derogation is permitted.") Since the infringement of such a compelling law involves the breach of an obligation to the international community of all states, there is no reason why one of those states should not make its courts available for a victim to sue any torturer who may come within its jurisdiction, especially since Article 2(3) of the ICCPR calls upon states to provide an effective remedy for victims of serious human rights abuses. This duty is fulfilled in the US by statutory provision: the 1789 Alien Tort Claims Act (ATCA) permits suit for any tort "committed in violation of the law of nations."[180]

The efficacy of civil remedies is limited by the doctrine of state immunity, which will preclude the state itself from being made a defendant, even in respect of acts of torture and murder which it has authorised. This means that a human defendant will have to be found, in the form of an individual who ordered or carried out the atrocity. It will not be often that Iranian political leaders or former Revolutionary Guards will travel or reside outside Iran and, if served with a writ on a visit to the US it is even less likely that they will stay around to contest the case. Civil actions, therefore, are only feasible in respect of torturers who are exiled or "on the run" from their own country and, like Ferdinand Marcos, have assets within the foreign jurisdiction that can be frozen or otherwise used to satisfy damages awards. Most foreign defendants to alien tort statute claims do not stay for the verdict. In the leading case of *Filartiga v Pena-Irala,* the relatives of a torture victim were awarded US$1 million against his torturer, who evaded payment by fleeing the US.[181] In 2000, a New York jury awarded US$745 million to victims of Radovan Karadzic who had been served with a writ while visiting the US in 1993 at the invitation of the UN. It is unlikely, once he is through with his present criminal trial in The Hague, that he will have the money to satisfy any part of the damages award.[182] At best, such civil actions *in absentia* give victims and relatives an opportunity to present their case in a legal forum and so have it assessed by a judge: they report that it helps them to grieve and to put their evidence on public record. A criminal prosecution would obviously be more effective, at least if brought against a real defendant and not *in absentia.*

11: Conclusion

My opinion on the facts and the international law issues to which they give rise may be shortly stated. Iran in 1988 was a nation of 40 million people (it now has 73 million), with prisons in over 100 cities. At least 20 of those prisons held political prisoners incarcerated for membership of groups opposed to the Islamic Republic. Some were members of the MKO, a group which opposed the Shah and after the revolution had lawfully operated until mid-1981, when hundreds of their supporters were killed by Revolutionary Guards at a demonstration. Thereafter some members went underground and engaged in terrorist violence against the state which in turn was violently suppressed. The other political parties were "leftists" mainly of different Marxist persuasions. On 20 July 1988 Ayatollah Khomeini, the Supreme Leader, reluctantly "drunk the cup of poison" and accepted the UN ceasefire in the war with Iraq. One week later a small force of *Mojahedin* coordinated with Iraqi air cover mounted an attack over the border. After an initial success, they were routed on 29 July 1988. The previous day, Khomeini had issued a *fatwa* ordering a death sentence for all imprisoned *Mojahedin,* and this was put into immediate operation through three-man "Death Committees" who confirmed the identity and "steadfastness" of *Mojahedin* prisoners prior to sending them for execution. By mid-August, several thousands, up to 3,800 according to Ayatollah Montazeri, of them had been killed. There was a lull in executions for ten days, but on 26 August a second wave broke, entailing brief trials of all "leftist" prisoners for the religious crime of apostasy. Those men from Muslim families who declined to say Islamic prayers were sent for execution, whilst female non-believers were tortured until they agreed to pray, and this torture was inflicted, more severely, on men who did not come from a devout Muslim family. The prison massacres stopped by November, when relatives began to be notified, in a cruelly slow and bureaucratic way, of the fact of a child or spouse's death, but they were refused any information about the place of burial and were forbidden to mourn. This prohibition is still enforced today.

I find that the state of Iran has committed four exceptionally serious breaches of *jus cogens* rules of international law which entail both state responsibility and individual accountability for war crimes and crimes against humanity, *viz*

1) The arbitrary killing of thousands of male and female prisoners pursuant to a *fatwa* that held them collectively responsible for the *Mojahedin* invasion, notwithstanding that they had been in prison and *hors de combat* for years, serving fixed term sentences for relatively minor offences. This was not the execution of a lawful sentence, because there was no trial, no charge and no criminal act other than adhering to a particular ideological group. It was dishonest of Iranian leaders to pretend that the executed prisoners had

all been given death sentences and had refused an opportunity to reform: this was a lie. So too was the suggestion that they had rioted or that they were all "terrorists and spies." None of those whom I interviewed had been charged with terrorism offences or with espionage, and most had been in prison since 1981-3. The immediate trigger for the massacre was tit-for-tat retaliation for the "Eternal Light" invasion and the pain of agreeing to a ceasefire, but the medieval defence of "reprisal" has long been abolished. The right to life, guaranteed by customary international law, by treaties to which Iran is a party and by the Geneva Conventions, was quite deliberately and barbarically breached, and all who bear international law responsibility for this mass murder should be prosecuted. An obligation to prosecute may also arise from the Genocide Convention, since the reason why MKO members were condemned as *moharebs* ("warriors against God") and exterminated was that they had adopted a version of Islam which differed from that upheld by the state.

2) The second wave of apostate killings was also a breach of the right to life, as well as the right to religious freedom. The male prisoners who were executed were given some kind of trial, but it was wholly deficient in compliance with legal safeguards and massively unfair. They were offered no time or facilities to prepare their defence and were taken by surprise by questions, the implications of which they did not understand. They were executed for a crime of conscience in that their only offence was to refuse to adopt the religious beliefs, prayers and rituals of the state. There is force in the argument that in this sense they comprised a distinct group exterminated not because of their left-wing political leanings but because of their beliefs about religion: they were in consequence victims of genocide. Apostasy in any event is not a crime for which the death penalty is permissible in international law – a position taken by most states a few months later when Khomeini purported to pass that sentence on Salman Rushdie. They were not, as the government later alleged, spies or terrorists or prison rioters. They were executed for no better reason than to rid a theocratic state of ideological enemies in post-war circumstances that could not possibly give rise to a defence of necessity or to any other defence.

3) The beatings inflicted on leftist women and on other men who were regarded as capable of religious compliance satisfied the definition of torture, which is absolutely prohibited even if it is consonant with national law. The beatings by electric cable on the soles of the feet, five times a day for weeks on end, together in many cases with beatings on the body, were calculated to and did cause excruciating pain and extensive suffering as well as humiliation and degradation. The mental anguish was heightened by the fact that the beatings were inflicted not for the purpose of punishment, but to make the prisoners adopt a religion that they had rejected, and thus surrender their freedom of conscience. Again, no defence of

necessity can possibly arise: the only object of the beatings was to break their will and their spirit and to make them more amenable to the state's version of Islamic governance.

4) Finally, the rights to know where close relatives have been buried and to mourn their deaths, have been and still are being denied by the state. These rights are implied from the right to life and (more logically) from the right of innocent families not to be treated inhumanely or cruelly. There is no possible justification, today, for denying information about burial locations or for prohibiting gatherings of mourners: there is no evidence to suggest that these gatherings would cause public disorder or breaches of the peace. What is being denied, two decades after the deaths, is the right of parents, spouses and siblings to manifest their feelings of devotion in respect of the memory of a family member: this is a denial of their rights to respect for home and family life (an aspect of privacy) as well as a denial of the right to manifest religious beliefs. It also amounts to discrimination, since no other class or category of the bereaved has been denied the opportunity to mourn. The refusal to identify mass graves implicitly involves a refusal to prevent DNA testing (which has proven reliable in war crimes investigations as a means of identifying the remains in mass graves) and, in consequence, the prevention of a proper burial.

So far as the state of Iran is concerned, these breaches of its treaty and customary law responsibilities have no criminal consequence.

States cannot be subjected to a penal sanction. But these breaches do give rise to two obligations: the state must cease the wrongful conduct and must make full reparation for the injury caused by its act.[183] Reparation should include damages where appropriate, which will be compensatory but not punitive.[184] The beneficiaries of holding Iran to these obligations would be relatives of the deceased, but action by them or by another state on their behalf would obviously have to be taken in a forum outside Iran. The difficulty will be in finding such a forum: the International Court of Justice might be activated by a UN organ or by a member state, but Iran would refuse to cede jurisdiction to it. That would not matter if the General Assembly or another UN organ were to seek an advisory opinion (e.g. on whether the prison killings amounted to genocide or to a crime against humanity): in such a case, the consent of Iran would not be required – the reason why Israel could not stop the ICJ from deciding the issue of the Palestinian wall. The prospect of a claims tribunal, or any other form of arbitration or negotiation under UN auspices, depends upon *realpolitik*. It may, for example, be urged that any concession to Iran in respect of its nuclear facilities should be contingent upon its atoning for past human rights abuses by providing information and compensation to survivors and relatives of those it has unlawfully massacred, and in opening mass graves so that DNA testing may establish and identify the remains.

The individuals against whom there is a *prima facie* case for prosecution for crimes against humanity, torture, genocide and war crimes, are those in the chain of command, from Supreme Leader to hangman. At the middle level, the members of the Death Committee are well known, as are the senior prison officials who organised and authorised the executions, and no doubt those Revolutionary Guards who acted as hangmen, firing squad members and gravediggers can also be identified. There is however, a good deal of opacity at the higher level: it is unclear to me, for example, which leaders were involved in advising Imam Khomeini to issue the *fatwa* on 28 July 1988 and which officials were involved in transmitting that decree to the prison governors and arranging the logistics of the first wave of executions. Different ministries would have had to give approvals and directions, most importantly the Ministry of Intelligence whose officials conducted interrogations, set questionnaires and kept tabs on every prisoner. There is evidence that, at some prisons, warders were supplanted by Revolutionary Guards who carried out the killings. When relatives were eventually notified, they were not in most cases informed by the prison authorities, but by Revolutionary Guards. There is a real mystery over the authority for the "second wave" of leftist/apostate executions, which were beyond the terms of the 28 July *fatwa*: was there another secret *fatwa*, as Montazeri suggests, in the first weeks of September, or was this a decision taken by the political leadership under pressure from hardliners in Qom and communicated through the High Judicial Council to the Death Committees? These questions must be answered before there can be any authoritative identification of all those criminally complicit in the massacres.

That said, the identification of those who directed the victims to the slaughterhouse in Tehran prisons is very plain. The *fatwa* was directed to **Hossein Ali Nayyeri**,[185] a religious judge at the time and currently Deputy Chief Justice of the Supreme Court. He was identified as presiding over Death Committees in Tehran prisons by many survivors permitted to take their blindfolds off when attending the committee, because he had presided over their earlier cases or was well-known from television appearances. He admitted to Montazeri on 15 August that he had already executed 750 prisoners in Tehran. Also named in the *fatwa* is **Morteza Eshraqi**, the Tehran Prosecutor and now a judge on the country's Supreme Court.[186] He was identified by many survivors as he had been involved in their initial prosecutions. Another prosecutor who took his place on occasion was his deputy, **Ebrahim Raisi**, who went on to become the Head of the General Inspection Organisation and is now the Deputy Head of the Judiciary.[187] The Intelligence Ministry Representative on the Tehran committee and Deputy to the Minister of Intelligence was **Mostafa Pourmohammadi**[188] who in 2005 was appointed as Minister of the Interior.[189] He is currently the Head of the General Inspection Organisation. **Ali Mobasheri** is another religious judge alleged to have substituted for Nayyeri on occasion at Evin Prison: he is President of the Revolutionary Courts in Tehran. **Esmail Shushtari**, who became Minister of Justice in 1989, is another alleged to have played an important role, as head of the State Prisons Organisation, in co-ordinating the implementation of the *fatwa*.[190] So too must **Mohammadi Gilani**, the outspoken Ayatollah who headed the Guardian Council and supervised Tehran's religious judges. In 2009, he was awarded the Medal of Justice by President Ahmadinejad for his service to justice in Iran.

These men all worked under the general supervision of **Chief Justice Ayatollah Mousavi Ardebili** whose blood-curdling Friday sermons as early as 5 August evidence his intentions all too plainly.[191] He certainly received the *fatwa* direct from the Supreme Leader on 28 July and immediately raised questions about its interpretation and implementation and he must have transmitted that interpretation to all members of the Death Committees. As head of the judicial system he presumably appointed the religious judges who headed the Death Committees in the provinces. **Ayatollah Mousavi Ardebili** is currently a grand ayatollah in Qom who is competent to issue *fatwas*. Another influential political jurist, who succeeded Mousavi Ardebili in 1989, was **Mohammad Yazdi.** He later became the Head of the Judiciary and is currently deputy-chairman of the Assembly of Experts (which appoints the Supreme Leader) and is a member of the Guardian Council.

All these individuals appear to have been directly responsible for approving the death and torture sentences that they must or should have known to have been contrary to international law. On the well-known principle established by the Nuremberg case of *US v Joseph Altstoeter and others* (the "Justice Case" dramatised in the film *Judgment at Nuremberg*) judges who contribute to crimes committed in the guise of legal process cannot themselves escape prosecution: as the Nuremberg prosecution put it, "men of law can no more escape... responsibility by virtue of their judicial robes, than the General by his uniform." Those defendants were convicted for "administering legislation which they must be held to have known was in

violation of international law."[192]

In considering the complicity of professionals in crimes against humanity, there is no good reason to exclude diplomats who, knowing the truth, nonetheless lie about them to UN bodies to whom they owe a duty of frankness. Iran's UN ambassador, **Jafar Mahallati,** consistently denied the massacres and claimed the allegations were propaganda; so did the Geneva representative **Sirous Nasseri** in his meetings with the UN Special Representative.[193] **Mahallati** is said to be living in the US, where he may be liable to civil action for aiding and abetting torture under the Alien Tort Claim Act. **Nasseri,** a businessman who lives in Europe, might be liable to prosecution on the same basis under the laws of some European countries.

Other individuals who feature in the witness statements as key figures in the interrogations and executions are senior prison officials, most zealously **Naserian** (real name **Mohammad Moghisei**), then the governor of Gohardasht and his Head of Security **Davoud Lashkari** (real name **Taghi Adeli**). Eyewitnesses tell grisly stories of both men enthusiastically supervising the death sentences and the tortures. They are described as bringing prisoners before the Death Committees and sometimes making critical remarks about them to the judges and are accused in a few cases of putting prisoners they disliked in the wrong queue for execution. **Naserian** is accused by several witnesses of actually hanging prisoners and participating in their torture. He is currently serving as Head of Branch 28 of the Revolutionary Courts in Tehran, which is responsible for sending those arrested during the 2009 demonstrations to prison. Similar allegations are made against **Sayed Hossein Mortazavi,** the Deputy Governor of Evin Prison, who is said to have personally supervised the executions there and the Ministry of Intelligence official known as **Zamani** (real name **Musa Vaezi**) who collected much of the intelligence upon which the Death Committees acted. If these allegations are proved – and the consistency and credibility of the witnesses who make them does amount to a *prima facie* case – then they are accountable on the same legal basis as prison guards at Omarska and at Nazi camps, convicted by the ICTY and the Nuremberg tribunals respectively. So too would be the individual guards – the Revolutionary Guards said to have taken control of executions in some prisons. A name which featured in one eyewitness's account of his torture was that of **Mahmoud Ahmadinejad,** whom he claimed to have been a member of a Revolutionary Guard torture team. I am instinctively sceptical of this allegation because of the unsuccessful efforts of *Mojahedin* propagandists to identify Ahmadinejad as a student hostage-taker at the US embassy, although it seems to be the case that he did serve as a Revolutionary Guard at the time of the massacres, which in the words of a biographer is one of the "periods in Ahmadinejad's past that remain mysteriously unaccounted for."[194]

There have been a number of high echelon figures accused by *Mojahedin* organisations of advising and supervising the implementation of the *fatwa*, although the evidence is sketchy. **Ahmad Khomeini,** the powerful but now deceased son of the Supreme Leader, wrote out the *fatwa* and was responsible for its delivery. **Mohammadi Reyshahri,** the Minister of Intelligence, must have played a role, at least to appoint his ministry's representatives on the Death Committees (until late 2009 he was the Supreme Leader's representative for the pilgrimage to Mecca). His autobiography makes no reference to these events despite his obvious knowledge of them. So too would **Mohammad Moussavi Khoeniha**, the General Prosecutor of Iran, responsible for appointing his Death Committee representatives. He has turned reformer and is now known as a spiritual advisor of the reform movement.

Ali Khamenei, as President of the Republic, had been closely involved in advising acceptance of the UN ceasefire resolution, and must be presumed to have played the same advisory role a week or so later in respect of the *fatwa*. His statements in December 1988 can be read as enthusiastic support for its implementation, and in that month he refused permission for Professor Pohl, the UNHRC Special Representative, to enter Iran to investigate. As Iran's current Head of State (he is now Supreme Leader) he would of course have immunity from prosecution in any court other than in one set up by the Security Council.

Ali Akhbar Hashemi Rafsanjani was the 'inner circle' member whom the Supreme Leader came to rely upon most.[195] He was Acting Commander and Chief of the Armed Forces and another key advisor of the ceasefire: he would have been responsible for the Revolutionary Guard detachments sent to the prisons and would have authorised the firing squads which in some provinces conducted the executions. He also led the Friday sermons in Tehran around this time, in which he led crowds in chanting slogans such as "Death to the *Monafeqin* prisoners." In December 1988 he too defended the executions, whilst pretending that "less than a thousand" prisoners had died. Several commentators have interpreted the prison massacres as part of the power struggle by Rafsanjani's faction to remove Montazeri as successor to the dying Khomeini – it is alleged they urged the killings in the knowledge that the more humane heir-apparent would earn the Supreme Leader's wrath by objecting.[196] This would make Rafsanjani a prime suspect. He is now Head of the Expediency Council and the Assembly of Experts, and these positions may not be sufficiently ministerial to attract the immunity approved by the ICJ in *DRC v Congo*. **Mohsen Rezai** was the actual commander of the Revolutionary Guards Corp and was one of the four candidates in the Presidential elections of 2009. He was likely to have been responsible for ordering the hardcore Revolutionary Guards who did the killings into the prisoners. Command responsibility might fall on **Mohsen Rafiqdust** who was Minister of the Revolutionary Guard at the time. He is now a frequently travelling businessman who comes on occasion to the UK.

There is more doubt over the role of **Mir Hossein Mousavi** who was Prime Minister at the time and in consequence held ministerial responsibility for the Intelligence Ministry. He joined the leadership chorus in December 1988 which sought to justify the massacres by reference to the Mersad operation when speaking to Austrian television. Some students were heard to chant "Eighty-Eight" at his 2009 election meetings but he has not given any account of his role at the time or his reaction to it today.[197] Mousavi responded to student questions about the massacres during his election campaign by stating that the executive branch had nothing to do with "trials." His struggle,

since being denied the presidency after the disputed election in June 2009, has won international admiration, but he cannot expect true respect unless and until he gives a full account of his conduct from July to November 1988, as the Prime Minister on whose watch barbarism became state policy. Now that Montazeri, the man of undeniable courage, can no longer testify in person, Mousavi must stand in his shoes to explain exactly what was done by senior officials around Khomeini, who implemented his *fatwa* and then covered up the crime.

The situation in Iran today illustrates the consequences of impunity for crimes against humanity that have never been properly investigated or acknowledged. Some of the perpetrators and their acolytes remain in powerful positions in the judiciary and the state, whose Supreme Leader Ali Khamenei has in the past year called upon the Revolutionary Guards to use violence against peaceful protests with the support of Ayatollah Mesbah Yazdi, who threatens that "[a]nybody resisting against the ruling system will be broken."[198] Those staged television show trials of the 1980s, with televised "confessions" by leftist prisoners wracked by torture and fear for their families, re-emerged in 2009, this time featuring 'Green Movement' reformists confessing to participation in an international conspiracy devised by the US and the British Embassy in collaboration with the BBC, Twitter, Facebook, George Soros, Human Rights Watch and Amnesty International. Once again, dissidents are being prosecuted for being *mohareb*s ("warriors against God") and some are being sentenced to death.[199] Evin Prison, scene of mass murder in 1988, remains a brutal environment for blindfolded prisoners picked up for no more serious offence than attending student demonstrations or contacting NGOs concerned about human rights.[200] There have been many casualties over the past year, and many ironic reminders of 1988, the year of impunity. Hundreds of protestors, including Ayatollah Khomeini's granddaughter, have been detained. Mir Hossein Mousavi's own nephew was shot and killed by Revolutionary Guards. One of Grand Ayatollah Montazeri's very last acts was to call on Iranians to accord three days of mourning to Neda Agha-Soltan, the young woman student shot dead by forces loyal to Ahmadinejad; and to support other victims of the repressive state which he helped to create, but then came to condemn.

The government of Iran was confident enough to table a massively dishonest "periodic review" report to the Human Rights Council in November 2009,[201] on the strength of which it sought election to the Council, a result which would have seriously damaged the Council's credibility had its candidacy not been withdrawn. The sanctions that have been applied to Iran in recent years have all been in response to its determination to develop nuclear power – a right that is in principle hard to deny, since many other nations use nuclear power for peaceful purposes, and some – Israel, India and Pakistan, for example – have already developed nuclear weapons.[202] Further sanctions are under discussion, although some proposed by the US (for example, on unrefined petroleum products) would hurt ordinary citizens whilst others (on communication technology) would actually have the result of inhibiting the organisation and reporting of protests. Europe (which does 24% of Iran's trade) has been slow to show support for these measures. There have

been recent calls for "targeted" sanctions on members of the elite, especially on the Revolutionary Guards, whose leaders have been enriched by a grateful government and allowed to take shares worth millions of dollars in privatised industries,[203] but who have no direct role in nuclear policy-making.

It would be more sensible to impose sanctions for the crimes against humanity that occurred in 1988, so long as they go uninvestigated and unpunished, than it would to impose them for alleged moves towards uranium enrichment. Given the evidence of international crimes, including one that the 1948 Genocide Convention makes subject to investigation and punishment without regard to limits of time, the Security Council would be perfectly entitled under its Chapter VII powers to establish an international court with a prosecutor who can quickly collect the incriminatory evidence and obtain access to the relevant state witnesses and records. After all, the most reasonable objection to Iran developing nuclear power for peaceful purposes is the fact that it is a regime that has already granted itself impunity for mass murder, and may do so again.

Many obvious suspects are still alive and well. They were men in Khomeini's inner circle; ministers and diplomats who knew what was happening; judges who betrayed their calling by zealously sentencing prisoners to death and torture without trial; prison governors and intelligence officers who shepherded the blindfolded victims to the queue for the gallows. There are many more who have been identified by survivors and are listed on dissident websites.[204] Although most of those judges and officials worked at Tehran's prisons, Evin and Gohardasht, where the main massacres took place, it is evident that there were hundreds and possibly thousands of prisoners killed in the provinces: Shiraz, Dezful, Tabriz, Qazvin, Arak, Khoramabad, Qom, Rasht, Esfahan, Mashhad, to name but ten local prisons. All would have had their trio of implacable judges, their willing executioners from among the prison officials and intelligence operatives and Revolutionary Guards. It is important to make the distinction between the long-detained *Mojahedin* prisoners who were the victims of the first wave of killings, and captured combatants from Rajavi's army, because the twain never met, other than in false claims by Iranian government officials that the only executed *Mojahedin* had been either captured on the battlefield or had been spying from the prison, an explanation that I firmly reject.

A few political quarters in Washington have regarded the *Mojahedin* in much the same mistaken light as they saw the Iraqi resistance prior to the 2003 US invasion, i.e. as a viable democratic alternative to an obsessively anti-Western government. But the reality is that the *Mojahedin* policy of "engagement with the masses" through Islam only worked for a short time among students in the early 1980s, and their armed alignment with Saddam in 1988 ended any hopes they may have entertained of

regaining popular support. And although some Westerners imagine the Green Movement of 2009 to be a reincarnation of the young left-wing radicals who revolted first against the Shah and then against Ayatollah Khomeini, most of the 2009 demonstrators were unborn or in their cradles when the leftist factional prisoners met their doom. There is little evidence that the latter's ideologies have much traction today. Iran's regime is now well established and must be accorded the recognition and respect owed to states under international law – but only if it complies with that law.

International law obliges all states to acknowledge and comply with their obligations under a human rights law which is fundamental and universal. It abominates systematic torture and summary executions – but that is what happened in the prisons of Iran in the middle of 1988. In the annals of post-war horrors the killings compare with the 1995 massacre at Srebrenica in terms of the vulnerability of the victims, and they exceed it when measured by the cold-blooded calculations made at the very pinnacle of state power. As long as the graves of the dead remain unmarked and relatives are forbidden from mourning, Iran will continue to contravene the rule of international law which its leaders so brutally defied in 1988.

GEOFFREY ROBERTSON QC
DOUGHTY STREET CHAMBERS
10 MAY 2010

Appendix A: Brief Chronology

A chronology of significant events in Iran mentioned in this legal opinion.

1907 Introduction of democratic constitution for Persia.

1921 General Reza Khan seizes power in military coup.

1926 Reza Khan crowned as Reza Shah Pahlavi. Mohammad Reza, his eldest son, proclaimed Crown Prince.

1935 Persia re-named Iran.

1941 Iran declares its neutrality in World War II, but the Shah's pro-Axis sympathies result in his deposition by the occupying British-Russian forces in favour of his son the Crown Prince.

1950 Negotiations between the Iranian government and the Anglo Iranian Oil Company (AIOC).

1951 Parliament votes unanimously to nationalise the oil industry and called on the Shah to make Mohammad Mossadeq, who had led the nationalization drive, Prime Minister. United Kingdom imposes blockade in reprisal.

1953 Shah temporarily leaves the country while military coup (backed by CIA and MI6) removes Mossadeq then returns to rule with military support.

1963 **January**

Shah announces the "White Revolution," a six-point program of reform. Ayatollah Khomeini along with other senior Ayatollahs of Qom publishes a protest letter against Shah's reforms.

June

5 June: Hundreds of demonstrators take to the streets to protest against the arrest of Ayatollah Khomeini who had criticised the Shah in a speech. Several demonstrators are killed by security forces.

1964 **November**

Khomeini is exiled from Iran after six months of house arrest.

1971 **August-September**

Arrest and torture of eleven *Mojahedin* student leaders. Brutality of SAVAK, the secret police, increasingly hardens opposition groups against the Shah.

October

Celebrations at Persepolis to celebrate 2,500 years of the Peacock Throne. The *Fadaiyan* Organisation (Marxist-Leninist) launches first guerrilla attack on police station, marking the beginning of armed resistance against the Shah..

1972 Trial and execution of *Mojahedin* leaders.

1978 The Shah frees a number of political prisoners but public dissent gains momentum.

September

Breakdown of civil order as all sections of society protest against the Shah.

Street demonstrations, strikes and riots all demand the return of Khomeini. Shah's imperial guards kill hundreds of protestors. Imposition of military law on "Black Friday."

1979 **January**

4 January: Shah appoints his long time opponent, Shapur Bahktiar, as Prime Minister. Bahktiar dissolves the political police, restores the freedom of the press and calls for free and fair elections as the only solution to the country's crisis.

16 January: the Shah leaves Iran, never to return.

February

1 February: Khomeini returns after 14 years in

exile and is hailed by the masses as the saviour and new leader. He refuses to submit his mandate to elections and demands Bahktiar's resignation.

5 February: Khomeini established the Provisional Islamic Revolutionary Government with Mehdi Bazargan as its Prime Minister. This new government draws on the Revolutionary *Komitehs,* armed Revolutionary Guards, and Provisional Council of the Revolution (also known as the Revolutionary Council), established in the months leading up to the revolution.

11 February: Bakhtiar's government is toppled by a popular uprising.

15 February: Summary executions of officials of former regime begin.

April

1 April: Khomeini declares victory in the referendum that establishes the Islamic Republic of Iran and declares April 1 "the first day of the Government of God."

May

15 May: Khomeini demands that the press conform to the principles of the Islamic Republic, further cementing the Islamisation of the media that had begun in February.

24 May: Ayatollah Khomeini announces that "anyone whose direction is separate from Islam" is an "enemy" of the revolution.

July

Foreign journalists are expelled from Iran for criticising the government.

2 July: The National Democratic Front (a coalition of leftist and nationalist groups) publishes an open letter to Khomeini calling his leadership a dictatorship.

11 July: A provisional Press Bill is implemented, providing for imprisonment for up to two years for anyone who slanders Islam, the revolution, or its leaders in writing.

August

3 August: Elections for an assembly of "Experts," instead of a Constituent Assembly, are held. The Assembly is charged with drafting a constitution for the Islamic Republic of Iran.

9-13 August: Demonstrations against the government's growing authoritarianism. Khomeini bans all demonstrations.

20 August: Twenty-two opposition newspapers, including that of the National Democratic Front, are ordered to close.

October

14 October: The Assembly of Experts approves a constitutional clause naming the Ayatollah head of the armed forces and giving him power of veto over the election of a president.

November

1 November: Khomeini urges students to "expand with all their might their attacks against the United States and Israel" in order to force the return of the Shah.

4 November: Armed students protesting the presence of the Shah in the US storm the US Embassy in Tehran and take 100 hostages.

6 November: Bazargan's provisional revolutionary government resigns. Khomeini orders the Revolutionary Council to take over the government.

December

2 December: Voters go to the polls to accept an Islamic Constitution that gives Khomeini total control over the body politic.

1980 January

24 January: Abolhassan Bani Sadr is elected President.

April

18 April: Khomeini gives a public speech attacking the "Westernisation" of universities.

Hezbollah militias injure hundreds of students.

June

12 June: Universities are shut down and will not re-open for two years during what is known as the "cultural revolution." Khomeini appoints a "Committee for the Islamisation of Universities" to ensure an 'Islamic atmosphere' in every subject taught.

September

22 September: Iraq launches several strikes against Iranian airfields, starting the Iran-Iraq war.

1981 January

US hostages released.

February

6 February: According to press reports, Hezbollah militias attack demonstrators from two Marxist-Leninist groups who are holding a rally in Tehran. At least 39 are reported to have been injured.

May

2 May : The *Mojahedin* take to the streets to protest the closure of Iran's universities. Three persons killed and 100 injured in clashes between the *Mojahedin* and Islamic extremists outside Tehran University.

June

20 June: Massive street demonstrations by *Mojahedin* supporters in favour of Bani-Sadr. Many killed.

22 June: Bani-Sadr dismissed and flees to Paris with Rajavi. The regime arrests and imprisons *Mojahedin* supporters.

28 June: Bomb at the Islamic Party headquarters; 73 killed. "Reign of Terror" against *Mojahedin* begins.

October

Rafsanjani calls for extermination of 'hypocrites', i.e. the *Mojahedin*. Many prisoners executed. Ayatollah Mohammadi Gilani declares that *bas-*

tinado when used as a religious punishment is not torture. Hossein Ali Nayyeri is appointed a religious judge in Tehran. Ali Khameini is elected President. Mir Hossein Mousavi is nominated as Prime Minister.

November

15 November: Hojatoleslam Musavi-Tabrizi says that 6,000-7,000 prisoners had been jailed for political offences since the fall of the Shah.

December

13 December: Amnesty International deplores the execution of at least 1,600 people between June and September 1981.

1982 January

30 January: Guidelines are sent classifying *Mojahedin* prisoners with a view to release repenters.

February-March

According to the Iranian media, Revolutionary Guards raid safe houses killing and arresting top leaders of leftist *Peykar* and FKO (Minority)

April

16 April: 1,000 people, including leading members of the Shi'a clergy, are arrested in connection with an alleged plot to assassinate Ayatollah Khomeini.

May

Heavy fighting continues between Iranian and Iraqi forces.

June

29 June: Iraq reports that the last of its troops have left Iran. Iranian officials say the withdrawal did not satisfy Iran's conditions for an end to the war.

November

Iran begins a major offensive against Iraqi troops.

7 November: Speaker of the Majlis Hashemi Rafsanjani said the communist *Tudeh* party was

a "disreputable party with a filthy record."

1983 February

7 February: *Tudeh* Party officials are arrested.

10 February: Iran's President Ali Khamenei says the "punishment of the leaders of the Iraqi regime" was the main goal of the war.

May

'May Day' televised confessions of communist (*Tudeh* party) leaders. Regime begins to arrest pro-Soviet leftists and dissolves the *Tudeh* party.

September

21 September: Universities reopen throughout Iran.

1984 Sentencing guidelines for political prisoners released.

February

8 February: Amnesty International charges Iran with large-scale abuses of human rights including over 5,000 executions since 1979.

May-June

Heavy fighting takes place across the Shatt al-Arab waterway; Iran attacks Basra and Iraq shells Abadan.

1985 March

Iran and Iraq continue fighting and shell cities and other civilian areas.

April-May

Anti-government and anti-war demonstrations in Tehran.

October

10 October: Khamenei is sworn in for a second four-year term and asks the Majlis to reappoint Prime Minister Mir Hossein Mousavi.

November

23 November: Ayatollah Hossein Ali Montazeri is selected by the Assembly of Experts as Khomeini's successor.

Fighting in Iraqi territory continues and cities in

both countries are targeted.

1986 May

20 May: A delegation headed by Iran's Deputy Prime Minister arrives in Paris, the first by such a high-ranking official since the 1979 revolution.

June

Rajavi and *Mojahedin* are expelled from France. They move to an armed camp on the Iraq border, under the protection of Saddam Hussein.

1987 June

The *Mojahedin* announce the formation of the Iranian National Liberation Army to overthrow the present regime.

July

7 July: The UN Security Council Resolution 598 suggests terms for a truce.

21 July: Iran calls the truce "null and void." Fighting continues throughout the year including attacks on civilian targets.

From September onwards the Ministry of Intelligence distributes questionnaires to political prisoners, testing their continued adherence to their political and religious beliefs.

1988 January

Government announces 'pardon committees' to determine early release of political prisoners.

March

The war of the cities continues with hundreds of casualties. Saddam uses chemical weapons against the Kurds in Halabja and Iranian villages in Marivan.

June

Ayatollah Khomeini appointed Majlis Speaker Ali Akbar Hashemi Rafsanjani Commander-in-chief of the armed forces.

July

3 July: USS *Vincennes* shoots down Iran-Air Flight 655, killing all 290 passengers and crew.

14 July: Rafsanjani chairs leadership meeting which decides to advise acceptance of ceasefire agreement along the lines of UN Resolution 598.

20 July: Khomeini broadcasts his bitter acceptance of a truce with Iraq ("more deadly than drinking poison").

25 July: The *Mojahedin* launch their "Eternal Light" invasion.

28 July: Khomeini's *fatwa* orders the execution of all 'steadfast' *Mojahedin* prisoners. Chief Justice Mousavi Ardebili asks for and is given clarification about the *fatwa*.

29 July: The *Mojahedin* army is beaten; it retreats to Iraq.

29 July - 10 August: Death Committee hearings and executions take place in Evin and Gohardasht and at least 20 provincial prisons.

August

"Trials" and executions of *Mojahedin* prisoners continue.

1 August: Judge Ahmadi complains to Khomeini and to Ayatollah Montazeri that he is being outvoted by prosecution and Intelligence Ministry members of the Death Committees.

4 August: Montazeri complains to Khomeini about the unfairness of the procedures.

5 August: Chief Justice Mousavi Ardebili announces that the public demands "to execute them all without exception."

13 August: Montazeri summons Death Committee members and tells them to stop executions for religious holiday. Nayyeri admits they have killed 750 in Tehran already.

15 August: Montazeri calculates that between 2,800 and 3,800 prisoners have been executed since the issuance of the fatwa.

20 August: Iran's acceptance of UN Resolution 598 formally brings an end to the Iran-Iraq War.

26 August: the Death Committees re-convene to begin the "Second Wave" of killings.

Week of Saturday, August 27: The High Judicial Council re-opens. Chief Justice Mousavi Ardebili orders prosecutors to confront the 'heathen' leftist groups.

September

The "Second Wave" of killings continues.

2 September: Amnesty International issues 'urgent action' in response to reports of the prison killings.

6 September: A second, secret, *fatwa* may have been issued approving the killing of leftist apostate prisoners.

6-8 September: In letters to Ali Khamenei and Mir Hossein Mousavi, the Supreme Leader relinquishes his power to impose Islamic punishments (*tazirat*) to the Exigency Council. The latter would determine how much of this prerogative would be left to the government.

October

Professor Reynaldo Pohl, UN Special Representative for Iran, reports to General Assembly that 200 *Mojahedin* were massacred in Evin Prison assembly hall and 860 buried in a mass grave in Tehran.

November

20 and 29 November: Professor Pohl meets with Iranian ambassador, Mahallati, who denies the allegation and says that the *Mojahedin* died on the battlefield.

December

Mousavi defends actions against leftists and *Mojahedin* in Austrian television broadcast.

1989 January

Rafsanjani admits that "less than one thousand" have been executed.

Professor Pohl reports to the Human Rights Commission, lists names of over 1,000 victims.

February

14 February: *Fatwa* on Salman Rushdie and his translators and publishers.

November

Professor Pohl report to the General Assembly confirms (paragraph 110) that mass executions of political prisoners took place in 1988.

December

Amnesty International report alleges 'perhaps thousands' of executions of political prisoners.

1990 Kasem Rajavi assassinated by Iranian agents in Switzerland.

1991 Assassination of Shapour Bahktiar by Iranian agents in Paris.

Appendix B: Bibliography

Ervarnd Abrahamian, *Tortured Confessions: Prisons and Public Recantations in Modern Iran* (University of California Press, 1999).

Ervarnd Abrahamian, *The Iranian Mojahedin* (Yale, 1989).

Nasrin Alavi, *We are Iran* (Portobello, 2005).

Said Amir Arjomand, *The Turban for the Crown: The Islamic Revolution in Iran* (Oxford, 1988).

Michael Axworthy, *Iran – Empire of the Mind* (Penguin, 2007).

Fakhreddin Azimi, *The Quest for Democracy in Iran* (Harvard, 2008).

Ronan Bergman, *The Secret War with Iran* (One World, 2009).

Antonio Cassese, *International Criminal Law* (Oxford, 2003).

Con Coughlin, *Khomeini's Ghost* (Macmillan, 2009).

Hamid Dabashi, *Theology of Discontent: The Ideological Foundation of the Islamic Revolution in Iran* (Transaction, 2005).

Adam Roberts and Richard Guelff (eds), *Documents on the Laws of War* (Clarendon Press, 2nd edn, 2002).

Haleh Esfandiari, *My Prison, My Home: One Woman's Story of Captivity in Iran* (Ecco, 2009).

Mohamed Heikal, *The Return of the Ayatollah: The Iranian Revolution from Mossadeq to Khomeini* (Andre Deutsch, 1981).

Dilip Hiro, *Islamic Fundamentalism* (Paladin, 1988)

Dilip Hiro, *The Longest War: The Iran-Iraq Military Conflict* (Paladin, 1990).

Ryszand Kapuscinski, *Shah of Shahs* (Harcourt, 1985).

Stephen Kinzer, *All the Shah's Men: An American Coup and the Roots of Middle East Terror* (John Wiley, 2008).

Sandra Mackay, *The Iranians: Persia, Islam and the Soul of a Nation* (Penguin, 1996).

Theodore Meron, *War Crimes Law Comes of Age* (Oxford, 1998).

Afshin Molavi, *The Soul of Iran: A Nation's Journey to Freedom* (WW Norton, 2002).

Tom Ginsberg and Tamir Mustafa (eds) *Rule by Law: The Politics of Courts in Authoritarian Regimes* (Cambridge, 2008).

Afar Nafisi, *Reading Lolita in Tehran* (Random House, 2007).

Kasra Naji, *Ahmadinejad: the Secret History of Iran's Radical Leader* (IB Taurus, 2008).

Marina Nemat, *Prisoner of Tehran* (John Murray, 2007).

William R Polk, *Understanding Iran: From Cyrus to Ahmadinejad* (Palgrave, 2009).

Geoffrey Robertson QC, *Crimes Against Humanity – The Struggle for Global Justice* (Penguin, 2006).

Geoffrey Robertson QC, *The Tyrannicide Brief* (Vintage, 2009).

Nigel S Rodley, *The Treatment of Prisoners in International Law* (Oxford, 3rd edn, 2009).

Majane Satrapi, *Persepolis* (Vintage, 2008)

William A Schabas, *Genocide in International Law* (Cambridge, 2nd edn, 2009).

Michael Newton and Michael Scharf, *Enemy of the State: The Trial and Execution of Saddam Hussein* (St Martin's Press, 2008).

Ray Takeyh, *Guardian of the Revolution: Iran and the World in the Age of the Ayatollahs* (OUP, 2009).

Yuma Tatoni, *The Tokyo War Crime Trial* (Harvard, 2008).

Endnotes

1 Amnesty International, *Iran: political executions*, UA235/88, MDE 13/14/88, 2 September 1988.

2 See Reynaldo Galindo Pohl, Interim Report annexed to Note by the Secretary General, ECOSOC Report, "Situation of Human Rights in the Islamic Republic of Iran," A/43/705, 13 October 1988 ("*Interim 1988 Report*"), paras 5-11, 59.

3 Iran Research Group, Iran Yearbook 89/90 (MB Medien & Bucher Verlagsgesellschaft mbH, 1989).

4 *Ettela'at*, 22 December 1988, 2.

5 *Kayhan*, 25 February 1989, 16.

6 The Baha'i Faith was founded in Iran in 1844 and is now its largest non-Muslim religious minority. While reaffirming the core ethical principles common to all religions, the founder of the Baha'i Faith, Baha'u'llah, was also said to have revealed new laws and teachings to lay the foundations of a global civilisation. The central theme of the Baha'i Faith is that humanity is one family and the time has come for its unification into a peaceful global society. After 1979, its adherents were treated as apostates and have been subjected to continual discrimination and repression.

7 Reynaldo Galindo Pohl, *Report on the Situation of Human Rights in Iran*, 28 January 1987, E/CN.4/1987/23, para 82(b). No Red Cross representatives were allowed to visit prisons in Iran until 22 January 1992: just 2 weeks later on 21 March 1992, all Red Cross representatives were expelled from the country. See Pohl, *Report on the Human Rights Situation in the Islamic Republic of Iran*, 28 January 1993, E/CN.4/1993/41, para 168.

8 Reynaldo Galindo *Pohl, Report on the Situation of Human Rights in Islamic Republic of Iran*, E/CN.4/1988/24, 25 January 1988, paras 82(7) and 82(8).

9 Reynaldo Galindo Pohl, *Interim 1988 Report*, above note 2, para 47.

10 Reported in *Kayhan,* 6 August 1988, 15.

11 Reynaldo Galindo Pohl, *Interim 1988 Report*, above note 2, paras 69 and 71.

12 Reynaldo Galindo Pohl, *Report on the situation of human rights in the Islamic Republic of Iran*, E/CN.4/1989/26, 26 January 1989, paras 15-18.

13 *Ibid* para 68.

14 See *ibid*, paras 6-10. The Iranian diplomats who blindsided Pohl in this period were ambassador Mahallati in New York and Ambassador Sirous Nasseri in Geneva. The latter is now a businessman in Europe and the former resides in the US; they may have a case to answer: see Chapter 11.

15 Ervand Abrahamian, *Tortured Confessions: Prisons and Public Recantations in Modern Iran* (University of California Press, 1999), 221.

16 One prisoner, Monireh Baradaran, in her memoirs *The Plain Truth: Memoirs of the Prisons of the Islamic Republic of Iran* (Independent Association of Iranian Women, 2006), 543-4, tells how she later met Pohl and discovered that he had been introduced to fake 'prisoners' in Evin, who had (unsurprisingly) praised their humane treatment. Other witnesses suggest that the Professor had been deceived, although the naivety shown in his reports does suggest that he lacked the experience and instinct to be an effective human rights investigator.

17 Reynaldo Galindo Pohl, *Report on the Situation of Human Rights in the Islamic Republic of Iran*, A/45/697, 6 November 1990, para 230.

18 *Ibid* para 240.

19 *Ibid* para 136.

20 *Ibid* para 142.

21 *Ibid* para 215.

22 *Ibid* para 256.

23 *Ibid* para 290.

24 Amnesty International, *Iran: Violations of Human Rights 1987-1990*, MDE 13/21/90, 1 December 1990, 14.

25 Professor Pohl seems to lose interest in the massacres: his report on 13 February 1991 makes no reference to them, despite the fact that Amnesty International published its detailed report just two weeks previously. See Pohl, *Report on the Human Rights Situation in the Islamic Republic of Iran*, E/CN.4/1991/35, 13 February 1991. In 1992, Pohl reports that 164 executions of political prisoners have taken place in 1992: see Pohl, *Final Report on the Situation of Human Rights in the Islamic Republic of Iran*, E/CN.4/1993/41, 28 January 1993, para 281. In the course of this year, the Iranian government officials realised that Pohl was obtaining his information on political executions from the local

media, which had been reporting the boastful statements of judicial authorities. So they took action to curtail reporting – a leaked government document expressed satisfaction that "one of the sources used by Galindo Pohl to provide documented and irrefutable reports was therefore neutralised;" see *Interim report on the situation of human rights in the Islamic Republic of Iran*, annexed to Note by the Secretary General transmitting the Pohl Report to the General Assembly, A/48/526, 8 November 1993, para 92.

26 Reynaldo Galindo Pohl, 8 November 1993, above note 25, para 25.

27 Amnesty International, above note 24, pages 12, 16, 14.

28 In some obituaries of Grand Ayatollah Montazeri it was wrongly stated that he alleged in his memoirs that 30,000 had been killed. See "The Cleric Who Dared To Defy The Regime," *The Times,* 21 December 2009; *The Australian,* 22 December 2009. The only figure that Montazeri gave was 3,800.

29 Abrahamian, *Tortured Confessions*, above note 15, 209.

30 Azar Nafisi, *Reading Lolita in Tehran* (Random House, 2003), 239.

31 Mohammad Hassan Zia'ifard, Secretary of the Islamic Human Rights Commission in *Payam-e Emrouz*, Issue 38, 21 March 2000, 34.

32 Iran Human Rights Documentation Centre (IHRDC), *Deadly Fatwa: Iran's 1988 Prison Massacre* (2009), 64.

33 See Anne Applebaum, "An Overlooked Force in Iran," *Washington Post*, 23 June 2009.

34 The funding for the Abdorrahman Boroumand Foundation is provided, among others, by the Oak Foundation, Sigrid Rausing Trust, Open Society and the National Endowment for Democracy (see http://www.ned.org/).

35 See Kasra Naji, *Ahmadinejad – The Secret History of Iran's Radical Leader* (IBTaurus, 2009), 119.

36 *Ibid* 20.

37 Film director Mohsen Makhmalbaf, Green Movement spokesperson, explains Montazeri's inspiration in his speech in London on 25 November 2009 accepting the "Freedom to Create" prize: see www.freedomtocreate.com.

38 Despite his pre-eminence as a theologian and a revolutionary, Montazeri's concern over the harsh treatment of prisoners and his increasing criticism of the intolerance of the regime and the greed of some of its key figures (he remained true to egalitarian ideals and was close to Bazargan) made him enemies who regarded him

as naive: see Fakhreddin Azimi, *The Quest for Democracy in Iran – A Century of Struggle against Authoritarian Rule* (Harvard University Press, 2008), 372.

39 See Con Coughlin, *Khomeini's Ghost – Ayatollah Khomeini's Islamic revolution and its enduring legacy* (Macmillan, 2009), 129.

40 The Muslim split, after the Prophet's death in 632AD, was between the Shia who favoured family succession to the leadership (i.e. his cousin Ali) and those who followed his close companion, Abu Bakr. These Sunni (a name derived from the Arabic word for tradition, *Sunna*) are now in the vast majority (about 87%) but 200 million remain Shia and predominate in Iran, Iraq and Bahrain. Sunni hardliners, including the Taliban and much of the religious establishment in Saudi Arabia, regard the Shia tradition as heretical. The Iranian theocracy, based on "the guardianship of the Islamic jurist" and constructed by Khomeini through controversial interpretation of religious texts, is disputed by many Shia theologians in Iran itself, and elsewhere.

41 See Stephen Kinzer, *All the Shah's Men: The American Coup and the Roots of Middle East Terror* (Wiley and Sons, 2008), 95.

42 For Taleqani's equivocal relationship with Khomeini, see Hamid Dabashi, *Theology of Discontent* (Iran, 2006), 267-270. His work inspired leftist groups and his sons were arrested for membership of the MKO.

43 The numbers killed on 5 June 1963 have been wildly overestimated ('thousands') by the Islamic Republic, to assist its demonization of the Shah. Emadeddin Baghi, *Review of Iran's Revolution* calculates that a total of 3,164 were killed between 1963 and 1979, under the Shah. Even this is said to be an over-estimate, for example by former UK ambassador Sir Denis Wright for one. However there is no doubt that many more were tortured by SAVAK.

44 Abrahamian, *Tortured Confessions*, above note 15, 220.

45 See Ervand Abrahamian, *The Iranian Mojahedin* (Yale University Press, 1989), 89 *et seq.*

46 Abrahamian, *Tortured Confessions*, above note 15, 106.

47 Said Amir Arjmand, *Turban for the Crown* (OUP, 1988), 137. Also see Khomeini's speech at the cemetery of Qom on 9 March 1979, *Sahifeh* Nur, Vol. 5 (Ministry of Islamic Guidance, 1983), 185.

48 Con Coughlin, *Khomeini's Ghost,* above note 40, 170.

49 Azimi, *The Quest for Democracy in Iran*, above note 39, 363.

50 *Ibid* 143.

51 See Abrahamian, *The Iranian Mojahedin*, above note 46, 220. Lingering suspicion still attaches to a pro-Soviet faction with the Islamist regime, since the most senior casualty, Beheshti, was the most powerful anti-communist among the Ayatollahs.

52 *Kayhan*, 4 July 1981, 14, reporting Ayatollah Khomeini's speech for the families of those killed at the bombing of the Islamic Party Headquarters. A fuller version, published on the same day in *Ettela'at*, page 10, can be read as a blood-curdling incitement to punish by death (the punishment God had set for them) the MKO, who are "corruptors who wade into the street and scare believers" by their Marxist-influenced interpretation of Islam: "They and we are not alike... They believe in class war. They think there is no day of resurrection and there is nothing beyond the material world. But you don't. The day they prevail, you (God forbid) shall be their sacrificial lamb."

53 *Ettela'at,* 4 July 1981, 10. The Chief Public Prosecutor of the Islamic Republic, Hojatoleslam Mousavi Tabrizi, clarifies in a speech, reported in *Jomhuri Eslami*, 21 September 1981, 11, the fate of dissidents mentioned by Ayatollah Khomeini: "If they arrest them, they will no longer wait for months while they [the arrested] eat, sleep, and use up the resources that belong to the people. [Instead,] they will be prosecuted in the streets. [Thus,] whoever held a [Molotov] cocktail in his hands and stood opposed to the institution of the Islamic Republic, was prosecuted on the spot. When they are arrested and by the time they are brought to the public prosecutor's office, they are already tried and their sentence is execution."

54 For Khomeini's speech see *Ettela'at* 4 July 1981, 10; for Rafsanjani's Friday Sermon, see *Jomhuri Eslami*, 4 July 1981, 3 & 8.

55 *Kayhan*, 3 October 1981, 15.

56 *Kayhan*, 19 October 1981, 14.

57 See Sayyid Muhammad Rizvi, *Apostasy in Islam,* http://www.al-islam.org/short/apostasy/, 8-12, and sources cited therein.

58 *Kayhan*, 4 March 1981, 3.

59 Mousavi Tabrizi, Chief Revolutionary Prosecutor in *Jomhuri Eslami*, 15 December 1981, 12.

60 Abrahamian, *Tortured Confessions*, above note 15, 125.

61 So I am informed by a number of survivors of the 1988 massacres who were arrested after participating in the *Mojahedin* demonstration of June 1981.

62 On 27 July 1981, Tehran radio announced that MKO central council member Mohammad Reza Sa'adati had been executed – apparently summarily (reported by NYTimes/Reuters).

63 The National Council for Resistance in Iran began as a cross-party group of exiles but evolved into an MKO body.

64 Abrahamian, *Tortured Confessions*, above note 15, 170.

65 *Jomhuri Eslami*, 21 February 1982, 12.

66 M. Rajavi in Abrahamian, *Tortured Confessions*, above note 15, 186.

67 *Jomhuri Eslami*, 8 January 1983, 5.

68 *Jomhuri Eslami*, 9 August 1982, 12.

69 Mohammad Reyshahri in *Kayhan*, 18 February 1985, 2.

70 Circular issued by Morteza Moqtada'i on behalf of the Supreme Judicial Council, 2 February 1984.

71 *Ettela'at*, 20 January 1982.

72 *Kayhan,* 7 January 1988, 17 and see *Ettela'at,* 3 January 1988, 2.

73 *Ettela'at,* 30 January 1988, 3.

74 National Council of Resistance of Iran (NCRI), *Crime Against Humanity* (2001), 68-9.

75 Fariba Sabet, interviewed in Paris, 24 June 2009.

76 See IHRDC, *Deadly Fatwa*, above note 32, 10- 14.

77 See Coughlan, *Khomeini's Ghost*, above note 40, 234-5.

78 Dilip Hiro, *The Longest War – The Iran Iraq Military Conflict* (Palladum, 1990), 244-245.

79 *Ettela'at*, 5 July 1988, 2.

80 Khomeini's letter to Montazeri (1986) in *The Political Memoirs of Reyshahri*. p.255, as quoted in Iraj Mesdaghi, *Neither Life nor Death, Volume 3: Restless Raspberries*, Alfabet Maxima Publishing: 2006 (second edition), 82.

81 Ayatollah Eslami in Resalat, 20 July 1987, 10.

82 Anonymous, interviewed in Europe, 30 June 2009.

83 Mehdi Aslani in IHRDC, *Deadly Fatwa*, above note 32, 12.

84 Rezvan Moqadam, interviewed in Berlin, 2 July 2009.

85 Manuchehr Eshqai, interviewed in Paris, 21 June 2009.

86 Shahab Shokuhi, interviewed in London, 14 June 2009.

87 *Unequal Battle: a report of 7 years imprisonment 1982-1989*, (Committee to Organise the Memorial of the Massacre of Political prisoners, 1994), translated by Shahla Sarabi, 52 and 53.

88 Mehdi Aslani, interviewed in Frankfurt, 1 July 2009.

89 Iraj Mesdaghi, Neither Life nor Death, above note 81, 66 and 100.

90 Several statements made to me confirm this and I do not

believe MKO denials. As an avid reader in my youth of World War II prison memoirs, I recall that there does not seem to have been a Stalag in which some hidden radio was not surreptitiously tuned to the BBC. Even the Baader-Meinhof gang, the most heavily guarded of terrorists, followed the fate of hijackers demanding their release via smuggled transistors. Many MKO members were engineering students. They were buoyed by what they heard, but there is no evidence that their radios were two-way or that they were giving or receiving commands from Iraq.

91   Dilip Hiro, above note 79, 242-3.

92   The numbers of casualties are disputed. See Baqer Moin, *Khomeini – Life of the Ayatollah* (Thomas Dunne Books, 2000), 278, which suggests that the casualties may have been in hundreds on both sides. The then Minister of Intelligence, Mohammad Mohammadi Reyshahri gives the figure of 3,400 Mojahedin killed, wounded or captured. See Mohammad Mohammadi Reyshahri, *Memoirs*, (The Centre for Islamic Revolution Documents, 2007 – in Persian), 171.

93   The *fatwa* itself is undated, but internal evidence from the Montazeri memoirs has pin-pointed this date.

94   Morteza Eshraqi in *Ettela'at*, 13 July 1988, 2.

95   Aftab, 6 May 2009, http://www.aftabnews.ir/vdcepw8v.jh8vzi9bbj.html, last visited: 27 January 2011.

96   Mohammad Ali Amani in The Iranian Student News Agency (ISNA), 21 August 2004.

97   See Moin, above note 92, 287-289.

98   *Kayhan,* 6 August 1988, 15.

99   Amnesty International, above note 1.

100 Initially by prison officials, although both MKO members and leftists insisted on being treated as political prisoners and separated from common criminals. Both groups demanded to be segregated from the "repenters" from their own group, who were under pressure to act as informers. Some MKO prisoners sought separation from leftists, because they were unbelievers.

101 There are reports that in some cases, *en route* to the gallows, prisoners were briefly held in waiting rooms and permitted to make their wills.

102 Ayatollah Hossein Ali Montazeri, *The Diaries* (Ketab Corporation, 2001), 357.

103 NCRI, *The Massacre of Political Prisoners*, (1999). In 2001 in its publication, *Crime Against Humanity*, the National Council of Resistance estimated 30,000 deaths nation-wide, although this figure is not convincingly explained and seems to me to be highly exaggerated; see above note

75.

104 NCRI, *Crime Against Humanity*, above note 75, 4 and 7. See also Montazeri, *The Diaries*, above note 102, 352-4.

105 Montazeri, *The Diaries*, above note 102, 352.

106 *Ibid* 357.

107 IHRDC, *Deadly Fatwa*, above note 32, 25-26.

108 *Ibid* 30.

109 *Ibid* 30 and 32.

110 *Ettela'at*, 1 September 1988, 14. Mousavi Ardebili refers to the same Koranic verse as used in Khomeini's *fatwa*. Statement reported to media by Moqtada'i, spokesperson of the High Judicial Council.

111 *Ettela'at*, 7 September 1988, 2.

112 *Ettela'at*, 26 September 1988, 2.

113 *Kayhan*, 11 December 1988, 14.

114 Iran signed Convention on the Prevention and Punishment of the Crime of Genocide on 8 December 1949 and ratification occurred on 14 August 1956.

115 Reza Shemirani, "Memoirs of the 1988 Massacre in Evin Prison, Parts 1-7," published on the Didgah website, http://www.didgah.net/maghalehMatnKamel.php?id=6312, last visited: 31 January 2011.

116 IHRDC, *Deadly Fatwa*, above note 32, 54.

117 Amnesty International, *Iran: Preserve the Khavaran Grave Site for Investigation into Mass Killings*, Index MDE 13/006/2009, 20 January 2009.

118 See above page 2, and above note 3.

119 IHRDC, *Speaking for the Dead: Survivor Accounts of Iran's 1988 Massacre*, 2010, 50.

120 See the NCRI, *Crime Against Humanity*, note 75, 81.

121 *Resalat*, 7 December 1988, 2 and 11.

122 See above page 2, and above note 4.

123 See Farhad Mogaddam, 'Death comes to a dissident: A young woman's struggle to stay alive', *The Guardian*, 13 January 1989.

124 See 'Iran: Double Standard?' *The Economist,* 29 August 1998, 45.

125 Mr. Moni'eh has agreed to provide his testimony to the present investigation solely in support of justice and accountability. Though he endorses the authors' legal assessment of the 1988 prison massacre, Mr. Moni'eh does not share the author's views on the MKO's ideology and policies.

126 Reyshahri in *Kayhan*, 18 February 1985, 2.

127 Mousavi Bojnordi in *Ettela'at*, 1 February 1988, 4.

128 A successor government is liable for contracts and other obligations concluded by its predecessor: *Western Electric Co. Inc. Claims* (1959) 30 ILR 166. Of course, a state may denounce a treaty (although Iran has not denounced the treaties above mentioned), but after doing so it still must respect treaty rights, especially human rights, that vested prior to the denunciation: see *Oppenheim's International Law*, 234-5.

129 "None shall kill an enemy who yields and throws down his arms, upon pain of death" was a rule of a) the King's Army in 1640, b) the Earl of Essex's Army in 1642 and c) the Army of the Kingdom of Scotland in 1643. The latter ordinance provided that "murder is no less unlawful and intolerable in the time of war, than in the time of peace, and is to be punished by death... if it shall come to pass that the enemy shall force us to battle and the Lord shall give us victory, none shall kill a yielding enemy." See a) Grosse, *Military Antiquities* (London, 1788) p.118 and b) Charles M Clode *The Military Forces of the Crown* (London 1869) Vol 1. P.422-5 and c) Grosse (above), 136.

130 See Geoffrey Robertson, *The Tyrannicide Brief: The Story of the Man Who Sent Charles I to the Scaffold* (Vintage, 2006), Chapter 10.

131 Holinshed, Shakespeare's source, mentions no such incident. The only justification ever suggested has been that the English army were vastly outnumbered by their French prisoners, who, if they had lived, might have fought another day and won. See Theodore Meron, *War Crimes Law Comes of Age* (Oxford, 1998).

132 H. Grotius, *De Jure Belli ac Pacis Liberi Tres,* Book iii, Chapter xi, Part xvi(i).

133 Lieber's Code *Instructions for the Government of Armies of the United States in the Field,* General Orders Number 100 (24 April 1863) Article 148. Article 28 of the Lieber code specifically provides "unjust or inconsiderate retaliation removes the belligerents further and further from the mitigating rules of regular war, and by rapid steps leads them nearer to the internecine wars of savages."

134 Meron, *War Crimes Comes of Age*, above note 131, 120.

135 See Yuma Tatoni, *The Tokyo War Crime Trial* (Harvard, 2008), 164-6.

136 ICRC Commentary, Fourth Geneva Convention (1958), 51.

137 See ICTY judgment, *The Prosecutor v Delalic et al*, IT-96-21-T, 16 November 1998, para 271.

138 *Military and Paramilitary Activities In and Against Nicaragua* (*Nicaragua v USA* (judgment)) ICJ Rep 1986, para 218. The ICTY Appeals chamber confirmed this in *Prosecutor v Tadic* (Decision on the defence motion for interlocutory appeal on jurisdiction) ICTY-94-1-AR72, 2 October 1995, para 102.

139 See *Legality of the Threat or Use of Nuclear Weapons* (Advisory Opinion) ICJ Rep 1995 [para 25] *Legal Consequences of the Construction of a Wall in the Occupied Palestinian Territory* (Advisory Opinion) ICJ reports 2004, para 106. In times of armed conflict, the protections provided by human rights law must be interpreted by reference to the *Lex Speciliae* of International Humanitarian Law. See Human Rights Committee General Comment 26 (61) on Issues Relating to the Continuity of Obligations to the ICCPR, UN doc CCPR/C/21/rev1add.8.rev.1, 8 December 1997, para 4. "The rights enshrined in the Covenant belong to the people living in the territory of the state party... once people are accorded the protection of the rights under the Covenant, such protection devolves with the territory and continues to belong to them, notwithstanding change in government of the state party..."

140 *Castillo-Pâes v Peru* HR (Series C) No. 34 para 90 (1997) see also *Velâsquez-Rodriquez v Honduras* Inter-American Court HR (ser. C) No.4. para 157 (1988).

141 *Schedko v Belarus*, Communication No. 886/1999, 28 April 2003.

142 *Tas v Turkey* Application No.24396/924, (2000) para 80. *Cyprus v Turkey*, Application No. 25782/924 ECHR paras 157-58 (2001).

143 See *Valesquez Rodriguez*, above note 140.

144 IAC 66, OAS/ser/L/V/3, 29 doc 4, and see Padilla "Reparations" in *Aloeboetoe v Suriname* HRQ 17 (1995), 541.

145 *"The Nuremberg Judgment"* (1947) 41 *American Journal of International Law* 172.

146 *Re Ohlendorf and Others* (1948) 15 ILR 656.

147 See Geoffrey Robertson, *Crimes Against Humanity: the Struggle for Global Justice* (Penguin and New Press, 2006), 260-61.

148 *United States v Ohlendorf* (Case 9, 1946-7) IV trials of war criminals before the Nuremberg military tribunals, 498.

149 *Case Concerning the Arrest Warrant of 11 April 2000 (Democratic Republic of the Congo v Belgium)* ICJ decision, 14 February 2002.

150 *R v Yamashita* (1946) 327 US1.

151 See *Prosecutor v Mitar Vasiljevic*, Case No. IT-98-32-T, para 227 (ICTY), 29 November 2002.

152 As the IHRDC seems to think – see its *Deadly Fatwa*

Report, above note 32, 61.

153 See Convention on the Prevention and Punishment of the Crime of Genocide, adopted by Resolution 260 (III) A of the U.N. General Assembly on 9 December 1948; entry into force: 12 January 1951, Article III.

154 See discussion in B Van Schaack, *The Crime of Political Genocide: repairing the Genocide Convention's Blind Spot* Yale Law Journal, Vol 106, No. 2259, 1997.

155 See William A Schabas, *Genocide in International Law* (Cambridge, 2nd edn, 2009), 147.

156 *Prosecutor v Kayishema*, 21 May 1999, para 98.

157 *Church of New Faith v Commissioner of Payroll Tax* (1983) 57 ALJR 785 (High Court of Australia).

158 See *Application of the Convention on the Prevention and Punishment of the crime of Genocide: Bosnia and Herzergovenia v Serrbia and Montenegro*, Case 91, ICJ judgement, 26 February 2007.

159 *The Prosecutor v Krstic*, Case No. IT-98-33-T, judgment, ICTY trial chamber, 2 August 2001, para 589.

160 Schabas, above note 155, 149.

161 Reservations to the Prevention on Genocide Case (1951) ICJ Rep. 15, 23.

162 This is ample to engage state liability, see *Prosecutor v Tadic* case No. IT-94-1-A Appeal Judgment, ICTY AC, 15 July 1999, para 131.

163 Imposing the death penalty for religious or political affiliation (or non-affiliation) is considered to violate the restriction of the death penalty to the "most serious crimes." See, for example, Concluding observations of the Human Rights Committee: Libyan Arab Jamahiriya, UN document CCPR/C/79/Add.101, 6 November 1998, para 8 and Concluding observations of the Human Rights Committee: Sudan, UN document CCPR/C/79/Add.85, 19 November 1997, para 8. Further, the Committee has, in particular, expressed concern about "very vague categories of offences relating to internal and external security" (Concluding observations of the Human Rights Committee: Kuwait, UN document CCPR/CO/69/KWT, 27 July 2000, para 13); about vaguely worded offences of opposition to order (Concluding observations of the Human Rights Committee: Viet Nam, UN document CCPR/CO/75/VNM, 26 July 2002, para 7); and about "political offences... couched in terms so broad that the imposition of the death penalty may be subject to essentially subjective criteria" (Concluding observations of the Human Rights Committee: Democratic People's Republic of Korea, UN document CCPR/CO/72/PRK, 27 August 2001, para 13).

164 *Ocalan v Turkey* No. 46221/99 ECHR 2005 paras 148-9.

165 See, for example, Concluding observations of the Human Rights Committee: Sudan, UN document CCPR/C/79/Add.85, 19 November 1997, para 8.

166 Newton and Scharf, *Enemy of the State: the Trial and Execution of Saddam Hussein* (St Martin's Press 2008).

167 See Geoffrey Robertson, *Crimes Against Humanity*, above note 147, 602-9.

168 *Prosecution v Kvocka et al*, Case No. IT-98-30/1-A, Appeal Judgment, 28 February 2005, 285-91.

169 (1969) 12 Year Book of European Convention Law 505.

170 See *Bati v Turkey* (No.33097/96;57834-00) ECHR, 3 June 2004, paras 114 and 117; *Mammadov v Azerbaijan* (No.34445/04) ECHR, 11 January 2007, paras 66, 68- 69; Nigel S Rodley *The Treatment of Prisoners under International Law* (Oxford, 3rd edn, 2009), 96.

171 European Court of Human Rights Series A No.25, paras 96-97.

172 *Selmouni v France* (No. 25803, 1994) European Commission of Human Rights Report 1999, paras 96-97.

173 *Prosecutor v Brdanin* (1 September 2004) Trial Judgment para 483, Appeal Judgment paras 243-252.

174 See respectively *Tyrer v UK* (No.5856/72) 1978 Series A, No 26; *Caesar v Trinidad and Tobago* 2005 Series C No.123 and *Curtis Francis Doebbler v Sudan* Communication 236/2000 16th Activity Report, 2002-3 VII.

175 See Rodley, above note 170, 445.

176 *Pinochet* No.3 [2000] 1 AC 147 at 198 per Lord Browne-Wilkinson

177 See *Al-Adsani v. Government of Kuwait* (1996) 107 ILR 536 and see also *Al-Adsani v United Kingdom (No.2)* (35763/97) European Court of Human Rights, 21 November 2001.

178 *DRC v Belgium* [2002] ICJ Rep 3 see para 61 in particular. A state may waive a high official's immunity – as the Philippines did for ex-president Marcos.

179 Ian Brownlie, *Principles of Public International Law* (OUP, 6th edn, 2003), 303.

180 The 1992 Torture Victim Protection Act extends the right to US victims or relatives in respect of acts of torture and summary execution permitted by officials in foreign countries, where there is no remedy.

181 *Trajano v Marcos* where a US Federal Appeals Court held

that immunity did not apply to acts of torture, kidnap and murder. *Trajano v Marcos* 878 F 2d 40 and 39 (9th Circuit) and *Re Estate of Ferdinand Marcos Litigation* (1992) 978 F 2d 493, 498 (9th Circuit).

182 *Filartiga* 1986 3OF 2d 876, *Kadic v Karadzic* (1995) 70 F 3d 232 (2nd Circuit).

183 *International Law Commissions, Articles on Responsibility of States for International Wrongful Acts* (2001) Articles 1, 30 and 31.

184 In *Velsquez Rodriguez*, above note 140, the Inter-American Court of Human Rights held that international law did not recognise the concept of punitive or exemplary damages (Series C No.7 1989). See also *Letelier v Moffitt*, (1992) 88 ILR 727.

185 Iranian law reports often refer to Hossein Ali (Jafar) Nayyeri.

186 He also has his own law firm on the corner of Vila and Sepand Avenue, Tehran.

187 Information provided by Iraj Mesdaghi, 11 March 2010.

188 During the Khatami period he was forced to resign from the Ministry because he was implicated in the "Chain Murders" (death squad murders of intellectuals and journalists), but he was taken under Khamenei's protection until he could return to work for Ahmadinejad and became a Cabinet minister.

189 Human Rights Watch Briefing, *Ministers of Murder: Iran's New Security Cabinet*, December 2005.

190 NCRI, *Crimes Against Humanity*, above note 75, 57.

191 On August 5, 1988, Mousavi Ardebili said at the Friday sermon, "People say they should all be executed... The judges are limited by some problems... such as trials. ... Most of all, I have to thank this miserable being [i.e. the leader of the *Mojahedin*] who made our work easy. Now we are trying them in groups of ten and twenty." *Jomhuri Eslami*, 6 August 1988, 10.

192 See Phillippe Sands *Torture Team – Deception, Cruelty and the Compromise of Law* (Alan Lane, 2008) 30.

193 See Pohl, January 1989 report, above note 12, and Kaveh Shahrooz, 'With Revolutionary Rage and Rancor: A Preliminary Report on the 1988 Massacre of Iran's

Political prisoners' (2007) 20 *Harvard Human Rights Journal* 227, 241. Shahrooz points out that another massacre denier at this time was Abdullah Nouri, Minister of the Interior, who a decade later became a leader of the reform movement and was jailed by the regime he had so enthusiastically served.

194 See Naji, *Ahmadinejad – The Secret History of Iran's Radical Leader*, above note 36, xiii and 34-36.

195 Moin, above note 92, 263.

196 See Reza Afshari, *Human Rights in Iran, the Abuse of Cultural Relativism,* University of Pennsylvania Press, (2001), 113; Shahrooz, above note 192, at 241-2.

197 Although, Mousavi's wife, Zahra Rahnavard, has vigorously condemned the *Mojahedin Khalq* as terrorists and traitors at meetings with students after the 2009 demonstrations. See Maziar Bahari, "Who is behind Tehran's Violence?" Newsweek Web Exclusive, 17 June 2009.

198 'Meet the Ayatollahs', *New Statesman*, 10 August 2009, 30.

199 See Catherine Philip, 'Iran executes alleged dissidents "to warn opposition"', *The Times*, 29 January 2010, 9.

200 See Haleh Esfandiari, *My Prison, My Home: One Woman's Story of Captivity in Iran* (Ecco, 2009). Esfandiari, an Iranian turned American who directs the Middle East Program at the Woodrow Wilson Center for Scholars in Washington, DC, was arrested on a visit to her mother in Tehran and incarcerated in Evin for some months in 2007. Her account is important evidence of the mindset of the Intelligence Ministry and its current establishment, which has convinced itself that the 'Green Movement' is really an emanation of a Zionist and Western conspiracy.

201 Iran National Report, 18 November 2009, A/HRC/WG.6/7/IRN1.

202 'Iran: Barricades and the Bomb', *The Economist*, 13 February 2010.

203 'US sees opportunity to press Iran on nuclear fuel', *New York Times*, 3 January 2010.

204 See, for example, the website of Iraj Mesdaghi: www.irajmesdaghi.com.

www.ingramcontent.com/pod-product-compliance
Lightning Source LLC
Chambersburg PA
CBHW051413200326
41520CB00023B/7212